EXPLORATIONS IN AMERICAN HISTORY

A SKILLS APPROACH

TEACHER'S EDITION

Complete Text with Instructor's Manual

MARK A. STOLER
University of Vermont

MARSHALL TRUE
University of Vermont

EXPLORATIONS IN AMERICAN HISTORY

A SKILLS APPROACH

VOLUME I
To 1865

Instructor's Manual Follows Text

ALFRED A. KNOPF
NEW YORK

For Charon
MT

For Those Who Helped Me Walk Again
MAS

AND TO OUR STUDENTS AT THE UNIVERSITY OF VERMONT

First Edition
98765432

Published in the United States by Newbery Award Records, Inc., a subsidiary of Random House, Inc., New York and simultaneously in Canada by Random House of Canada Limited, Toronto. Distributed by Random House, Inc.

Library of Congress Cataloging-in-Publication Data

Stoler, Mark A.
Explorations in American History.

Contents: v. 1. To 1865 -- v. 2. Since 1865.
1. United States--Historiography. 2. United States--History--Sources. I. True, Marshall. II. Title.
E175.S76 1986 973'.032 86-10458
ISBN 0-394-35281-5 (v. 1)
ISBN 0-394-35471-0 (v. 2)
ISBN 0-394-36567-4 (Teacher's Edition, v. 1)
ISBN 0-394-36568-2 (Teacher's Edition, v. 2)

Text design by Susan Phillips

Manufactured in the United States of America

PREFACE

What is history? Usually, it is defined simply as the study of the past. Actually, it is much more.

History is, first of all, the study of humankind's *entire* past, the study of *all* events—political, social, economic, cultural, scientific, intellectual, material, or abstract—that have taken place over the thousands of years of recorded time. History is also a way of thinking and a way of interpreting the present as well as the past. As such, it is not only one of the oldest disciplines to which men and women have turned their minds and efforts but also an extremely rich, complex, and exciting one. It demands a high level of knowledge, thought, creativity, and skill. In return, it offers much.

History can help you rediscover past ideas with continued relevance for the present. These ideas range from the technological (as evidenced by our new interest in the ancient windmill and wind power as an alternate energy source) to the ideological (as shown by our continued belief in the concepts articulated in the centuries-old Declaration of Independence and Constitution). History can also help you see parallels between past and present and the interconnectedness of human beings over time as well as space. It is interesting to note, for example, that our generation is by no means the first in American history to be faced with numerous political, economic, social, and international problems. Corruption and abuses of power, unemployment and high interest rates, racism and sexism, the Cold War and the nuclear arms race with the Soviet Union are indeed "current events." Yet they are also symptomatic of broader problems that were as evident and important in 1886, or 1786, or 1686 as they are in 1986.

Perhaps most important, the study of history can explain the processes by which our society has reached its present state and even the processes by which you as an individual have become what you are. The importance of such knowledge cannot be overemphasized, for it is impossible to know where you are, or where you are going, unless you are first aware of where you have been and how you got from that point to the present. The continuing popularity of genealogy, or tracing one's "roots," is impressive testimony to public awareness of this truth. In the broadest sense, then, history is a way of learning about the present as well as the past.

Finally, history is inevitable. We are all forced to live in it and relate to it. Consciously or not, each individual is both an actor on the historical stage and a historian. We all interpret the past in light of our own present and we all act on the basis of our knowledge, or lack thereof, regarding that past. The only questions are how we accomplish these processes and how aware we are of them. To be ignorant of history is not to avoid it but to become its victim.

This does not mean that historical knowledge is the universal panacea. The study of history has not solved—nor can it solve—the world's problems. Neither can it predict the future. But as this preface attempts to show, history is much more than simple storytelling and the presentation of irrelevant facts from the past, and it involves much more than mere rote memorization. It is not something simple, linear, one-dimensional, or completely objective.

A survey course is designed to introduce you to these numerous facets of history and to provide you with a useful, basic overview of the historical process (in this case as it has applied to the United States). It can also enable you to develop a series of skills that are of basic importance to the study not only of history but also of other aspects of the humanities and social sciences; that are, in fact, vital to a successful undergraduate education and, we believe, to life itself.

This particular volume is unique in its emphasis on the acquisition of those skills. It is primarily devoted to learning and applying them, and it has been designed to mesh with your textbook readings, lectures, and class discussions.

The most important skills for historical study are those of clear and critical reading, thinking, and writing. Each chapter in this book contains both explanations and exercises designed to develop your abilities in these areas, and your instructor may ask you to complete some or all of these exercises. You should realize in this regard that reading and thinking clearly are inseparable from writing clearly, that poor writing is often a reflection of incomplete reading and illogical thinking, and that efforts to clarify your writing will often help to improve your reading and clarify your thoughts. You should also realize that the value of historical knowledge depends on the ability to *communicate* that knowledge to others, and that such communication requires the ability to compose prose that others can follow.

Along with such general skills, this volume will introduce you to a series of more specific skills, the mastery of which is essential to the study of history. These include the ability to understand and use a university library; to identify, question and analyze different types of secondary and primary sources; to cite historical material correctly; to present historical data using maps, charts, and graphs; to work with a range of nontraditional sources, from architectural drawings to films; to form intelligent hypotheses; to deal with cause-and-effect relationships over time; and to understand and use conflicting historical interpretations of the past. The acquisition of these skills will give you a deeper understanding of the material studied in this course and will show you the breadth of the discipline of history. It should also teach you a great deal about gathering and using the information you need to live in a complex world.

We originally wrote this volume in 1978 as part of a general revision of our U.S. history survey courses at the University of Vermont. Since then we have consistently revised it in response to student and faculty suggestions as well as our own experiences in the courses. This edition incorporates our most recent revisions. Many of them have been added so as to make the volume usable in any U.S. history survey course, rather than simply our own.

From the inception of this project we have been indebted to the University of Vermont's Instructional Development Center. In 1978, it provided both encouragement for this new project and financial assistance through an Instructional Incentive Grant. In 1980, the Center's newly established Curriculum Publication Series produced our first formal edition of this volume, and in 1983–1984 the Center provided financial assistance for additional revisions. We would like to express our thanks to John Clarke, Barbara Collins, David Holmes, Alton Roberts, and Lynn Tarbutton of the Center for all their help and support.

Numerous colleagues on the University of Vermont campus provided invaluable assistance, comments, and criticisms in the preparation of this volume. Within our own department, we are particularly indebted to Connie McGovern, Jerry Felt, Sam Hand, Susan Jackson, and Neil Stout for team-teaching the courses with us, suffering through some of our early experiments and mistakes, making contributions to individual chapters, and offering numerous suggestions. We would also like to thank our chairpersons past and present, Wolfe Schmokel and Bill Metcalfe, for their encouragement and support. In other departments, Mary Jane Dickerson, Karen LeFevre, and Frank Manchel (of English), Ted Miles and Hal Meeks (of Geography), and the entire reference staff at Bailey-Howe Library offered important insights and suggestions in the preparation of individual chapters. Our deepest appreciation goes to all of them, as well as to Stuart Johnson of Addison-Wesley for his interest and support in the early preparation of these volumes, and to Fred H. Burns of Alfred A. Knopf, Inc., who guided them through the final stages of publication.

Finally, we would like to thank the students in our U.S. history survey courses between 1978 and 1986 who participated in, and sometimes suffered from, our numerous experiments with the skills approach. Their comments, criticisms, and detailed suggestions proved invaluable in preparing these volumes. These volumes are thus not only *for* our students, but also partly and genuinely *by* them. Encouraging student participation in their own learning is in large measure the reason we wrote *Explorations in American History* in the first place, and it is therefore appropriate that this volume be dedicated to them.

MARSHALL TRUE
MARK A. STOLER

CONTENTS

INTRODUCTION
HOW TO USE THIS VOLUME

This volume is designed to help you learn a series of important skills associated with the study of history in general, and United States history in particular. It consists of ten chapters. Each chapter is divided into three basic sections and is linked by title, introductory material, and examples to specific time periods examined within any introductory course surveying the history of the United States.

The first section of each chapter introduces and explains the skills being discussed within the context of historical events and issues that took place during one of those time periods. Often, this section is accompanied by supplementary material (such as documents, maps, excerpts, or essays) provided either within or at the end of the chapter. This supplementary material offers you examples of the types of historical evidence being analyzed in the chapter. It also forms the basis for the two other sections of the chapter (the written assignments and the additional questions to consider), and it should be read carefully.

The second section of each chapter contains numbered instructions for written assignments. Your professor will tell you which of the numbered assignments to complete, and he or she may very well change some of them and provide you with more specific guidance. If you do not receive instructions, we advise you to complete the written assignments on your own as a way of practicing and mastering the skills under discussion. Since most of these assignments are essays, you can also improve your writing skills. Where specific short answers are required, your professor should be able to provide you with a list of the correct ones. At all times you should make sure you understand any specific instructions given by your professor before you proceed with a written assignment.

The third section of each chapter contains numbered additional questions for you to consider regarding the skills and written assignments you have just completed studying. As in the previous section, your professor may give you directions about how to handle these questions. In large lecture courses, you may be asked simply to think about them on your own, or to be prepared to talk about them in weekly discussion groups. In smaller courses, your instructor may lead a discussion of some or all of them in class, or ask you to lead such a discussion. As in the previous section, you should make sure you understand any instructions given by your professor before proceeding.

We hope that you will be interested in examining some of the historical problems and skills presented in this volume in greater depth. Just as the course you are taking is an introduction to historical study, so is this volume. The hope shared by your instructors and by us is that your experiences with both this volume and this course will encourage you to pursue your studies in greater depth on your own.

1

EXPLORATION AND COLONIZATION

QUESTIONING, USE OF THE LIBRARY, HISTORICAL RESEARCH, AND FORM

Your textbook readings for this week discuss the European discovery, exploration, and settlement of the Western Hemisphere in general terms and the establishment of England's North American colonies in more specific terms. In the process, your text deals with numerous famous "facts" associated with these activities, from the voyages of Columbus to the founding of Harvard College by the Puritans.

Despite what many believe, history is not merely the rote memorization of these facts. Nor do they "speak for themselves." They make sense only when placed in a context, a framework of interpretation that can explain why they occurred, what they meant, how they relate to each other, and why they are important. By itself, a fact is only a piece of random data and is valueless.

As a student of history, you must seek to place facts in a framework of interpretation. This requires the ability to ask questions of the evidence. You also need to know where to go to find answers to questions and how to present answers in a form others can understand. This chapter will explain how to ask historical questions, where to begin to find answers, and how to present them clearly.

QUESTIONING

Historians ask numerous questions of the events they examine. Of course they ask *what* happened, *when* and *where* it happened, and *who* was involved. But these are by no means the only or even the most important questions asked. After answering these basic points, historians attempt to figure out *how* and *why* an event occurred. And sometimes, the very act of asking these two questions leads to even more questions of the what, where, when, and who variety.

Obviously, you cannot find the answer to any question until you know how to ask it, and this is by no means as easy as it may appear. It is, however, essential to any serious study of history. And in practical terms, you will find the ability to generate questions extremely valuable in helping you to master the material in this and other courses.

Begin by reading the assigned pages of your textbook, keeping in mind as you read that this volume is only a survey introduction and that such introductions generally raise many questions without fully answering them. For example, your text explains the founding of the New England colonies in what appears to be sufficient detail. Upon close examination, however, you should be able to see that it leaves many questions unanswered. Does it explain Puritan theology or tell you *what* role that theology played in the success of the Massachusetts Bay Company? Does it tell you *where* besides Massachusetts it was practiced, or *when* and *why* it developed? In the political realm, does it mention who besides John Winthrop held political leadership in Massachusetts, *who* supported Anne Hutchinson against him, *why* they did so, or *how* they organized and attempted to take power?

Because of their limited scope, most textbooks will not answer these questions. And those that do so will not answer other questions of a similar nature. Only a critical reader can recognize this fact, however, and with it the limitations of a textbook. Such critical reading is essential for all historical study. You should thus be constantly questioning what you read and in the process become aware of the limitations and biases of all written material. In future chapters, this skill will be emphasized. To help develop it on the most basic level, try composing a series of questions on colonial history that are not answered in your textbook.

THE LIBRARY

After raising a series of questions, you need to know *where* and *how* to find the answers. Where to find them is clear—the library. This building is the heart of any institution of higher education and should be the focal point of your intellectual endeavors. In and of itself, however, the library is only a building. By learning to use it intelligently, you will increase dramatically the benefits to be derived from your work as a student. And intelligent use requires knowledge of what the library contains, how it is organized, and how to find what you want.

The first area to explore is the *public* or *card catalogue,* a compilation of thousands of index cards listing all the books and periodicals in your library along with their location by *call number.* (Many university libraries are replacing their card catalogues with computers. These computers should increase the speed and efficiency with which you can use the library's holdings.) The drawers holding these cards are usually located in a prominent and easily accessible section of the library; they may be arranged in two alphabetized sections, one by author and title and one by subject. The author/title section is used when you know the author and/or title of a book and need merely to discover its library location; the subject section is used when you want to explore the library's holdings on a particular topic. When using the author/title catalogue to find the location of a book, you will be wise to double-check under the author's name if you do not find a title entry, and vice versa. When using the subject catalogue, you should first consult the large red volumes nearby, the *Library of Congress Subject Headings,* to discover the terms used in the catalogue for the area you are studying.

While the subject catalogue appears to be the most appropriate place to find materials capable of answering questions, you can usually obtain more relevant information in a shorter period of time by using the author/title catalogue to find the location of specialized *reference* works. In most libraries, these works are located in a special *reference section* containing a large number of noncirculating volumes of exceptional value to you. You can often find specific data far more quickly by using reference encyclopedias and dictionaries than by starting with the subject catalogue. Reference bibliographies and indexes can give you a full listing of scholarly articles and books in your area of interest as well as valuable information about the contents of these works. We therefore recommend consulting the appropriate reference works *first,* using the card catalogue only to find their location, and then, after you have completed your reference research, to discover whether and where your library has the specific books and articles that the reference volumes have shown to be relevant to your topic. If your library does not have a work you desire, the reference section can often be used to order specific materials via interlibrary loan. The librarian can help you with this and with finding specific reference works of value; you should consult this individual when you need assistance.

For the study of history, there are literally thousands of reference works available. Many of these are listed and explained in Helen J. Poulton, *The Historian's Handbook: A Descriptive Guide to Reference Works* (Norman, Okla.: University of Oklahoma Press, 1972), and in the history sections of Eugene Sheehy's *Guide to Reference Works,* rev. 8th ed., C. M. Winchell, ed. (Chicago: American Library Association, 1976) and Carl M.

White's *Sources of Information in the Social Sciences,* 2nd ed. (Chicago: American Library Association, 1973). For the study of American history on a survey level, however, the number of pivotal works is substantially smaller and quite manageable. These works are explained directly below.

If you want to check or obtain specific facts about events in U.S. history, you should consult Thomas H. Johnson, *The Oxford Companion to American History* (New York: Oxford University Press, 1966) or Louise B. Ketz, ed., *Dictionary of American History,* rev. ed., 8 vols. (New York: Scribner's, 1976). For a listing and explanation of facts in chronological as opposed to alphabetical order, see Gordon Carruth, ed., *The Encyclopedia of American Facts and Dates,* 7th ed. (New York: Crowell, 1979) or Richard B. Morris, ed., *Encyclopedia of American History* 16th ed. (New York: Harper & Row, 1982).

For biographical research, Allen Johnson and Dumas Malone, eds., *Dictionary of American Biography,* 20 vols., supplements 1–7, and complete index guide (New York: Scribner's, 1944–1981), commonly known as the *DAB,* is indispensable. It provides biographical sketches of thousands of prominent figures in American history, and each sketch closes with a discussion of the best sources for additional research on that person's life. A newer work, edited by Edward T. James, Barbara Sicherman, and Carol Hurd Green, is *Notable American Women,* 4 vols. (Cambridge: Harvard University Press, 1971, 1980); it fills some notable gaps in the *DAB* and should be the first work you consult if your subject is a woman.

If you need to research a topic or individual in depth, the information provided in these works will not be adequate. Instead, you should consult specific bibliographies and indexes of works in U.S. history so that you can compose a preliminary list of appropriate sources to look up in the card catalogue and read. The *first* such bibliography to consult for books and articles in U.S. history is Frank Freidel, ed., *The Harvard Guide to American History,* 2nd rev. ed., 2 vols. (Cambridge: Belknap Press of Harvard University Press, 1974). If you need more extensive coverage, use the New York Public Library's *Dictionary Catalogue of the History of the Americas,* 28 vols. and 9-vol. supplement (Boston: G. K. Hall, 1961, 1973) and the U.S. Library of Congress's *A Guide to the Study of the United States of America* (Washington, D.C.: U.S. Government Printing Office, 1960, 1976). Special bibliographies on specific subjects in U.S. history are also available and are described in the previously cited works by Poulton, Sheehy, and White.

One of the most important but commonly ignored sources of detailed information consists of *articles* published in *scholarly journals.* These articles are particularly useful because they deal with very specific subjects in depth and often summarize in twenty to fifty pages an analysis also published in a book-length study. They are commonly ignored because individual articles are not listed in the card catalogue; therefore many students do not know how to find them. Here specific reference works can be exceptionally valuable.

One common mistake that many students make is to confuse a *schol-*

arly with a *popular* article and to consult a key index for popular articles, the *Reader's Guide to Periodical Literature,* when they really need a guide to scholarly journals. The *Reader's Guide* lists only articles in mass-circulation magazines; while these magazines are often valuable as primary sources (see Chapter 2), their articles are in no way valid historical analyses and should not be used as such.

Numerous indexes list and comment on scholarly articles published in historical journals. For the study of U.S. history, the most valuable index is *America: History and Life.* In addition to being limited to American history, this annual index provides summaries, or *abstracts,* of individual articles. These abstracts enable you to tell, before reading it, whether a specific article is truly relevant to your topic. One section of *America: History and Life* also lists book reviews that will help you to tell whether a particular book is relevant. Abstracts of some of these reviews can be found in the annual *Book Review Digest.*

To make full and proper use of these or any article index, you should read in their introductory sections how they are organized and the meaning of their abbreviations. Since the card catalogue lists only periodicals, not specific articles within them, you will also need to copy from the index the article author and title, the name of the journal, and the volume number, date, and page numbers for the specific article you wish to consult. You can then use the card catalogue to find the call number of the journal you need, locate the appropriate volume, and look up the article. Many libraries have separate periodical sections and listings of journals that will enable you to bypass the card catalogue. Keep in mind, however, that *only* the periodical index can provide you with information on the article itself.

Other important reference works provide detailed information on specific types of historical material. *The New York Times Index* is invaluable for finding information in America's "newspaper of record." For geographic information, consult Charles Oscar Paullin's *Atlas of the Historical Geography of the United States* (Washington, D.C., and New York: Carnegie Institute and American Geographical Society, 1932); W. Kirk Reynolds, ed., *Atlas of American History,* 2nd rev. ed. (New York: Scribner's, 1984); or Clifford L. and Elizabeth H. Lord, *Historical Atlas of the United States,* rev. ed. (New York: Holt, 1953). Statistical information can be found in the U.S. Census Bureau's *Historical Statistics of the United States* (Washington, D.C.: U.S. Government Printing Office, 1975), a two-volume work with updates entitled *Statistical Abstracts of the United States.* For a one-volume overview of government documents, consult Laurence F. Schmeckebier, *Government Publications and Their Use* (Washington, D.C.: Brookings Institute, 1969). The most comprehensive guide to congressional documents is the massive *U.S. Serial Set Index* published by the Congressional Information Service. Additional guides are available on specific types of government documents. Many libraries have special sections and librarians for government documents that you should consult prior to undertaking any document research.

Many college and university libraries have additional sections for special manuscript collections, maps, microfilm, new books, and photocopying. Most also have a *reserve* section, an area set aside for books and articles placed there by professors because they will be used by large numbers of students. Works on reserve can usually be taken out only for a few hours or days; you should check on the specific rules and procedures used by your library. In most libraries, reference works, periodicals, and documents must be read in the library; only books can be checked out.

FORM: BIBLIOGRAPHIES, FOOTNOTES, AND STYLE MANUALS

In addition to knowing how to use the library, you need to know the correct form to use when presenting the results of your research. In this regard, you should realize that the finest research in the world is worthless if it cannot be clearly communicated to others. The ability to do this rests not only on correct grammar and organization but also on proper citation form for footnotes and bibliographies.

There ought to be no mystery about footnotes and bibliographies. They are part of all research papers and serve to guide your reader to your sources of information and interpretation. It is very important that your *citations,* as footnotes and bibliographies are called, be clear and uniform and that they follow the specific rules that govern their use.

A *footnote* or *end note* is used to credit the source of every quotation, paraphrase, fact, or idea you use in a paper and to give the reader the exact location of each item. A *bibliography* simply lists all the sources used in the preparation of a given work.

The primary purposes of footnotes and bibliographies are to provide your readers with information regarding your sources, should they wish to consult them for additional information, and to give proper credit to authors and sources you have used. Not to give such credit is falsely to claim it for yourself, a very serious and punishable academic offense known as *plagiarism.* Bluntly stated, plagiarism is a form of theft. If you do not provide a bibliography and footnotes (as well as quote marks whenever direct quotes are used), you are falsely claiming by this omission that the words and ideas you use are your own. Unless otherwise instructed by your professor, you should therefore include proper footnotes and bibliographies with *all* written assignments, with footnotes being placed either at the bottom of the page or the end of your paper. They can be single-spaced with double spacing between entries or double-spaced with triple spacing between entries; ask your professor which form to use.

Footnotes *must* be used for all direct quotations *or* paraphrases; for charts, diagrams, graphs, and statistics taken from another work; and for interpretations made by others. They should also be used to cite sources for little-known facts and can, on occasion, be used to discuss a tangential issue (this is known as a "discursive" footnote). If you have numerous citations to the same source in one paragraph, you can usually simplify matters by placing a single footnote at the end of the paragraph.

Footnotes and bibliographies are governed by a set of very specific but evolving rules regarding the information to be provided and the order in which it is to be presented. The purpose of these rules is to ensure that your reader will be able to find the work or works you cite. It is thus essential for you to provide all the information required, and in the proper order. Should you omit some of the information or decide to change the order of presentation, you will only confuse your readers and make it impossible for them to go back to your sources. In citing scholarly articles, for example, standard form requires you to put the title of the article in quote marks, to underline the title of the journal, and then to provide the volume number of the journal, the date (in parentheses), and the page number or numbers. Suppose you choose instead to underline the article title and put the journal title in quote marks, or to put the page number before the volume number, or not to include the date. Could your reader possibly find the information you cite? Could *you* find that information again?

Proper form for books and articles is fairly straightforward. Footnotes are indicated in the text by consecutive, raised arabic numerals half a space above the line and immediately after a reference to another source, as shown at the end of this sentence.[1] The footnote is then presented at the bottom of the page or the end of your paper. The first line of the note is indented and preceded by the raised arabic numeral. Information is then provided according to the following forms. (Titles of books and journals, italicized below, are underlined when typewritten.) For books:

> Author's first and last name, *Title of Book* (Place of Publication: Publisher, year), p. and page number.

For articles in journals:

> Author's first and last name, "Title of Article," *Title of Journal,* volume number (date), page number.

For articles in a book-length collection:

> Author's first and last name, "Title of Article," in *Title of Book,* ed. Name of Editor (Place of Publication: Publisher, year), p. or pp. and page number(s).

Proper footnotes for books and articles that could answer the questions raised at the opening of this chapter would thus be presented as follows:

[1]Edmund S. Morgan, *The Puritan Dilemma: The Story of John Winthrop* (Boston: Little, Brown, 1958), pp. 140-143.

[2]Babette M. Levy, "Early Puritanism in the Southern and Island Colonies," *American Antiquarian Society Proceedings,* 70 (1960), 69.

[3]Darret B. Rutman, "The Mirror of Puritan Authority," in George A. Billias, ed., *Law and Authority in Colonial America* (Barre, Mass.: Barre Publishers, 1965), p. 163.

These so-called "full" citations need be given only once for each source. For later references, you should use a shortened form that includes only the author's last name and the page number (i.e., [4]Morgan, p. 145). If you are using more than one book or article by the same author, however, include a shortened version of the title of the work (i.e., [4]Morgan, *Dilemma,* p. 145). Please note that *ibid.* ("the same") and *op. cit.* ("cited elsewhere") are no longer used, though you will see them in older works.

In a bibliography, basically the same information is given as in a footnote but with a different ordering and punctuation. Bibliographies should include all works consulted for your paper, not merely those cited in the footnotes. The citations are arranged alphabetically by author's last name, and the last name is therefore given first. The second and following lines, instead of the first, are indented to make the author's last name stand out, and periods replace commas. In book citations, parentheses and page numbers are deleted. For the works previously cited as footnotes, proper bibliographic form would look like this:

Levy, Babette M. "Early Puritanism in the Southern and Island Colonies." *American Antiquarian Society Proceedings.* 70 (1960), 69-130.

Morgan, Edmund S. *The Puritan Dilemma: The Story of John Winthrop.* Boston: Little, Brown, 1958.

Rutman, Darret B. "The Mirror of Puritan Authority." In *Law and Authority in Colonial America.* Ed. George A. Billias. Barre, Mass.: Barre Publishers, 1965, pp. 149-167.

While proper form is thus fairly simple, it is important to realize that variations exist; that different forms are used for other types of sources such as government documents, newspapers, and so on; and that form occasionally varies with the discipline involved. Because of these variations and complexities and because of the importance of clear and correct citations, you should have a detailed guide to consult for proper footnote and bibliographical forms. All *style manuals* contain such guides in the form of special chapters on citation. They also contain important information on preparing and writing papers (see Chapters 2 and 5), and many provide more detailed information on use of the library. You should therefore plan to purchase one of these manuals as a key reference work and to consult it whenever you are preparing a paper.

The most commonly used and cited manual is Joseph Gibaldi and Walter S. Achtert, *MLA Handbook for Writers of Research Papers,* 2nd ed. (New York: Modern Language Association, 1984). Also popular are *The Chicago Manual of Style,* 13th ed. (Chicago: University of Chicago Press, 1982) and its student complement by Kate L. Turabian, *Student's Guide for Writing College Papers,* 3rd ed. (Chicago: University of Chicago Press, 1976). Joan H. Garrett-Goodyear et al., *Writing Papers: A Handbook for Students at Smith College,* a concise and inexpensive manual, is now available to students at other colleges. Of the numerous manuals available from commercial publishers, the most comprehensive and up to date are Robert V. Daniels, *Studying History: How and Why,* 3rd ed. (Englewood Cliffs, N.J.: Prentice-Hall, 1981); James D. Lester, *Writing Research Papers: A Complete Guide,* 4th ed. (Glenview, Ill.: Scott, Foresman, 1984); and Melissa Walker, *Writing Research Papers: A Norton Guide* (New York: Norton, 1984).

Since these manuals vary in content and recommended form and since many others are available, you should consult your professor before purchasing one to find out if he or she has any preference or recommendation.

ASSIGNMENTS

1. Compose six questions on a colonial-era topic that are not answered in your textbook. Each question should begin with a different word of inquiry ("what," "when," "where," "who," "how," and "why") and all should deal with the same general topic.
2. Take your list of questions to the library. If a librarian or self-guided tour is available, take it. If not, examine the library areas and reference works discussed in this chapter and complete the exercise given at the end of the chapter. Your instructor may collect this exercise or provide you with the answers.
3. How many of your questions could be answered by consulting only reference works? Which ones would you use?
4. Using the appropriate reference bibliographies and indexes, find at least two books and two scholarly articles that would provide detailed answers to the questions you have asked. Then, make use of the abstracts and book reviews (or summaries) available to choose the one book and one scholarly article that would be most appropriate for answering your questions.
5. Use the card catalogue, the stacks, the periodicals section, and/or the periodicals list to find the book and the article chosen. Cite each in correct footnote *and* bibliographic form and place the appropriate call number in the left-hand margin. If your library does not have the book or article, choose another.

ADDITIONAL QUESTIONS TO CONSIDER

1. What shortcomings in the textbook are revealed by the questions you have raised? How do you account for these shortcomings? Does your textbook appear to have particular strengths and weaknesses in terms of coverage or particular biases in terms of interpretation?
2. On what specific occasions would you use footnotes in a paper? When are they not necessary?
3. Exactly how would you go about preparing a preliminary bibliography for a research paper in colonial history? Which reference works would you consult, and in what order? How would you use the card catalogue? What circumstances would lead you to add or delete specific works?

LIBRARY EXERCISE

1. Look in the subject card catalogue under "Women—History." Find the book by Page Smith. What is its title, place of publication, and date of publication?
2. In the author/title card catalogue, find the call numbers for the *Dictionary of American History,* the *Dictionary of American Biography,* the *Harvard Guide to American History,* and *America: History and Life.* Write these down in the order given.
3. Locate the *Dictionary of American History* and read the article on women's suffrage. What notable early results of the Women's Suffrage Amendment of 1920 does it mention?
4. Locate the *Dictionary of American Biography* and read the entry for Dolly Madison. It indicates that during the evacuation of the White House in 1814 she salvaged a portrait of George Washington. What else did she save?
5. Locate the *Harvard Guide to American History.* In Volume 2, which chapter lists books and articles on English colonization of the New World before 1688, and what is the title of the chapter? What are the author, title, and date of the first *book* listed under the subheading that deals with the establishment of the Massachusetts Bay Colony?
6. Locate *America: History and Life.* Take out the retrospective volume covering the years 1954–1963 (Volume 0) and turn to the heading "House of Burgesses" in the index at the end of the volume. What number is given for this entry? Locate that number in the main part of the volume and write down the following: author, article title, journal abbreviation, full journal title, volume number, issue number, pages, and date.
7. Does your library own this journal? How did you find out? Does the library own the volume you need? If yes, where is the volume located and what is its call number?
8. Turn back to the index section at the end of Volume 0 of *America: History and Life.* The article you found in question 6 may be listed under additional subject headings to give you other points of access to the same information. Which of the following subject headings will lead you to the same article you found in question 6 (look for the same entry number!): "Virginia—Aristocracy"; "Virginia—Provincial and Colonial Government"; "Provincial and Colonial Government—Virginia"; "Colonial Government."
9. To locate, in the subject catalogue, a book on colonial government in the United States, what is the *best* subject heading to use?

2

COLONIAL SOCIETY

ANALYZING PRIMARY SOURCES AND WRITING

Although you are spending only a few weeks studying the colonial era, you should realize that it spans more years (1607–1776) than the rest of this course and is filled with numerous important events and issues. Understanding these events and issues is sometimes difficult, not only because of the large number of years involved but also because of the equally large number of years that separate us from this era and its values.

Our knowledge of the colonial world, indeed of all worlds from the past, is governed by the artifacts and documents available from that era. Historians refer to these artifacts and documents as *primary* sources, for they were produced by the participants in the era under study and are the basic raw material of history. Historical writing itself is labeled *secondary,* because it is derived from a careful study of the primary material.

Historians use primary sources not only as evidence but also to generate answerable questions. To do the latter they have to pay careful attention to the evidence within a source and to its historical context. In the last chapter you were asked to pay such attention to the information provided within a secondary source, your textbook, and to use that information to generate a series of questions. In this chapter you will be asked to examine the evidence provided in a broad range of primary sources and to use these materials to generate additional questions about the past. You will also be asked to think about ways of analyzing the reliability of these materials and to produce your first piece of historical writing.

PRIMARY SOURCES AND THEIR RELIABILITY

Studying American history, you will be exposed to numerous primary and secondary sources. Your textbook, this explanation, and the library works you examined and cited in the last chapter are all secondary in nature, while the documents and artifacts reproduced here and in later chapters are primary.

Clearly, an enormous variety of primary material is available to students of history. Poetry, literature, song, painting, architecture, and maps, to suggest some examples, can all be used as primary sources. Even secondary writing done by historians can be a primary source provided the right questions are asked of it. Historian George Bancroft's early-nineteenth-century writings, for example, while basically secondary in nature, could become primary sources for an investigation of how nineteenth-century historians perceived American history. So could your textbook for some future investigation of how twentieth-century historians perceived the American past.

Working with primary sources demands careful thought and analysis. These sources vary substantially not only in form but also in reliability. Moreover, different types of primary sources provide different kinds of information. And unfortunately, all primary sources are biased and incomplete. The historical witness cannot see everything, and even the best witness can tell the historian only what he or she perceived. Questions about limited knowledge and biased perception are profoundly important to the student of history.

Historians assess the reliability of documents in a variety of ways. A good way to begin is to consider some basic questions for any primary source. How much evidence does it supply? How believable is this information? Is there any evidence of bias in this source? Why does this source exist at all? In examining the primary sources at the end of this chapter, keep these and related questions constantly in mind.

To illustrate the importance of such questions, examine Figure 2.1, an engraving that appeared in a 1792 memoir by Scottish adventurer John William Stedman (1745–1796) entitled *A Narrative of a Five Year Expedition Against the Revolted Negro in Surinam.* To illustrate his memoir, Stedman had over eighty engravings done by the leading artists of Britain. This particular engraving was one of four done by the English poet William Blake. It is entitled "Flagellation of a Female Samboe Slave." If one merely looks at the engraving, the "evidence" provided is quite clear. But is it believable, and is there bias involved? Realize in this regard that this is a view of *Dutch* slavery done by an Englishman, who may have been reflecting abolitionist sentiments, in a memoir by a Scotsman who was a hired mercenary for the Dutch. Its accuracy as a depiction of slavery in the New World in general, and in the English colonies in particular, is therefore questionable. However, it may offer a very accurate view

FIGURE 2.1

of English and/or abolitionist *sentiments* regarding slavery in general or Dutch slavery in particular. In this regard, it is important to remember that the accuracy of a primary source is partly determined by the questions asked of it.

WRITING

In addition to asking questions and assessing the reliability of primary sources, the historian must be able to express his or her conclusions in effective prose, so that those conclusions can be clearly communicated to others. Good writing is one of the trademarks of the historian and of the educated person in general; it is mandatory for effective communication.

Good writing is hard work. George Orwell acknowledged this in his essay "Politics and the English Language" (1946). Orwell suggested that good writers asked four questions about *every sentence* they wrote. "What am I trying to say? What words will express it? What image or idiom will make it clearer? Is this image fresh enough to have an effect?" Orwell was writing to protest the stale language of postwar politics, but his advice still applies in a world where television, politics, and much else provides us with ready-made phrases and slogans that we can employ as a substitute for our own words or ideas.

One of the most important goals of this volume is to encourage you to work on your writing skills—to use your own words and ideas in writing history. Since good writing is largely the product of practice and effort, we urge you to regard the written assignments in this book, essay exams in this and other courses, and indeed all of your written work as opportunities to practice effective writing.

What is effective writing? Books have been written to answer this question, but—sadly—the magic formula has not been found. Yet, at the simplest level, good writing is characterized by clarity, coherence, and liveliness. You must make your meaning clear; you cannot expect your reader to guess at your meaning. Your ideas must be well organized. Coherence requires that your argument should be logical and proceed in an orderly way from beginning to end. Liveliness is vital. No writer wants readers to fall asleep or to lose track of the argument. Liveliness also demands that the writer include vivid, concrete details. These are essential to good historical writing because they are the evidence that supports your generalizations.

As you begin to work on the assignments in this book, you should discover the necessity of revising your written work. Since we often write to find out what we think, rewriting is an integral part of our thinking process. You should be aware that this revising process is complex and difficult; nobody likes to change the words that seemed so appropriate when they were first written. Revision is worthwhile, however, since only by discovering what you think can you communicate your ideas and convictions to others (see Chapter 5 for additional comments on revising).

We would advise that you take the task of communicating *your* ideas to others seriously. Too much student writing is marred by students' successful efforts to imitate bad academic writing. If you are trying—as you should—to discover your own ideas, you handicap yourself inordinately if you attempt to imitate someone else's prose style.

If there are no magic formulas, there *are* some solid rules and guideposts. In his essay, George Orwell offered the following six rules to effective writing:

1. Never use a metaphor, simile or other figure of speech which you are used to seeing in print [or hearing on television].
2. Never use a long word where a short one will do.
3. If it is possible to cut a word out, always cut it out.
4. Never use the passive [voice] when you can use the active [voice].
5. Never use a foreign phrase, a scientific word, or a jargon word if you can think of an everyday English equivalent.
6. Break any of these rules sooner than say anything outright barbarous.

We think Orwell offered good advice. You will find these rules valuable as you work on your writing skills.

The style manuals discussed in Chapter 1 present detailed guidelines for effective writing; we therefore once again recommend that you purchase and use one of them. If you desire further advice beyond what is offered in these manuals, there are a number of good books about writing which you might consult. We would recommend two books by Peter Elbow, *Writing Without Teachers* (New York: Oxford University Press, 1973) and *Writing With Power* (New York: Oxford University Press, 1981). Elbow is particularly good at suggesting solutions to writers' problems. William Zinsser's *On Writing Well* (New York: Harper & Row, 1966), is a masterful commentary on the ingredients of good prose. Finally, William Strunk and E. B. White, in *Elements of Style,* 3rd ed. (New York: Macmillan, 1978), provide a witty and wise guide to the rules of effective writing.

In addition to a style manual, the library of every student writer should include a good dictionary. Webster's *New Collegiate Dictionary,* 9th ed. (Springfield, Mass.: Merriam-Webster, 1983) is still the standard desk dictionary, but there are also reasonably good soft-cover dictionaries, including those published by American Heritage and Oxford. As with the style manuals, you should see if your professor has any advice or preferences in this regard.

ASSIGNMENTS

1. Read or examine carefully each primary source reproduced below. Ask yourself whether the evidence it provides supports or contradicts information you have received from the text or in class.
2. After reading each source, summarize its contents for your own later use. You should note the essential points this source makes, jot down any details you find interesting, and list any questions the source suggests to you.
3. Choose *one* of these sources as instructed by your professor or at your own discretion and prepare a list of *four* historical questions generated from it. You may apply the "who, when, where, what, why, how" formula used in the last chapter, or you may simply raise the questions that occur to you as you read and think about the source.
4. Using the questions you listed, write a brief statement (about a hundred words) on the reliability of your source. Remember that the accuracy of a source is partly determined by the questions asked of it.

ADDITIONAL QUESTIONS TO CONSIDER

1. Be prepared to discuss the reliability of all the primary sources listed below.
2. Can you deduce any general rules for determining the reliability of a primary source? Is there such a thing as a completely reliable primary source? Why or why not?

3. In light of the problems you have encountered with reliability, how should an individual go about using primary sources to write a good history?

SOURCE 1

Those abstemious Puritans of Massachusetts Bay displayed considerable artistic interest in gravestone carving. The gravestone in Figure 2.2 is dated 1748 and features the "heart mouth" design, found preponderantly on children's gravestones.

SOURCE 2

Much present-day folk wisdom originated in the colonial era. This folk saying has been traced to Connecticut in approximately 1700:

Use it up, wear it out
make it do or do without.

SOURCE 3

John Winthrop delivered this sermon aboard the *Arbella* in 1630. In it, he expressed the hopes and aspirations of the Puritans migrating to Massachusetts Bay.

FIGURE 2.2

A MODELL OF CHRISTIAN CHARITY, 1630

Written on Board the Arbella, *on the Atlantic Ocean*

God almighty in His most holy and wise providence hath so disposed of the condition of mankind, as in all times some must be rich, some poor, some high and eminent in power and dignity, others mean and in subjection.

Reason: First, to hold conformity with the rest of His works, being delighted to show forth the glory of His wisdom in the variety and difference of the creatures and the glory of His power, in ordering all these differences for the preservation and good of the whole.

Reason: Secondly, that He might have the more occasion to manifest the work of His spirit. First, upon the wicked in moderating and restraining them, so that the rich and mighty should not eat up the poor, nor the poor and despised rise up against their superiors and shake off their yoke. Secondly, in the regenerate in exercising His graces in them, as in the great ones, their love, mercy, gentleness, temperance, etc., in the poor and inferior sort, their faith, patience, obedience, etc.

Reason: Thirdly, that every man might have need of other, and from hence they might be all knit more nearly together in the bond of brotherly affection. From hence it appears plainly that no man is made more honorable than another, or more wealthy, etc., out of any particular and singular respect to himself, but for the glory of his creator and the common good of the creature, man.

Thus stands the cause between God and us. We are entered into covenant with Him for this work, we have taken out a commission, the Lord hath given us leave to draw our own articles, we have professed to enterprise these actions upon these and these ends, we have hereupon besought Him of favor and blessing. Now if the Lord shall please to hear us, and bring us in peace to the place we desire, then hath He ratified this covenant and sealed our commission, [and] will expect a strict performance of the articles contained in it, but if we shall neglect the observations of these articles which are the ends we have propounded, and dissembling with our God, shall fall to embrace this present world and prosecute our carnal intentions seeking great things for ourselves and our posterity, the Lord will surely break out in wrath against us, be revenged of such a perjured people, and make us know the price of the breach of such a covenant.

Now the only way to avoid this shipwreck and to provide for our posterity is to follow the counsel of Micah, to do justly, to love mercy, to walk humbly with our God. For this end we must be knit together in this work as one man, we must entertain each other in brotherly affection, we must be willing to abridge ourselves of our superfluities for the supply of others' necessities, we must uphold a familiar commerce together in all meekness, gentleness, patience, and liberality, we must delight in each other, make others' conditions our own, rejoice together, mourn together, labor and suffer together, always having before our eyes our commission and community in the work, our community as members of the same body. So shall we keep the unity of the spirit in the bond of peace. The Lord will be our God and delight to dwell among us as His own people, and will command a blessing upon us in all our ways, so that we shall see much more of His wisdom, power, goodness, and truth than formerly we have been acquainted with. We shall find that the God of Israel is among us, when ten of us shall be able to resist a thousand of our enemies, when He shall make us a praise and glory, that men shall say of succeeding plantations, the Lord make it like that of New England. For we must consider that we shall be as a city upon a hill, the eyes of all people are upon us. So that if we shall deal falsely with our God in this work we have undertaken and so cause Him to withdraw His present help from us, we shall be made a story and a byword through the world, we shall open the mouths of enemies to speak evil of the ways of God and all professors for God's sake, we shall shame the faces of many of God's worthy servants, and cause their prayers to be turned into curses upon us till we be consumed out of the good land whither we are going. And to shut up this discourse with that exhortation of Moses, that faithful servant of the Lord in His last farewell to Israel, Deut. 30., Beloved, there is now set before us life and good, death and evil, in that we are commanded this day to love the Lord our God, and to love one another, to walk in His ways and to keep His commandments and His ordinance, and His laws, and the articles of our covenant with Him that we may live and be multiplied, and that the Lord our God may bless us in the land whither we go to possess it. But if our hearts shall turn away so that we will not obey, but shall be seduced and worship other Gods, our pleasures, our profits, and serve them, it is propounded unto us this day we shall surely perish out of the good land whither we pass over this vast sea to possess it. Therefore let us choose life, that we, and our seed, may live, and by obeying His voice, and cleaving to Him, for He is our life, and our prosperity.

SOURCE 4

These excerpts are taken from the Proceedings of the General Assembly of the Colony of Rhode Island and Providence Plantations, held at Newport on the first Wednesday of February, 1770. They are interesting chiefly for the variety of issues dealt with by the Assembly.

Whereas, Messrs. John Jenckes, Moses Brown, John Brown, David Harris, William Smith, John Updike, Knight Dexter, Ebenezer Thompson, Joseph Lawrence, Zephaniah Andrews, Elijah Bacon, Noah Mason, John Smith, Jonathan Ellis, Jonathan Hamman, Thomas Greene and James Lovett, in behalf of themselves and their associates, preferred a petition, and represented unto this Assembly, that from a regard to the instruction of youth, in the most necessary parts of learning, they, with the town of Providence, have caused to be built within the said town, a commodious brick school house, two stories high; the upper part of which, containing two rooms, belongs to them and their associates; that, for the better carrying their design in building the said rooms into execution, they have formed themselves into a society, known by the name of the Proprietors in the Town School House; and thereupon, for the well ordering and governing the said school, in the upper part of said house, and for the better establishing the rules and orders already made; and also all future regulations respecting the same, they pray this Assembly to grant and extend to the said society, their heirs and assigns, a full and ample power, at all times hereafter, to order, ordain and enact all such rules and regulations, as may from time to time, appear to them necessary for the well ordering all prudential affairs of the said society; and that all rules, acts, orders and regulations so made, as may (not repugnant or disagreeable to the laws of this colony, or the acts and orders of the said town of Providence), be, to all intents and purposes, valid and binding upon the said society, and each individual thereof; on consideration whereof,—

Be it enacted by this General Assembly, and by the authority thereof it is enacted, that the prayer of the petitioners, in the foregoing petition contained, be, and the same is hereby, granted.

At the special request of the inhabitants of the town of Providence, made by their representatives,—

It is voted and resolved, that the inhabitants of the said town of Providence, be, and they are hereby, permitted and authorized to sell all kinds of spirituous liquors, in any quantities not less than one quart; provided, that the same be not drank in the house of the retailer; any law of this colony to the contrary, in any wise, notwithstanding.

It is voted and resolved, that the petition preferred to this Assembly, praying that all that part of the town of Providence, lying westward of Weybosset Bridge, and the harbor or bay, may be set off and incorporated into a new township, be referred to the next session; and that, in the mean time, the town of Providence be cited to appear and show cause (if any they have), why the same should not be granted.

Whereas, Mr. John Greene and others, preferred a petition, and represented unto this Assembly, that Nathaniel Greene and Company, John Greene and Company, Griffin Greene and Christopher Greene, have been at a very great expense in erecting and building dams, forges, anchor works and saw mills upon the south branch of Pawtuxet river, in providing a very considerable stock, and employing a great number of hands, to prosecute the business; the emolument arising from which, is the principal support of themselves and their dependants, amounting to upwards of one hundred in number; that there is a law of this colony, directing that suitable fish-ways be made and kept open on the said south branch of said river, from the 21st of April to the 1st of June, annually; that if the said law be carried into execution, it will render it almost impossible for them to pursue their business; that the number of fish coming up to those dams, is so small and contemptible, that the benefit arising from them, is by no means to be compared with the great advantages derived to the public from their works; and thereupon, they prayed this Assembly, that the dams above enumerated, standing on the said south branch of Pawtuxet river, may be established by act of government, and totally exempted from preparing and providing fish-ways, in the same manner as the dams on the north branch of the same river are now established, and exempted from preparing and providing fish-ways; on consideration whereof,—

Be it enacted by this General Assembly, and by the authority thereof, it is enacted, that the prayer of the petitioners, in the foregoing petition contained, be, and the same is hereby, granted.

Whereas, Moses Brown, presented the following memorial unto this Assembly, to wit:

MEMORIAL OF MOSES BROWN, RELATIVE TO THE NORTHERN BOUNDARY LINE OF RHODE ISLAND.

To the Honorable the General Assembly:

Gentlemen:—Agreeably to the vote of this Assembly, at their last session, I received and have taken copies of the plats and papers respecting the northern boundary line of this colony; by which papers, it appears that the colony had made application in conjunction with the colony of Connecticut, to Mr. Partridge, then agent for both colonies, to pursue the settlement of the said line; and it appears that this colony, in the month of April, 1753, formed a petition to His Majesty, upon this subject; whether it was forwarded or not, or what further was done, does not appear by the papers I have yet been able to collect; but am informed by one of the commissioners, who conferred with the commissioners of the colony of Connecticut, upon this matter, in April, 1752, that the two colonies agreed to prosecute the case jointly; and as this government had expended a considerable sum in running the line, procuring evidence, and fitting the case to go home, Connecticut was to pursue it at home until they had laid out the same sum that we had; after which, the expense for any more, should be necessary, was to be paid by both governments equally.

This being the case, and it appearing clear to me, that the colony had a just right to a strip of four miles and fifty-six rods; the width of the colony being about twenty-two miles, I propose and desire this Assembly to appoint some proper person or persons to make application to the Governor or secretary of the colony of Connecticut, and procure information how the case was left; and if they are unable to inform us, to write to the agent of this colony, who, about the time this matter was in agitation in England, lived with Mr. Partridge, and without doubt, hath the papers respecting this matter, that belong to the colony, and request him to examine the papers, and inform us of the circumstances this affair was under at the commencement of the late war; which I suppose was the occasion of its not being determined.

As Joseph Harrison, Esq., one of this colony's committee to run the line; and Col. Lyman, who was one of Connecticut's committee, are both in London, and are acquainted with all the circumstances of this case, I apprehend a more favorable opportunity for the colony to get information in this matter, could not happen.

I am obliged to the General Assembly for their confidence in depositing the papers in my hands, and herewith return them.

I am, gentlemen, &c., &c.,

MOSES BROWN.

On consideration whereof,—

It is voted and resolved, that the said memorial be accepted; that Moses Brown, be, and he is hereby, appointed to make the inquiry therein mentioned; and when he shall have obtained the best information he can procure, that he make report thereon, to the General Assembly.

Whereas, Esther Sachem (calling herself queen of the tribe of Indians in this colony), Thomas Sachem, her husband, and Henry Harry, with others, as her council, who preferred a petition unto this Assembly, praying that she, with her husband and council, and James Helme, Joseph Haszard and Sylvester Robinson, Esqs., (who were a committee appointed by this Assembly, to dispose of the estate of Thomas Ninegret, deceased, late sachem of said tribe, for the payment of his debts,) may make a deed or deeds of the estate of the said Thomas Ninegret, for the payment of his just debts in the same manner as the said Thomas Ninegret, in his life time, with his council, and the said committee, by act of Assembly, might have done; and whereas, Samuel Niles and others (calling themselves a council, appointed by said tribe, for transacting their public affairs), did appear before this Assembly, and for the settlement of the disputes and differences subsisting in said tribe, did mutually agree that the Hon. Joseph Wanton, Esq., the Hon. Stephen Hopkins, Esq. and Joseph Haszard, Esq., or any two of them (by their consent, and by order of this Assembly), should be empowered to inquire into the subject matter of their disputes, and in particular to ascertain and to set off all the lands which shall, upon inquiry and examination, appear to them to have been the lands or estates of the said Thomas Ninegret, deceased, for the payment and satisfaction of the debts due to his creditors and to his heirs, after such debts as are paid and satisfied; that the expense of such inquiry and examination be equally paid by the said two parties; and that the said report be made to this Assembly at the next session; and the premises being duly considered,—

Be it enacted by this General Assembly, and by the authority thereof, it is enacted, that the above recited agreement be, and hereby is, approved; and that the said Joseph Wanton, Stephen Hopkins and Joseph Haszard, or any two of them, be empowered to do, and transact every thing submitted to them, by said agreement.

And be it further enacted by the authority aforesaid, that the above named James Helme, Joseph Haszard and Sylvester Robinson, or any two of them, be empowered to take into their care and possession, all such lands as shall be set off as the estate of the said Thomas Ninegret, deceased, and the same to improve, in such manner as they shall think most for the interest of his heirs and creditors, until so much of them shall be disposed of, as will be sufficient to satisfy and pay his just debts.

God save the King.

SOURCE 5

Domestic life in the colonies was subject to regulation, as the following acts of the Virginia House of Burgesses from 1661 to 1691 attest.

THE LAWS OF VIRGINIA

March 1661–62

Against Ffornication

FOR restraint of the ffilthy sin of ffornication, *Be it enacted* that what man or woman soever shall commit ffornication, he and she soe offending, upon proofe thereof by confession or evidence shall pay each of them five hundred pounds of tobacco fine, *(a)* to the use of the parish or parishes they dwell in, and be bound to their good behavior, and be imprisoned untill they find security to be bound with them, and if they or either of them committing ffornication as aforesaid be servants then the master of such servant soe offending shall pay the said ffive hundred pounds of tobacco as aforesaid to the use of the parish aforesaid, for which the said servant shall serve half a yeare after the time by indenture or custome is expired; and if the master shall refuse to pay the ffine then the servant to be whipped; and if it happen a bastard child to be gotten in such ffornication then the woman if a servant in regard of the losse and trouble her master doth sustaine by her haveing a bastard shall serve two yeares after her time by indenture is expired or pay two thousand pounds of tobacco to her master besides the ffine or punishment for committing the offence and the reputed father to put in security to keep the child and save the parish harmelesse.

December 1662

Women Servants got with Child by Their Masters . . .

WHEREAS by act of Assembly every woman servant haveing a bastard is to serve two yeares, and late experiente shew that some dissolute masters have gotten their maides with child, and yet claime the benefitt of their service, and on the contrary if a woman gott with child by her master should be freed from that service it might probably induce such loose persons to lay all their bastards to their masters; *it is therefore thought fitt and accordingly enacted, and be it enacted henceforward* that each woman servant gott with child by her master shall after her time by indenture or custome is expired be by the churchwardens of the parish where she lived when she was brought to bed of such bastard, sold for two yeares, and the tobacco to be imployed by the vestry for the use of the parish.

Men Servants Getting Any Bastard Child . . .

WHEREAS by the present law of this country the punishment of a reputed father of a bastard child is the keeping the child and saving the parish harmlesse, and if it should happen the reputed father to be a servant who can noe way accomplish the penalty of that act, *Be it enacted by the authority aforesaid* that where any bastard child is gotten by a servant the parish shall take care to keepe the child during the time of the reputed fathers service by indenture or custome, and that after he is free the said reputed father shall make satisfaction to the parish.

Negro Women's Children . . .

WHEREAS some doubts have arrisen whether children got by any Englishman upon a negro woman should be slave or ffree, *Be it therefore enacted and declared by this present grand assembly,* that all children borne in this country shalbe held bond or free only according to the condition of the mother, *And* that if any christian shall committ ffornication with a negro man or woman, hee or shee soe offending shall pay double the ffines imposed by the former act.

April 1691

. . . For prevention of that abominable mixture and spurious issue which hereafter may encrease in this dominion, as well by negroes, mulattoes, and Indians intermarrying with English, or other white women, as by their unlawfull accompanying with one another, *Be it enacted by the authoritie aforesaid, and it is hereby enacted,* that for the time to come, whatsoever English or other white man or woman being free shall intermarry with a negroe, mulatto, or Indian man or woman bond or free, shall within three months after such marriage be banished and removed from this dominion forever, and that the justices of each respective countie within this dominion make it their perticular care, that this act be put in effectuall execution. *And be it further enacted by the authoritie aforesaid, and it is hereby enacted,* That if any English woman being free shall have a bastard child by any negro or mulatto, she pay the sume of fifteen pounds sterling, within one moneth after such bastard child shall be born, to the Church wardens of the parish where she shall be delivered of such child, and in default of such payment she shall be taken into the possession of the said Church wardens and disposed of for five yeares, and the said fine of fifteen pounds, or whatever the woman shall be disposed of for, shall be paid, one third part to their majesties for and towards the support of the government and the contingent charges thereof, and one other third part to the use of the parish where the offence is committed, and the other third part to the informer, and that such bastard child be bound out as a servant by the said Church wardens untill he or she shall attaine the age of thirty yeares, and in case such English woman that shall have such bastard child be a servant, she shall be sold by the said church wardens, (after her time is expired that she ought by law to serve her master) for five yeares, and the money she shall be sold for divided as is before appointed, and the child to serve as aforesaid. . . .

SOURCE 6

In Figure 2.3 we see an interesting portrait of Indian King Philip done by Paul Revere, America's most prominent colonial engraver, for the second edition of Thomas Church's *History of King Philip's War,* published in Newport in 1772. Although it was done a hundred years after King Philip's War, it is one of the few Indian portraits of the colonial period done by an American.

SOURCE 7

On February 10, 1676, during King Philip's War, Mary Rowlandson was abducted by Narragansett Indians. She was held captive for almost twelve weeks and then ransomed. Her account of her captivity, published in 1682, was a seventeenth-century best-seller that helped to establish the captivity narrative as a genre in early American literature.

THE NINETEENTH REMOVE

They said, when we went out, that we must travel to Wachusett this day. But a bitter weary day I had of it, traveling now three days together, without resting any day between. At last, after many weary steps, I saw Wachusett Hills, but many miles off. Then we came to a great swamp, through which we traveled up to the knees in mud and water, which was heavy going to one tired before. Being almost spent, I thought I should have sunk down at last and never got out; but I may say, as in Psalm 94:18, *When my foot slipped, thy mercy, O Lord, held me up.*

Going along, having indeed my life but little spirit, Philip, who was in the company, came up and took me by the hand and said, "Two weeks more and you shall be mistress again." I asked him if he spake true. He answered, "Yes,

FIGURE 2.3

PHILIP. *KING* of Mount Hope.

and quickly you shall come to your master again" (who had been gone from us three weeks).

After many weary steps we came to Wachusett, where he was, and glad I was to see him. He asked me when I washed me. I told him not this month. Then he fetched me some water himself, and bid me wash, and gave me the glass to see how I looked, and bid his squaw give me something to eat. So she gave me a mess of beans and meat, and a little groundnut cake. I was wonderfully revived with this favor showed me, Psalm 106:46, *He made them also be pitied of all those that carried them captives.*

My master had three squaws, living sometimes with one and sometimes with another one. One was this old squaw at whose wigwam I was, and with whom my master had been those three weeks. Another was Wettimore, with whom I had lived and served all this while. A severe and proud dame she was, bestowing every day in dressing herself neat as much time as any of the gentry of the land; powdering her hair and painting her face, going with necklaces, with jewels in her ears and bracelets upon her hands. When she had dressed herself, her work was to make girdles of wampum and beads. The third squaw was a younger one, by whom he had two papooses. By that time I was refreshed by the old squaw, with whom my master was, Wettimore's maid came to call me home, at which I fell a-weeping. Then the old squaw told me, to encourage me, that if I wanted victuals I should come to her, and that I should lie there in her wigwam. Then I went with the maid, and quickly came again and lodged there. The squaw laid a mat under me and a good rug over me—the first time I had any such kindness showed me. I understood that Wettimore thought that if she should let me go and serve with the old squaw, she would be in danger to lose not only my service but the redemption pay also. And I was not a little glad to hear this, being by it raised in my hopes that in God's due time there would be an end of this sorrowful hour.

Then came an Indian and asked me to knit him three pair of stockings, for which I had a hat and a silk handkerchief. Then another asked me to make her a shift, for which she gave me an apron. Then came Tom and Peter with the second letter from the Council about the captives. Though they were Indians, I gat them by the hand and burst out into tears; my heart was so full that I could not speak to them.

But recovering myself, I asked them how my husband did, and all my friends and acquaintances. They said, "They are all very well but melancholy." They brought me two biscuits and a pound of tobacco. The tobacco I quickly gave away. When it was all gone, one asked me to give him a pipe of tobacco. I told him it was all gone. Then began he to rant and threaten. I told him when my husband came I would give him some. "Hang him rogue," says he, "I will knock out his brains if he comes here." And then again in the same breath they would say that if there should come an hundred without guns they would do them no hurt: so unstable and like mad men they were. So that fearing the worst, I durst not send to my husband, though there were some thoughts of his coming to redeem and fetch me, not knowing what might follow. For there was little more trust to them than to the master they served.

When the letter was come, the sagamores met to consult about the captives, and called me to them to inquire how much my husband would give to redeem me. When I came I sat down among them, as I was wont to do, as their manner is. Then they bade me stand up, and said they were the "General Court." They bid me speak what I thought he would give. Now knowing that all we had was destroyed by the Indians, I was in a great strait; I thought if I should speak of but a little, it would be slighted, and hinder the matter, if of a great sum, I knew not where it would be procured. At a venture, I said, "Twenty pounds," yet desired them to take less. But they would not hear of that, but sent that message to Boston, that for twenty pounds I should be redeemed. It was a Praying Indian that wrote their letter for them.

There was another Praying Indian who told me that he had a brother that would not eat horse, his conscience was so tender and scrupulous (though as large as hell for the destruction of poor Christians). Then, he said, he read that Scripture to him, 2 Kings 6:25, *There was a great famine in Samaria; and, behold, they besieged it, until an ass's head was sold for fourscore pieces of silver, and the fourth part of a cab of dove's dung for five pieces of silver.* He expounded this place to his brother and showed him that it was lawful to eat that in a famine which is not at another time. "And now," says he, "he will eat horse with any Indian of them all."

There was another Praying Indian who, when he had done all the mischief that he could, betrayed his own father into the English hands, thereby to purchase his own life. Another Praying Indian was at Sudbury fight, though, as he deserved, he was afterward hanged for it. There was another Praying Indian so wicked and cruel as to wear a string about his neck, strung with Christians' fingers. Another Praying Indian, when they went to Sudbury fight, went with them, and his squaw also with him, with her papoose at her back.

Before they went to that fight, they got a company together to powaw; the manner was as followeth. There was one that kneeled upon a deerskin, with the company round him in a ring, who all kneeled, striking upon the ground with their hands and with sticks, and muttering or humming with their mouths. Besides him who kneeled in the ring, there also stood one with a gun in his hand. Then he on the deerskin made a speech, and all manifested assent to it; and so they did many times together. Then they bade him with the gun go out of the ring, which he did, but when he was out, they called him in again; but he seemed to make a stand. Then they called the more earnestly, till he returned again. Then they all sang. Then they gave him two guns, in either hand one. And so he on the deerskin began again; and at the end of every sentence in his speaking they all assented, humming or muttering with their mouths, and striking upon the ground with their hands. Then they bade him with the two guns go out of the ring again; which he did, a little way. Then they called him in again, but he made a stand, so they called him with greater earnestness; but he stood reeling and wavering, as if he knew not whether he should stand or fall, or which way to go. Then they called him with exceeding great vehemency, all of them, one and another. After a little while he turned in, staggering as he went, with his arms stretched out, in either hand a gun. As soon as he come in, they all sang and rejoiced exceedingly awhile. And then he upon the deerskin made another speech, unto which they all assented in a rejoicing manner; and so they ended their business, and forthwith went to Sudbury fight.

To my thinking they went without any scruple but that they should prosper and gain the victory. And they went out not so rejoicing, but they came home with as great a victory. For they said they had killed two captains and almost an hundred men. One Englishman they brought along with them; and he said it was too true, for they had made sad work at Sudbury, as indeed it proved. Yet they came home without that rejoicing and triumphing over their victory which they were wont to show at other times, but rather like dogs (as they say) which have lost their ears. Yet I could not perceive that it was for their own loss of men. They said they had not lost above five or six, but I missed none, except in one wigwam. When they went, they acted as if the Devil had told them that they should gain the victory; and now they acted as if the Devil had told them they should have a fall. Whether it were so or no I cannot tell but so it proved, for quickly they began to fall, and so it held on that summer, till they came to utter ruin. They came home on a Sabbath day, and the powaw that kneeled upon the deerskin came home (I may say, without abuse) as black as the Devil.

When my master came home, he came to me and bid me make a shirt for his papoose, of a Holland-laced pillowbere. About that time there came an Indian to me and bid me come to his wigwam at night and he would give me some pork and groundnuts. Which I did, and as I was eating, another Indian said to me, "He seems to be your good friend, but he killed two Englishmen at Sudbury, and there lie their clothes behind you." I looked behind me, and there I saw bloody clothes, with bullet holes in them; yet the Lord suffered not this wretch to do me any hurt. Yea, instead of that, he many times refreshed me; five or six times did he and his squaw refresh my feeble carcass. If I went to their wigwam at any time, they would always give me something, and yet they were strangers that I never saw before. Another squaw gave me a piece of fresh pork, and a little salt with it, and lent me her pan to fry it in; and I cannot but remember what a sweet, pleasant, and delightful relish that bit had to me, to this day. So little do we prize common mercies when we have them to the full.

SOURCE 8

Martha Emons's will, although far less dramatic than Rowlandson's narrative, also affords insight into the social and economic history of the colonial period.

I, *Martha Emons,* of Boston, widow, being sicke & weake in body, but of p^{r}fect memory, make this my last will. Debts to be paid. I give vnto my sone, *Obadiah Emons,* all that my messuage tenem^{t}. or dwelling house, with the land thereto belonging, wherein he now dwelleth, being in Boston. Vnto my sone, *Samuel Emons,* my dwelling house wherein I now live, wth. the land thereto belonging, situate in Boston. Vnto my sone, *Joseph Emons,* £20, to be paid him by my executo^{rs}, at such times as the ou^{r}seers to this my will shall judg meet, (that is to say) when he doth take such good corses as to live orderly & to follow the Trade of a Cordwaine^{r}. & is clear of such debts as he now owes by following the imploy he now hath taken up. Vnto my Sone, *Benjamin Emons,* Foure score pounds, to be paid him by my executo^{rs}, as followeth, £60 thereof in such pay as will p^{r}duce him lether & other things w^{c}h he may need. I will that the £20 given my Sone, *Benjamin,* by his fathers will, be paid to him, in the moneth of June, w^{c}h shall be in the year 1667, by my executo^{r}s; & for the £60 aforesaid, to be paid unto him £40, by my sone, *Obadiah,* out of the value of the house I have hereby bequeathed him, & £20 by my sone, *Samuel,* out of the value of the house I have bequeathed him, & £20 by *Obadiah,* & £10 by *Samuel,* to pay the said *Benjamin* in June 1668; the other £30 to be paid in specie in the moneth of June thence next ensuing; the other £20 to be paid my sone, *Benjamin,* to make up the sume of Fourscore pounds to be paid vnto him by the value thereof, of my goods, viz. that Fether bed w^{c}h he best liketh, with the Bolster & pillow, the new Cou^{r}led, a paire of Blankets, Curtins, hangings, the bedstead I now ly on, Two paire of my best sheets, a paire of pillow beers, my Silver Beker & Silver Spoon; & of other my goods, as pewter, Brasse & old bedding, to make up the value of £20; said goods to be paid him when he receives the legacie of £20, aforesaid, given him by the will of his father or soone^{r} if his occasions cale for it, & the plate & bedding immedyatly after my Decease. Vnto my son, *Samuel,* my Cloth Gound to make him a sute, & to his wife my best cloth petticote. To my dau. *Alice Emons,* my Turkey moehaire coate & my finest paire of new pillowbers. Vnto my grandsone, *Thomas,* 40^{s}·; vnto my Grand Dau. *Martha Emons,* my Gold ring & my silue^{r} bodkin; to my grandson, *Samuel,* my Silver wine cup & Dram cup; vnto my grand dau. *Mary,* 20^{s}, to be paid her in pewter; to my grand dau. *Elizabeth* 10^{s}· to buy her a silue^{r} spoon. Vnto my grandson, *Samuel Crab,* £18, to be paid him by my executo^{rs} when he shall be 20 years of age; vnto my Kinswoman, *Martha Winsor,* £8, to be paid vnto her at her age of 21, or day of Marriage, wch of them shall first be, & my hire Calliminco gound, & my old Moehaire petticoate & a red taminy petticoate & a new cloth wastcoate, wch lyeth in my chest, & a sute of my linning complete, (except a white Apron) & my bible & box. To Goodman *Prat,* of Charlestowne, 10^{s}; vnto my Kinswoman, *Hannah Winsor,* Two platters to be paid her at her Marriage. Vnto Goodwife, *Cop,* & goodwife, *Goold,* 10^{s} apeece; vnto my loving neighbo^{rs} Goodwife *Stanes* & goodwife *Winsor,* each of them, a dresing of my best, after that my dau. *Alice* hath take her choice. My will is, that such of my waring lining not disposed of, my dau^{rs} to Devid between them. My will is, that my Sone, *Samuel,* shall have the refuse of such implem^{ts} in my house wch he shall desire, paying for it as it is prized. Vnto my sons, *Obadiah & Samuel,* all my goods, Debts & estate not hereby bequethed, to be devided between them, whom I make joint executo^{rs} of this my last will & testament. I intreat my loving friends, *Mr John Wiswell* & *Mr William English* to be overseers, whom I do hereby also impower, that in case my executo^{rs} be remisse in p^{r}forming this my will, that then, upon such neglect, they shall have power over the before bequeathed dwelling houses to dispose of them for time, till my debts & legacies be paid, anything before expressed to the Contrary there of notwithstanding. Vnto my before named friends, *Mr Wiswell & Mr English,* 40$^{s.}$ a peece for theire paines. I have here vnto set my hand & seale the second day of April in the year above written. In Case my houshold goods & debts will not amount to pay my debts & legacies hereby ordered & bequeathed, then the same shall be made up & paid by my executo^{rs} out of the Value of the houses respectively, hereby to them bequeathed, *Obadyah* paying two parts & *Samuel* one part thereof.

MARTHA EMONS

SOURCE 9

As Source 5 indicates, slavery was a presence in colonial America, as it would be well into the nineteenth century. Blacks, however, did not accept servitude gladly, as the following excerpt from a 1712 letter from the colonial governor of New York, Robert Hunter, to the Lords of Trade attests.

I must now give your Lordships an account of a bloody conspiracy of some of the slaves of this place, to destroy as many of the Inhabitants as they could, It was put in execution in this manner, when they had resolved to revenge themselves, for some hard usage, they apprehended to have received from their masters (for I can find no other cause) they agreed to meet in the orchard of Mr Crook the middle of the Town, some provided with fire arms, some with swords and others with knives and hatchets, this was the sixth day of April, the time of meeting was about twelve or one o'clock in the night, when about three and twenty of them were got togeather, one coffee and Negroe slave to one Vantilburgh set fire to an out house of his Masters, and then repairing to the place where the rest were they all sallyed out togeather wth their arm's and marched to the tune, by this time the noise of fire spreading through the town, the people began to flock to it upon the approach of severall the slaves fired and killed them, the noise of the guns gave the alarm, and some escaping their shot soon published the cause of the fire, which was the reason, that not above nine Christians were killed, and about five or six wounded, upon the first notice which was very soon after the mischeif was begun, I order'd a detachment from the fort under a proper officer to march against them, but the slaves made their retreat into the woods, by the favour of the night, having ordered centries the next day in the most proper places on the Island to prev^t their escape, I caused the day following the Militia of this town and of the county of west Chester to drive the Island, and by this means and strict searches in the town, we found all that put the design in execution, six of these having first laid violent hands upon themselves, the rest were forthwith brought to their tryal before ye Justices of this place who are authorized by Act of Assembly, to hold a Court in such cases, In that Court were twenty seven condemned whereof twenty one were executed, one being a woman with child, her execution by that meanes suspended, some were burnt others hanged, one broke on the wheele, and one hung a live in chains in the town, so that there has been the most exemplary punishment inflicted that could be possibly thought of, and which only this act of assembly could Justify, among these guilty persons severall others were apprehended, and again acquitted by the Court, for want of sufficient evidence, among those was one Mars a negroe man slave to one Mr Regnier, who was to his tryall and acquitted by the Jury, the Sheriffe the next day moving the Court for the discharge of such as were or should be soe acquitted, by reason hee apprehended they would attempt to make their escape but Mr Bickley who y^{n} executed the office of the Atter: Generall, for Mr Rayner opposed his motion, telling the Court that at that time, none but Mars being acquitted, the motion could be only intended in his favour, against whom he should have some thing further to object, and therefore prayed he might not be discharg'd. so the sheriff did not obtain his motion, Mars was then indicted a second time and again acquitted, but not discharg'd, and being a third time presented was transferr'd (the Court of Justices not designing to sit again) to the supream Court, and there tryed and convicted on ye same evidence, on his two former tryals, this prosecution was carryed on to gratify some private pique of Mr Bickleys against Mr Regnier, a gentleman of his own profession, which appearing so partial, and the evidence being represented to me as very defective, and being wholly acquitted of ever having known any thing of the Conspiracy by the Negroe witnesses, who were made use of in the tryals of all the criminals before the Justices, and without whose testimonies very few could have been punished, I thought fit to reprieve him till Her Majesties pleasure be known therein. if this supream court were likewise tryed, one Husea belonging to Mrs Wenham, and one John belonging Mr Vantilbourgh and convicted, these two are prisoners taken in a Spanish prize this war and brought into this Port by a Privateer, about six or seven years agoe and by reason of their colour which is swarthy, they were said to be slaves and as such were sold, among many others of the same colour and country, these two I have likewise reprieved till Her Majesties pleasure be signified. soon after my arrival in this government I received petitions from several of these Spanish Indians as they are called here, representing to me that they were free men subjects to the King of Spain, but sold here as slaves, I secretly pittyed their condition but haveing no other evidence of w^{t} they asserted then their own words, I had it not in my power to releive them, I am informed that in the West Indies where their laws against their slaves are most severe, that in case of a conspiracy in which many are engaged a few only are executed for an example, In this case 21 are executed, and six having done that Justice on themselves more have suffered than we can find were active in this bloody affair which are reasons for my repreiving these, and if your Lordships think them of sufficient weight, I beg you will procure Her Majesty's pleasure to be signifyed to me for their pardon, for they lye now in prison at their masters charge, I have likewise repreived one Tom a Negroe belonging to M[r] Van Dam and Coffee a Negroe belonging to M[r] Walton these two I have repreived at the instance of the Justices of the Court, who where of oppinion that the evidence against them, was not sufficient to convict them.

SOURCE 10

William Byrd (1674–1744) was a wealthy Virginia planter whose wide-ranging interests led him to collect the largest (approximately four thousand volumes) library in the colonies and to become a member of the British Royal Society for men of cultural distinction. His diaries—one of which is excerpted below—were written in cipher and not intended for publication.

Dec. 25, 1710

I rose at 5 o'clock and read a chapter in Hebrew and some Greek in Lucian. About 7 o'clock the negro woman died that was mad yesterday. I said my prayers and ate boiled milk for breakfast. The wind blew very strong and it rained exceedingly. . . . About 11 o'clock we went to church where we had prayers and the Holy Sacrament which I took devoutly. We brought nobody home to dinner. I ate boiled venison. The child was a little better. In the afternoon I took a long walk and I saw several parts of the fence blown down with the wind, which blew very hard last night. In the evening I read a sermon in Mr. Norris but a quarrel which I had with my wife hindered my taking much notice of it. However we were reconciled before we went to bed, but I made the first advance. I neglected to say my prayers but not to eat some milk. I had good health, good thoughts, and indifferent good humor, thank God Almighty.

Feb. 5, 1711

I rose about 8 o'clock and found my cold still worse. I said my prayers and ate milk and potatoes for breakfast. My wife and I quarreled about her pulling her brows. She threatened she would not go to Williamsburg if she might not pull them; I refused, however, and got the better of her, and maintained my authority. About 10 o'clock we went over the river and got to Colonel Duke's about 11. There I ate some toast and canary. Then we proceeded to Queen's Creek, where we found all well, thank God. We ate roast goose for supper. The women prepared to go to the Governor's the next day and my brother and I talked of old stories. My cold grew exceedingly bad so that I thought I should be sick. My sister gave me some sage tea and leaves of [s-m-n-k] which made me mad all night so that I could not sleep but was much disordered by it. I neglected to say my prayers in form but had good thoughts, good humor, and indifferent health, thank God Almighty.

October 20, 1711

I rose about 6 o'clock and drank tea with the Governor, who made use of this opportunity to make the Indians send some of their great men to the College, and the Nansemonds sent two, the Nottoways two, and the Meherrins two. He also demanded one from every town belonging to the Tuscaroras. About 9 the Governor mounted and we waited on him to see him exercise the horse and when all the militia was drawn up he caused the Indians to walk from one end to the other and they seemed very much afraid lest they should be killed. The Governor did nothing but wheel the foot, and Colonel Ludwell and I assisted him as well as we could. About noon the Governor ordered lists to be taken of the troops and companies that the people might make their claim to be paid, because they had been on the service five days. When this was done he gave liberty to the people to go home, except a troop and company for the guard that night. Then we went and saw the Indian boys shoot and the Indian girls run for a prize. We had likewise a war dance by the men and a love dance by the women, which sports lasted till it grew dark. Then we went to supper and I ate chicken with a good stomach. We sat with the Governor till he went to bed about 11 o'clock and then we went to Major Harrison's to supper again but the Governor ordered the sentry to keep us out and in revenge about 2 o'clock in the morning we danced a g-n-t-r dance just at the bed's head. However we called for the captain of the guard and gave him a word and then we all got in except Colonel Ludwell and we kept him out about quarter of an hour. Jenny, an Indian girl, had got drunk and made us good sport. I neglected to say my prayers and had good health, good thoughts, and good humor, thank God Almighty.

October 21, 1711

I rose about 6 o'clock and we began to pack up our baggage in order to return. We drank chocolate with the Governor and about 10 o'clock we took leave of the Nottoway town and the Indian boys went away with us that were designed for the College. The Governor made three proposals to the Tuscaroras: that they would join with the English to cut off those Indians that had killed the people of Carolina, that they should have 40 shillings for every head they brought in of those guilty Indians and be paid the price of a slave for all they brought in alive, and that they should send one of the chief men's sons out of every town to the College. I waited on the Governor about ten miles and then took leave of him and he went to Mr. Cargill's and I with Colonel Hill, Mr. Platt, and John Hardiman went to Colonel Harrison's where we got about 3 o'clock in the afternoon. About 4 we dined and I ate some boiled beef. My man's horse was lame for which he was let blood. At night I asked a negro girl to kiss me, and when I went to bed I was very cold because I pulled off my clothes after lying in them so long. I neglected to say my prayers but had good health, good thoughts, and good humor, thank God Almighty.

January 9, 1712

I was a little displeased at a story somebody had told the Governor that I had said no governor ought to be trusted with £20,000. . . .

January 15, 1712

I rose about 7 o'clock but read nothing because I wrote some letters and one especially to Will Randolph concerning what I understood the Governor had [been] informed concerning my saying no governor ought to be trusted with £20,000, and he owned he had told it because I had said it and he thought it no secret, for which I marked him as a very false friend. . . .

January 24, 1712

I was a little perplexed what to say to the Governor to extenuate what I had said but I was resolved to say the truth, let the consequence be what it would. About 10 o'clock, I and my brother [in-law] went to town and lighted at my lodgings. Then I went to the coffeehouse where I found Mr. Clayton and he and I went to the Governor. He made us wait half an hour before he was pleased to come out to see us and when he came he looked very stiff and cold on me but did not explain himself. . . .

March 2, 1712

I rose about 7 o'clock and read a chapter in Hebrew but no Greek because Mr. G-r-l was here and I wished to talk with him. I ate boiled milk for breakfast and danced my dance. I reprimanded him for drawing so many notes on me. However I told him if he would let me know his debts I would pay them provided he would let a mulatto of mine that is his apprentice come to work at Falling Creek the last two years of his service, which he agreed. I had a terrible quarrel with my wife concerning Jenny that I took away from her when she was beating her with the tongs. She lifted up her hands to strike me but forbore to do it. She gave me abundance of bad words and endeavored to strangle herself, but I believe in jest only. However after acting a mad woman a long time she was passive again. I ate some roast beef for dinner. In the afternoon Mr. G-r-l went away and I took a walk about the plantation. At night we drank some cider by way of reconciliation and I read nothing. I said my prayers and had health, good thoughts, and good humor, thank God Almighty. I sent Tom to Williamsburg with some fish to the Governor, and my sister Custis. My daughter was indisposed with a small fever.

SOURCE 11

No selection of colonial documents would be complete without something from Benjamin Franklin, one of the most accomplished men of his era. Franklin's achievements in literature, politics, science, and business also made him perhaps the best-known American of his time. This famous woodcut (Figure 2.4), one of the earliest American political cartoons, expressed Franklin's support for the Albany Congress of 1754.

FIGURE 2.4

3

LIVES OF THE AMERICAN REVOLUTION

ASSESSING EVIDENCE AND SUMMARIZING

Although no public opinion polls existed during the 1760s and 1770s, it was obvious to people at the time and to later historians that the American colonists disagreed sharply over the proper response to British acts. According to John Adams, only one-third of the colonists finally concluded that revolution was the answer; the other two-thirds split evenly between loyalty to the king and neutrality in the struggle. Even within these rough divisions, sharp differences of opinion separated the colonists throughout the revolutionary era. In this chapter we will study how and why they disagreed.

History concerns itself not only with the "what" of past events but also with the "why," and one of its endless fascinations is to figure out the reasons that individuals behaved as they did in specific situations. The fascination is endless because a clear answer is seldom possible. The situation itself, the times, self-interest, deeply held beliefs, and personal status and history all play a role in determining individual behavior. Even when all these factors are considered, one can seldom predict with accuracy how an individual will behave; the variables and intangibles are simply too numerous. Furthermore, many individuals do not take clear or consistent stands; for numerous reasons, they may attempt to confuse and mislead their contemporaries and later historians. In May of 1774, for example, Benjamin Franklin offered the following "solution" to the colonial problem in a letter to a London newspaper:

> Permit me . . . to convey to the Premier . . . my own opinion, and that of many of my Brethren . . . of the most feasible Method of humbling our rebellious Vassals of North America. As we have declared by our Representatives that we are the supreme Lords of their Persons and Property, and their occupying our Territory at such a remote Distance without a proper Controul from us, except at a very great Expence, encourages a mutinous Disposition, and may, if not timely prevented, dispose them in perhaps less than a Century to deny our Authority . . . more especially when it is considered that they are a robust, hardy people, encourage early Marriages, and their Women being amazingly prolific, they must of consequence in 100 years be very numerous, and of course be able to set us at Defiance. Effectually to prevent which, as we have the undoubted Right to do, it is humbly proposed . . . that a Bill be brought in and passed, and Orders immediately transmitted to G[enera]l G[ag]e, our Commander in Chief in North America, in consequence of it, that all the Males there be c[a]st[rat]ed. . . . There may be a Clause in the Bill to be left at the Discretion of the General, whose Powers ought to be very extensive, that the most notorious Offenders, such as Hancock, Adams, &c. who have been Ringleaders in the Rebellion of our Servants, should be shaved quite close. . . . It is true, Blood will be shed, but probably not many Lives lost. . . . The Advantages arising from this Scheme being carried into Execution are obvious. In the course of fifty years it is probable we shall not have one rebellious Subject in North America.

Franklin was obviously being satiric here. But beyond the humor, does the piece help to explain his beliefs in 1774, or to mask them?

This week you are to learn about the lives and ideas of nine Americans of the revolutionary era. Included at the end of this chapter are short biographical sketches of these individuals as well as unattributed quotations taken from their writings—one quotation from each. By carefully reading the biographical material, you should be able to determine which of the numbered and randomly arranged quotations can be attributed to each author; and you should be able to explain the reasons for your conclusions.

In this exercise, the accuracy of your attributions is not nearly as important as your thinking—why you made the choices you did. Although problems do occur, like those exemplified in the Franklin excerpt above, biographical data generally provide enough information for you to reach thoughtful and intelligent (if not necessarily correct) conclusions. What matters most is the development of your thought processes, your ability to understand what you read and to link facts in an individual's life to statements of policy and belief.

Your comprehension will be greatly improved if you take notes on what you have read in the form of a *written summary.* For selections of the size included in this chapter, the easiest method is simply to list the major points in each quote and/or biographical sketch. For example, summary notes on the Franklin quote previously presented might look like this:

1. It will be difficult to humble rebellious colonists because the colonial population is growing so rapidly.
2. To quell the rebellious spirit, this population growth must be stopped. Therefore, a bill should be introduced to castrate the male colonists.
3. Such a "solution" will involve less loss of life than putting down an actual rebellion.

However, because we know that Franklin delighted in making his points humorously—remember his 1733 *Poor Richard's Almanac* ("After three days men grow weary of a wench, a guest, and rainy weather")—we should not take this excerpt literally. In doing so, we would miss some of the basic ideas beneath Franklin's rhetoric and would thus have a total misunderstanding of his position in 1774. Based on what we know of that position, a summary of what Franklin wanted his readers to infer would be quite different from the summary given above, and would look like this:

1. The real reason for colonial rebelliousness is England's insistence on ruling and subjugating a fast-growing population thousands of miles away.
2. This problem will simply get worse as the colonists continue to multiply and England continues with her policies.
3. England can successfully rule the colonies only by preventing their growth, but such a policy would be absurd because it would destroy the American prosperity which England seeks to control.
4. Implicitly, England's cause is hopeless.

As this example illustrates, the meaning of a quotation can—and often will—be found only by going beyond its *literal* meaning (i.e., what the words say). Thus you should be able to draw inferences and to read carefully enough to make judgments about the actual meaning of words used.

To help prepare yourself for the completion of the assignment, you should make a summary of each of the biographical sketches and quotes provided. As you should realize, making summary notes can be most useful for everything you read for this and for other courses. Indeed, making written summaries is an excellent method of note-taking both for lectures and for assigned readings; in the long run, it may be more helpful and less time-consuming than underlining in your textbook.

After you have summarized the key ideas of the material that follows, look carefully through these summaries to see which themes are repeatedly articulated and which quotes convey principles that you have found in the biographies. In other words, look for similarities between your summaries of the biographical sketches and your summaries of the direct quotations. Then use a process of elimination by matching the most obvious pair first and proceeding to the more elusive combinations later.

ASSIGNMENTS

1. Identify the author of each of the nine quotes given at the end of the chapter.
2. Reproduce your summary for one of the quotes. Your professor may give you a specific quote to summarize in writing, or you may have your choice.
3. Write a 100- to 250-word essay explaining why you chose a specific author for the quote you have summarized. Be sure to include specific facts and details as well as some insight into your reasoning process.

ADDITIONAL QUESTIONS TO CONSIDER

1. Be prepared to summarize, orally, the other eight quotes.
2. Be prepared to explain, orally, your choices of authors for the other eight quotes.
3. How do you account for the lack of direct correlation between the socioeconomic status of the nine individuals and the stand of each on the question of independence? What factors aside from wealth and class might explain the stand each individual took?
4. Could the factors cited in answer to the previous question for these nine individuals provide sufficient evidence to disprove a class analysis of the American Revolution? Why?

BIOGRAPHICAL SKETCHES

MOSES BROWN

Moses Brown was an early American manufacturer, philanthropist, and humanitarian reformer of sound judgment, unblemished integrity, and liberal spirit. Born in 1738, he was apprenticed at an early age to his uncle (following the death of his father). When his uncle died, Moses and his brothers used the uncle's estate to develop the mercantile firm of Nicholas Brown and Company in Providence, Rhode Island. During the 1760s, the rapidly rising Brown also became active in politics and philanthropy. From 1764 to 1771, he was a member of the Rhode Island Assembly; in 1770, he took a leading step in moving Rhode Island College to Providence by endowing it with $1,000. Under continued benefactions from Brown's family, it would later be renamed Brown University.

The death of his wife in 1773 was a crushing blow to Brown and led to some major changes in his life. A year later he became a Quaker, freed his slaves, and helped start the Rhode Island Abolition Society. For the duration of the revolutionary era, he continued to mourn his wife and to pay attention to his business. He took no part in the Revolution itself, regarding it his duty as a Quaker and a businessman to remain neutral in the conflict.

After the war, Brown continued to be active in business. He became one of the first Americans to interest himself in cotton manufacturing and in 1789 induced Samuel Slater to come to America to build a cotton mill. "Come and work our machines and have the credit as well as the advantage of perfecting the first water mill in America," Brown wrote. Evading the stringent British laws prohibiting the export of patents or the emigration of skilled tradesmen, Slater came to America and, under Brown's patronage, built and put into operation a frame with twenty-four spindles. This began the first successful cotton manufacturing in America and added to Brown's already large estate.

Brown also became involved in a host of religious, philanthropic, and reform activities during the remainder of his life. He helped to establish and support a Quaker school and founded numerous educational, religious, and reform societies. These included the Providence Athenaeum library, the Rhode Island Bible Society, and the Rhode Island Peace Society, to name but a few. He died in 1836 at the age of ninety-eight.

JOHN DICKINSON

Throughout the 1760s and 1770s, John Dickinson was the foremost American spokesman against British parliamentary taxation of the colonies, yet he refused to sanction separation from England. Although he eventually supported the War for Independence, this initial refusal severely diminished his reputation both at that time and in later years.

Dickinson was born in 1732 to a family of wealthy colonial farmers. After study in England, he opened a law practice in Philadelphia and quickly won success and respect. He was elected to the Delaware Assembly in 1760 and to the Pennsylvania legislature two years later; he was heavily involved in the prerevolutionary debates from the start.

Dickinson's first major work was a 1765 pamphlet, *The Late Regulations Respecting the British Colonies Considered,* which urged repeal of the Sugar and Stamp Acts. As a result of this pamphlet and his knowledge of the subject, he was appointed to the Stamp Act Congress in New York, where he authored that body's *Declaration of Rights and Grievances.* In 1768, he started publishing his most famous writings, the highly popular and influential *Letters From a Farmer in Pennsylvania to the Inhabitants of the British Colonies.* Using simple, straightforward language, Dickinson pointed out the evils of British policy, argued against any form of parliamentary taxation, and called for a revival of the nonimportation agreements which had been used against the Stamp Act.

The *Letters* brought Dickinson fame and support in both America and England. He continued to help organize the colonists against parliamentary taxation and during the 1770s was appointed to both Continental Congresses. However, he refused to sanction any drastic action and consistently urged moderation and conciliation. Although he recognized the problems in the colonial system under British domination, Dickinson was more fearful of the popular, radical factions within the colonies and the dangers inherent in their calls for revolution and separation.

When Boston called for intercolonial aid in response to British closure of the port in 1774, Dickinson thus sent only his sympathy. At both Continental Congresses he drafted conciliatory petitions to the king and urged peaceful methods on his colleagues. Fearful of leading America into full-scale war without a strong central government or any allies, he voted against the Declaration of Independence at the Second Congress in 1776.

Despite Dickinson's opposition to declaring independence, Parliament's continued refusal to compromise regarding taxation—even in the face of his logical arguments on the subject—did lead Dickinson eventually to cast his lot with the revolutionaries. While still urging conciliation at the Second Continental Congress, he simultaneously took responsibility for the military preparedness of the colonies and for writing the Congress's official rationale for its decision to fight. After passage of the Declaration of Independence over his negative vote, Dickinson became one of only two members of the Congress to take up arms in defense of the adopted measure.

During the remaining years of his life, Dickinson became increasingly disillusioned with politics and gradually withdrew from the national scene. His last significant act was participation in the 1787 Constitutional Convention as a delegate from Delaware. After that he held no public office, and in 1808 he died in Delaware.

MERCY OTIS WARREN

Mercy Otis Warren was a playwright, poet, and historian. In her first play, published in 1772, she caricatured Thomas Hutchinson as Rapatio, a ruthless tyrant determined to destroy "the love of liberty" in the country that he governed. Later, in her history of the American Revolution (published in three volumes as the *History of the Rise, Progress and Termination of the American Revolution* in 1805), she portrayed a prideful and ambitious John Adams who was lukewarm in defense of liberty and other basic tenets of the American Revolution. Her criticism led Adams to conclude sourly, "History is not the province of the Ladies." Nevertheless, Mercy Otis Warren is remembered today both for her ardent defense of liberty and for her trenchant judgments of some of the leading figures of her day.

Mercy Otis was born into a comfortable, well-established Massachusetts family in 1728. Her father, a prosperous lawyer, merchant, and farmer, served his community as a colonel in the local militia and as a judge in a county court. Although the Otis family believed in public service, they shared the conviction common to their time that this service should be done only by men. Consequently, while the Otis sons were prepared for college, Mercy and her sisters had to be content with the scraps of knowledge they managed to pick up as they listened to their brothers being tutored. Evidence from her later writing suggests, however, that despite her lack of formal schooling, Mercy Otis was a literate young woman with a penetrating mind.

In 1754, Mercy Otis married James Warren, a Harvard-educated merchant and farmer, and the couple set up housekeeping in Plymouth. Despite the responsibilities of a growing family (Mercy and James produced five sons in nine years), the Warrens found themselves increasingly drawn into public affairs as the crisis between Great Britain and the colonies deepened. Their house was a frequent meeting place for opponents of royal policy like Samuel Adams, John Adams, and Mercy's older brother, James Otis.

While her husband served in the Massachusetts legislature, Mercy Warren served the revolutionary cause with her pen. During the 1770s, she produced a number of political satires in the form of plays. Featuring characters like Judge Meagre, Brigadier Hateall, and Hum Humbug, Warren's work poked fun at Tories and British alike. While her plays were not particularly good literature, they were a substantial achievement for a woman who had lived all her life in small Massachusetts towns and who, most likely, had never seen a play in her life.

Although the Warrens were committed to the rebel cause, the achievement of independence did not lead to their political advancement; therefore they soon withdrew from politics. In 1787–88, Mercy and James led the family's last political campaign by actively opposing Massachusetts' ratification of the new federal Constitution. Mercy Warren's arguments, published in 1788 as *Observations on the New Constitution,* revealed her to be an adroit political thinker with an abiding faith in people's ability to govern themselves. Warren believed that all nations are likely to pass through a "paroxysm of vice at some period or other" and warned that if "your government is not secure upon a solid foundation, and well-guarded against the machinations of evil men, the liberties of the country will be lost—perhaps forever." Although the Warrens lost their campaign and Massachusetts ratified the Constitution, Mercy Warren's warning anticipated some of the crises, particularly that over slavery and much later over Watergate, which would beset America's republican institutions in the years ahead.

After 1790, Mercy Warren continued to work on the history of the American Revolution that she had started in the 1770s. After completing that monumental work, she continued an active literary and political correspondence until her death in 1814 at age eighty-six.

THOMAS HUTCHINSON

Thomas Hutchinson was in every way a colonial aristocrat. His family was descended from the original Massachusetts Bay settlers and already held considerable wealth and influence when he was born in Boston in 1711. He was educated at Harvard, married into another aristocratic family, and soon amassed a fortune in commerce and trade. Like other colonial aristocrats, he entered politics at an early age. After many years in the Massachusetts Assembly, he was given a series of prestigious and lucrative appointments as an agent of the king and Parliament. By 1760 he was lieutenant governor and chief justice of Massachusetts. When he was appointed governor of the colony in 1771, Hutchinson was the most learned and distinguished colonial-born official in America. He was also, or would soon become, the most hated.

Hutchinson's unpopularity was a result of his long-held conservative views and the positions in which he found himself during the revolutionary era. As early as 1748, he had gained the enmity of debtor groups in Massachusetts by successfully pushing through the Assembly a measure that eliminated unsound land banks and their bills of credit. Although this victory made him a leader of conservative, creditor forces, the ensuing contraction of credit ruined many other people and led to Hutchinson's defeat for reelection in 1749. Suspicion of him only increased when he then received lucrative appointments.

Hatred of Hutchinson reached the boiling point during the Stamp Act crisis of 1765. Although he objected to the act because it injured trade, he refused to question Parliament's absolute authority to tax and govern the colonies. To the contrary, he soon made it clear that his allegiance as a public official was to the Crown, and he worked to strengthen the act and weaken colonial opposition. These efforts, combined with the fact that his brother-in-law was a stamp distributor, convinced popular leaders that Hutchinson was a puppet of the king. On August 26, 1765, an angry mob sacked his home.

This incident embittered Hutchinson and reinforced his previously held convictions that democracy was dangerous and that colonial opposition to British acts had to be met with a strict policy. His appointment as governor in 1771 enabled him to put such a strict policy into effect against the radical leaders of Boston. In the press, he openly debated Sam Adams and argued for the absolute supremacy of Parliament over the colonists. As chief executive of Massachusetts, he did not hesitate to call out troops to break up public demonstrations and disorder. The result was the Boston Massacre. The ensuing animosity towards Hutchinson was only increased by the publication of his private letters (procured by Benjamin Franklin in England), which urged the British government to be even stricter in enforcing its authority over the colonies.

In line with his belief that firmness was the correct policy, Hutchinson insisted, in 1773, that the tea brought into Boston Harbor by the East India Company be unloaded, despite massive popular opposition. This inspired the Boston Tea Party. Several months later, Hutchinson departed for England, leaving General Thomas Gage, commander of British troops in North America, as governor.

Hutchinson reported to the king on the situation in America and was prepared to return home to resume his post as soon as Gage had succeeded in quieting the colonists. However, Gage did not succeed; in fact, there was the outbreak of full-scale war, so Hutchinson was forced to remain in England for the rest of his life. He now urged reconciliation, but to no avail. Homesick for his native New England, a land to which he could not return, Hutchinson died and was buried in Croyden, England, in 1780.

HENRY LAURENS

A rich merchant and planter from South Carolina, Henry Laurens, was a moderate who would hold numerous important posts on both state and national levels during the revolutionary era. Born in Charleston on May 6, 1724, the son of a prosperous saddler, Laurens received the best education possible in the colony at that time, inherited his father's business, and visited England in order to learn more about commerce and make the "proper" contacts. Upon his return to Charleston, he joined an active mercantile house and quickly prospered by trade in slaves, wine, indigo, and rice. After 1765, however, his business interests shifted from commerce to the acquisition and management of plantations. Again he prospered. By the time of the Revolution, his holdings totaled some 20,000 acres, including the 3,000-acre home estate of Mepkin.

With his increasing wealth Laurens became involved in politics and was elected to the South Carolina Assembly. As a rich merchant and landholder, he advocated organized opposition to parliamentary acts but simultaneously feared the colonial mob and its radical calls for independence. As a result, Laurens soon found himself under attack from two directions. During the Stamp Act crisis, an armed colonial band searched his house for stamps, while the British seized two of his ships for technical violations of the Navigation Acts.

In 1771, Laurens traveled to England to arrange for the schooling of his three sons. Disgusted by the corruption he witnessed in the English ruling classes, he moved to Geneva; in 1774, he returned to Charleston. He was soon elected to South Carolina's first Provincial Congress, and because of his status and ability became its president a year later. From 1775 to 1776, he helped draft South Carolina's temporary constitution, defend Charleston against British attack, and prevent a civil war from breaking out between loyalists and patriots.

A few months later, Laurens was appointed one of the American peace commissioners in Paris. He also served as an unofficial minister to England and did not return to Charleston until 1785. With his health broken by the ordeals of the past five years, his property severely damaged, and his heart saddened by the death of his son in the war, Laurens retired to Mepkin and died in December of 1792.

GOUVERNEUR MORRIS

As an intelligent young member of the landed aristocracy of New York, Gouverneur Morris seemed an unlikely candidate for revolutionary leader in 1775. Born in 1752 on the family estate of Morrisania, graduated from King's College (now Columbia University) at the age of sixteen, and admitted to the New York bar three years later, Morris appeared to be on his way to a distinguished, conservative career in law and politics when the war began. He had previously opposed calls for revolution, but after fighting began at Lexington, despite formidable family opposition, he unexpectedly attached himself to the patriot cause.

Morris was at first active in New York's provincial congress and constituent assembly, where he attempted to prevent civil war between radicals and loyalists determined to destroy each other. He successfully argued for religious toleration, and worked determinedly, though unsuccessfully, for the abolition of slavery. He was most interested, however, in national politics, and was an early proponent of strong powers for the Continental Congress. After being elected to that body in 1777, he specialized in financial, military, and diplomatic affairs, chairing several committees and drafting numerous important documents. As military inspector for the Congress, he also visited Valley Forge and became a friend and defender of George Washington.

Chiefly because he would not support New York's claims to Vermont in the Continental Congress, Morris was defeated for reelection in 1779. He then moved to Philadelphia, where he practiced law and wrote a series of brilliant articles on continental finance. These articles led to his appointment as assistant to Superintendent of Finance Robert Morris (no relation) in 1781. He held the position until 1785 and is best remembered for his plans for a decimal system of coinage.

In 1787, Morris was chosen to serve as a delegate to Pennsylvania's Constitutional Convention. There, he argued actively for a strong, centralized government in the hands of the rich and well born. He wanted a president elected for life, severely limited suffrage ("Give the votes to the people who have no property and they will sell them to the rich"), and the overthrow of all existing state governments. Morris was defeated on all these points, but he accepted the bundle of compromises that emerged as the Constitution and worked loyally for its ratification.

From 1792 to 1794, Morris served as minister to France. In 1800, he filled out an unexpired term in the U.S. Senate but was defeated for reelection in 1802, and returned to Morrisania. He spent the remaining thirteen years of his life cultivating his friends and his estate, promoting the Erie Canal as chairman of the canal commission, and writing bitterly critical letters about contemporary politics. He died in 1816, not at all sure that the United States would long survive.

JAMES OTIS

A pivotal and brilliant figure in Massachusetts politics during the crises of the 1760s, James Otis is considered by many to have been the true father of the American Revolution. His early challenge to British acts, his organization of the Popular party in Massachusetts, and his numerous political pamphlets all played crucial roles in preparing the ground for the struggle of the 1770s. Beyond that, his political theories became the mainstay of American political thinking both during and after the revolutionary era. Only a freak accident cut short Otis's brilliant career and prevented him from taking his place as one of the giants among the Founding Fathers.

Otis was born in February 1725 in West Barnstable, Massachusetts, the son of a respected colonial lawyer. He received a private education, studied law at Harvard, and then developed a respected and profitable practice in Boston. In addition to law, he was very well versed in the ancient classics, English literature, and political theory.

Otis's abilities were recognized by the royal governor of Massachusetts and he was chosen as the king's advocate general of the vice-admiralty courts in Boston. In this position, he was expected, in 1760, to aid in the enforcement of the Sugar Act by applying for search warrants—called writs of assistance—to aid customs collectors in their search for evidence of violations. Instead, Otis resigned his lucrative post in protest and supported the Boston merchants who were opposing the writs. In February 1761, he argued their illegality before the superior court by invoking the doctrine of fundamental law, embodying natural law as superior to the acts of Parliament. According to John Adams, "Otis was a flame of fire" in the courtroom who "hurried away everything before him. American independence was then and there born."

Two months later, Otis was chosen as one of four representatives from Boston to the Massachusetts House of Representatives. His father was at that time speaker of the House, and the two soon organized a popular bloc against Crown officials. Otis was also active in the Sons of Liberty and began to write powerful political pamphlets that defined the constitutional rights of the colonies and supported the natural law theory of the rights of man. His doctrines were adopted by the Massachusetts House, and he was appointed chairman of a committee to correspond with other colonial assemblies. In 1765, he was chosen as a delegate to the Stamp Act Congress. Afterward, he continued to write political pamphlets espousing his natural rights theory. These pamphlets and their arguments had more influence in America and England than those of any other American except John Dickinson.

From 1766 to 1768, Otis and his political allies directed the majority of the Massachusetts House in opposition to Governor Barnard. This led to a showdown in 1768, when Barnard negated the election of Otis as speaker and of six councilors who supported him. Otis countered by presiding over the Boston town meeting that launched the nonimportation movement. He also joined with Sam Adams to write the Massachusetts circular letter, which did more to unify the colonies than any measure since the Stamp Act. In the ensuing months, word spread that Otis and Adams were threatened with trial for treason in England and that troops were being sent to Boston. Despite such rumors, Otis opposed violent opposition and revolt and repeatedly urged his followers to restrain themselves.

Otis's career as an activist came to an abrupt end on September 5, 1769, when he received a severe blow on the head during a brawl with Crown officers in a coffee house. Although he lived, Otis never regained lasting control of his mental faculties, and his conduct thereafter made people question his sanity. "He wanders and rambles like a ship without a helm," John Adams noted.

A temporary recovery led to Otis's reelection to the Massachusetts House in 1771, but this recovery lasted only six months. By the end of the year, his brother had been named his guardian, and he made no more political statements of any consequence. He did take up arms and helped fight the British at Bunker Hill, but for the most part his last years were spent quietly in the care of his family. He died on May 23, 1783, when a bolt of lightning struck him as he watched a thunderstorm at a friend's farm in Andover.

THOMAS PAINE

More than any other individual in the late eighteenth century, Thomas Paine fit the classic definition of radical "outside" agitator. His cause was world revolution for the "rights of man" against all forms of tyranny, and his weapon was an inflammatory pen. He had no permanent home and would hold citizenship in three separate countries: England, France, and the United States. He played an important role in the revolutions that swept two of those countries and tried to start one in the third. His repayment was banishment from England, imprisonment in France, and ostracism in the United States.

Paine was born in 1737, in Thetford, England, the son of a poor Quaker corset maker. Forced to leave school at age thirteen because of family poverty, he became an apprentice to his father and soon learned to hate both the monotony of his work and the ugliness of his poverty. These feelings would have a tremendous impact on his thinking and writing.

Between 1737 and 1774, Paine was married twice and worked as a corset maker, schoolteacher, tobacconist, grocer, and tax collector, or exciseman. His earliest political activity involved one of the first attempts to organize labor when he served as an agent for the excisemen in an attempt to get Parliament to raise their wages. For this effort he was summarily fired. Facing bankruptcy and ruin, Paine left for the New World in 1774.

Upon his arrival in Philadelphia, Paine was swept up in the revolutionary crisis and the radical thinking it generated. He became a prorevolutionary journalist and soon showed the world his brilliance. In January 1776, he published *Common Sense,* a pamphlet urging the colonists to declare their independence from a vicious, irrational British monarchy in order to maintain their natural liberties and to serve as a model for people throughout the world. As revolutionary as was this idea, so was the style of *Common Sense.* Eschewing the standard, aristocratic rules of writing, Paine used extremely simple and inflammatory rhetoric in an attempt to reach as wide an audience as possible. As a result, *Common Sense* sold an unprecedented 120,000 copies in the first few weeks after publication and 500,000 copies in total; it played a major role in coalescing public support for the Declaration of Independence.

During the war years, Paine also wrote a series of articles entitled *Crisis.* His opening statement, "These are the times that try men's souls," helped to hearten colonial spirits during the depressing first year of the war. He also supported the war effort by donating about a third of his salary to a relief fund for the Continental Army and by actually joining that force during its retreat through New Jersey.

Although he was financially rewarded for his work after the war, Paine, restless, returned to Europe in 1787 to promote an invention and world revolution against monarchies. He actively supported the French Revolution, and in his famous *The Rights of Man* argued that only a republican form of government could be trusted to ensure the individual his natural rights of life, liberty, property, security, and resistance to oppression.

Paine had hoped that *The Rights of Man* would convince the English to overthrow their king and follow the examples of the United States and France. Instead, it led to his being outlawed from his native land. He fled to France, where in 1792 he was granted citizenship and elected to the revolutionary French Assembly. But when his political allies fell from power in 1793, Paine was thrown into prison on the grounds, ironically, that he was a citizen of an England then at war with France. At the request of James Monroe, then American minister to Paris, he was released in 1794.

While in prison, Paine had composed the first part of his famous treatise *The Age of Reason;* in 1796, he completed it. A deist in religion, like many of his revolutionary contemporaries, Paine in his treatise attacked Christianity as irrational while promoting an enlightened, analytical, and rational approach to life.

By now an internationally known political writer, Paine returned to the United States in 1802. The reception was anything but friendly. His radical views on politics and religion, as well as his criticism of George Washington during the 1790s, had by this time lost him much of his popular support in America, and he spent the last seven years of his life fighting social ostracism as well as poverty and poor health. He mixed with radical rationalists but wrote no more major treatises before his death in New York in 1809.

SAMUEL SEABURY

Samuel Seabury was born in November 1729, the son of a Connecticut Congregational minister. Despite this background of being among dissenters in religion, Seabury became an active propagandist during his lifetime for both the Anglican Church and British sovereignty in North America. While his efforts for the latter cause ended in failure, he was highly successful after the Revolution in helping to establish the Episcopal Church in the United States.

Seabury had entered Yale, in 1744, with interests in both theology and medicine. He then studied at Edinburgh, where, in 1753, he completed studies in both areas and was ordained a priest in the Anglican Church. That body sent him to New York as a missionary for its Society for the Propagation of the Gospel.

The next few years were of great importance for Seabury's personal and professional life. He married, settled in Jamaica, and later moved to Westchester, New York. Along with his church duties, he also practiced medicine, opened a school, and actively promoted the cause of Anglicanism. Such promotion involved him in controversy over which church would control the proposed new King's College in New York (now Columbia University), in a campaign to secure American bishops for the English church, and in attacks upon those who dissented against a strong Anglican Church in America.

As the conflict with Parliament arose in the 1760s, Seabury and his colleagues also led a literary struggle to keep the colonists loyal to the Crown. In an important pamphlet that he signed "A. W. Farmer," he tried to convince Americans that their greatest freedom and good lay in submission and peaceful, orderly appeals to the British government. Alexander Hamilton, then a seventeen-year-old student at King's College, publicly attacked Seabury's writings and defended the patriot cause.

By 1775, Seabury was an active loyalist. He and his supporters tried first to prevent the election of committees to provincial and continental congresses and then to nullify the measures those bodies enacted. With the news of Lexington and Concord, Seabury and his colleagues were forced into hiding. Unwilling to remain confined, he surfaced and was taken prisoner and confined in New Haven for a month. Nine months later, in September 1776, he entered the British line on Long Island. Soon thereafter, he moved his family to New York City. For the remainder of the war, he would aid the British as a guide to army excursions on Long Island and in Westchester and as chaplain of the king's American regiment.

Despite the achievement of colonial independence, Seabury decided to stay in America and resume his efforts to build a strong Anglican Church. In 1784, he became the first American bishop of that church and began at once its revival and reorganization in the New World. His efforts led to the unification of the Scottish and English branches as the Episcopal Church.

Devoting himself wholeheartedly to building up the Episcopal Church in America, Seabury took no part in national politics. He died suddenly, in 1796, while making parish calls in New London, Connecticut.

Quote 1

Gentlemen, I have taken and repeatedly taken the oath of allegiance to King George the Third. I now profess to be one of his Majesty's most dutiful and loyal subjects, willing at all times to do my utmost in defense of his person, crown and dignity; I neither wish his death nor to remove him from the throne. . . . I pray for his life, that he may at a long distant day transmit the crown and sceptre to the only true and legal hereditary heir in the line of the royal house of Hanover. By convenanting in this paper "to go forth, to bear arms, and to repel force by force," I mean to act in terms of my oath of allegiance. His majesty has been misinformed, ill advised by some of our fellow subjects, who are his Majesty's enemies and the enemies of his faithful Americans. Against these I am willing, and shall be willing to bear arms and to repel force by force in any command suitable to my rank, when ever such shall appear in hostile acts against my country. Against every invader of our rights and liberties, I shall be ready to make all possible opposition.

Quote 2

Government by kings was first introduced into the world by the heathens, from whom the children of Israel copied the custom. It was the most prosperous invention the Devil ever set on foot for the promotion of idolatry. The heathens paid divine honors to their deceased kings, and the Christian world has improved on the plan by doing the same to their living ones. How impious is the title of sacred Majesty applied to a worm, who in the midst of his splendor is crumbling into dust! . . . It is repugnant to reason, to the universal order of things, to all examples from former ages, to suppose that this continent can long remain subject to any external power.

Quote 3

Will you be instrumental in bringing the most abject slavery on yourselves? Will you choose such Committees? Will you submit to them, should they be chosen by the weak, foolish, turbulent part of the country people? — Do as you please but, by HIM that made me, I will not — No, if I must be enslaved, let it be by a King at least, and not by a parcel of upstart, lawless Committee-men. If I must be devoured, let me be devoured by the Jaws of a lion, and not *gnawed* to death by rats and vermin.

Quote 4

The Parliament unquestionably possesses a legal authority to regulate the trade of Great Britain and all her colonies. Such an authority is essential to the relation between a mother country and her colonies; and necessary for the common good of all. . . . I have looked over every statute relating to these colonies from their first settlement to this time, and I find every one of them founded on this principle, till the Stamp Act administration. All before are calculated to regulate trade and preserve or promote a mutually beneficial intercourse between the several constituent parts of the empire. And though many of them imposed duties on trade, yet those duties were always imposed with design to restrain the commerce of one part that was injurious to another, and thus to promote the general welfare. The raising a revenue thereby was never intended . . . . Never did the British Parliament, till the period above mentioned, think of imposing duties in America for the purpose of raising revenue.

Quote 5

The Colonists being men, have a right to be considered as equally entitled to all the rights of nature with the Europeans, and they are not to be restrained, in the exercise of any of these rights, but for the evident good of the whole community.

By being or becoming members of society, they have not renounced their natural liberty in any great degree than other good citizens, and if tis taken from them without their consent, they are so far enslaved.

They have an undoubted right to expect, that their best good will ever be consulted by their rulers, supreme and subordinate, without any partial views confined to the particular interest of one island or another. Neither the riches of Jamaica, nor the luxury of the Metropolis, should ever have weight enough to break the balance of truth and justice. Truth and faith belong to men as men, from men, and if they are disappointed in their just expectations of them in one society, they will at least wish for them in another. If love of truth and justice, the only spring of sound policy in any state, is not strong enough to prevent certain causes from taking place, the arts of fraud and force will not prevent the most fatal effects.

Quote 6

The town of Boston is the source from whence all the other parts of the province derive more or less troubled water. When you consider what is called its constitution, your good sense will determine immediately that it never can be otherwise for a long time together, whilst the majority, which conducts all affairs, if met together upon another occasion, would properly be called a mob, and are persons of such rank and circumstance as in all communities constitute a mob, there being no sort of regulation of voters in practice; and as these will always be most in number, men of weight and value, although they wish to suppress them, cannot be inducted to attempt to do it for fear not only of being outvoted, but affronted and insulted. Call such an assembly what you will, it is really no sort of government, not even a democracy, at best a corruption of it. There is no hope of a cure [except . . .] to compel the town to be a corporation. The people will not seek it, because everyone is sensible his importance will be lessened. If ever a remedy is found, it must be by compelling them to swallow it, and that by an exterior power—the Parliament.

Quote 7

But as the Americans in general have lost sight of their object, and Congress have in some measure out-lived their dignity, and vested most of their powers in the hands of artful and avaricious men, it may be long before we see a nervous, equal, systematical administration of government. This people are marked with characters too distinct for unison; we talk high of the excellency of the republican system, and our legislatures are established on this liberal plan, while in principles and manners and in fashion, monarchic habits mark many characters.

The consequences of this absurdity appear at once in the want of consistency and decision in design, and uniformity and vigour in execution through the higher departments; as well as in that servility of mind and that insolence of imagined independence which has nearly destroyed the proper ideas of subordination, decency, and civility among the lower classes. The truth is, so far has this country deviated from the principles, manners, and spirit that instigated an opposition to Britain, and so dazzled are many with the splendor of courts, the parade of armies, the pride and pomp of war, the soft indulgencies of sudden affluence, and the reigning taste for luxurious and expensive pleasures, that they are prepared to ask a King, though a voice from heaven denounced as to the ungrateful Israelites that their sons should run before his chariots.

You have doubtless seen by the American papers that there has been a project for a tax through the Continent by an impost of five per cent of all articles of commerce, this to be payed by the importer on the arrival of his goods. It was to have been a permanent revenue to be appropriated without controul or inquiry as Congress should see fit.

This measure was not to be inforced without the consent of the representatives of the people by each legislature making it an act of their own. There has been little difficulty to obtain a compliance except in the small state of Rhode Island, who have stood alone in opposition till most of the other States begin to be sick of the project.

This country is at present under a cloud that may not suddenly be dissipated—the morals of the people are depreciated, private engagements evaded and public credit suffers:—but as the conduct of mankind in all ages depends much on the character and genius of their leaders, there may yet appear some in America who have capacity enough to form the manners of the people and virtue enough to save their contemporaries from irretrievable ruin in consequence of the inexperience, the weakness, the extravagance, the venality and supple complaisance of their predecessors.

But the political stars either in the southern or more northern hemisphere do not at present augur such an happy revolution in favour of purer morals or more energetic government; the cities are setting up the work of their own hands and making for themselves Gods, regardless of the secret Hand that directs the wheels of revolution and throws down the proudest Empires. Yet the modern idols differ in one point from the favorite images we have read of in sacred story, for the heads of most of them seem to be of the same clay materials with the feet—and if I am not mistaken in the prophecies, several of them will be scattered as the chaff of the summer threshing floor.

The history of all ages has taught us that the wind of popular fame is much less stable than the hurricane that sweeps down both the cedar and the thistle; yet by a strange concurrence of circumstances we often see, after the most violent struggles in favour of civil liberty, all authority is vested in the hand of the weakest or the wickedest, who perhaps were only called in the beginning of the conflict to aid in pulling down the more gigantic abetters of tyranny;—men who are better qualified for the glare of royal pageantry, the managers of a play-house, or the patrons of a ball room than for the first magistrates of a free republic whose manners ought to be simple and their morals uncorrupt.

Quote 8

The spirit of the English constitution has yet a little influence left, and but a little. The remains of it, however, will give the wealthy people a superiority this time, but would they secure it they must banish all school-masters and confine all knowledge to themselves. This cannot be. The mob begin to think and to reason. Poor reptiles! It is with them a vernal morning; they are struggling to cast off their winter's slough, they bask in the sunshine, and ere noon they will bite, depend upon it. The gentry begin to fear this. Their committee will be appointed, they will deceive the people and again forfeit a share of their confidence. And if these instances of what with one side is policy, with the other perfidy, shall continue to increase and become more frequent, farewell aristocracy. I see, and I see it with fear and trembling, that if the disputes with Great Britain continue, we shall be under the worst of all possible dominions; we shall be under the domination of a riotous mob.

Quote 9

Dear Brother,

When I came home from Newport and heard of a Vessel or Two being Armd & fitted & gone Out to Cruise for Vessels &c I feard whither thou Might not be Still led further a Side from thy Duty by the Same Delusive Spirit and have Sinse heard that thou hast been so far Concernd therein as greatly to

Affect Me as well as thy Self which is the more Imediate Ocation of this Letter As I have not claimd any Merrit to Myself thro My Journey to Boston, I will yet avoid it as far as Possible and only lay the Case before thee for Determination weither or know My Character as a person profesing Religion will not suffer and insted of that Sincerity & Honnesty thou knows I was tho't to have in Boston I shal not be thot to be a Deciver & Hippocrite if thy Conduct Turns out so Contrary to What thou Engaged and I was a Voucher & Surety for? this Hurt to me as a Man only I could bear, but my religious profession & faithful Brethren which are nearer than any thing in my Life to Me are by me in this View Reproachd allso and which at this time when We as a people can not Stand between the Violence of Two parties but by Our Sincerity and faithfulness to the Leadings of that Divine Principal of Truth which we profess to follow is truely a distressing Consideration to Me. . . .

4

THE FOUNDING FATHERS AND THE AMERICAN STATE PAPERS

DOCUMENT ANALYSIS FROM THE CONSTITUTIONAL ERA

By historical standards, the United States is a young nation. Yet it is governed by the oldest written constitution in the world. No other country has used a single frame of government for close to two hundred years, and few societies have been so devoted to constitutionalism or the rule of law in institutionalizing change.

This raises a host of fascinating questions regarding the American political system. However, before any of those questions can be answered properly, a detailed knowledge of the form of government set up by the Founding Fathers, and of the reasons for their action, is first necessary.

Your textbook describes the factors that led to the calling of the Constitutional Convention, the conflicts that emerged during that convention, and the compromises that ensued. One purpose of this chapter is to make sure you understand the constitutional system *as the Founding Fathers created it and envisaged it working* (it works quite differently today).

The writers of the Constitution wanted to create a system of government strong enough to protect their newly won republican liberties against any internal or external threats but not so strong as to become tyrannical itself and thereby destroy the very freedoms it had been designed to protect. Their unique solution to this old problem was to concentrate power in the hands of a central government while simultaneously dispersing that power *within* its different branches and *between* the new central and the old state governments. The dispersion within the government's branches is known as the *separation* of powers; that between it and the states is known as the *division* of powers.

The logic behind this system of "checks and balances," and with it the reasoning of the Founding Fathers, was best described in an extraordinary series of newspaper articles written in 1787–88 by Alexander Hamilton, John Jay, and James Madison in an effort to convince New Yorkers to ratify the new Constitution. Known today as the Federalist papers, these eighty-five articles are among the most brilliant constitutional and political expositions in American history. They are also an extraordinary primary source capable of providing exceptional insights into the minds of the writers of the Constitution. Reprinted at the end of this chapter are four of the most famous of these papers, numbers 10 (Madison), 15 (Hamilton), 23 (Hamilton), and 51 (Madison).

As with many primary sources, the Constitution and the Federalist papers are often misunderstood by later generations because they fail to take into account the attitudes and beliefs of the era in which the documents were written or the specific events that heavily influenced the authors of the documents. These attitudes, beliefs, and events are quite different from the ones that influence us today, and any effort to understand past documents without recognizing the influence of these factors will lead to distortion and misunderstanding. When the Founding Fathers used the word "democracy," for example, it called up images of mass tyranny or mob rule, a hysterical society willing to trample on the rights of individuals and eventually to give up its own rights to a tyrant who made grandiose promises. Similarly, their definitions of "republicanism," "liberty," "federalism," and "factionalism" differed from those we hold today, as did their reactions to paper money, mortgage foreclosures, boundary disputes, and trade restrictions. To understand the meaning of any document, one must read it in the context of these past definitions and reactions, not our own.

Documents, as you learned in Chapter 2, must be understood within their *historical context*. To rip them out of that context and read them from our own vantage point today is to create not history but a self-serving mythology. The Founding Fathers did indeed have posterity in mind when they wrote, but their primary purpose was to serve the needs of their own people in their own time, and the primary influences on them were of eighteenth, not twentieth-century origin. The exercises that follow are designed to make you aware of these influences and thus capable of understanding the constitutional system as envisaged by the Founding Fathers.

ASSIGNMENTS

1. After completing your assigned textbook reading, carefully read the Declaration of Independence and the original Constitution, which are reprinted in the back of your textbook, and the four Federalist papers reproduced at the end of this chapter. Summarize the key points in those papers as they relate to the need for a new frame of government and to the general principles behind the checks-and-balances system. To make sure you understand the Federalist papers in their own as opposed to our context, define the differences Madison and Hamilton would make between a democracy and a republic and between a confederation, a national government, and a federal government. To make sure you understand the workings of their checks-and-balances system, compare and contrast the constitutional provisions for the different branches of the federal government in terms of the following: who is eligible to hold the offices set up, who selects the individuals to hold these offices, how often they are selected and by what process, what powers each branch of government holds, what checks each possesses over other branches, and what powers are specifically prohibited.
2. Your written assignment is to apply your knowledge of the constitutional system to a specific problem. Listed below are four hypothetical situations. Choose one or more of them as instructed by your professor and use the information from the text, the Constitution, and the reprinted Federalist papers to answer the four specific questions pertaining to that situation. Since this assignment concerns understanding the Constitution within the context of its time, you are *not* to consider any of the amendments as part of the document or any government practices that developed at a later date as part of the original system.

HYPOTHETICAL SITUATIONS

1. Farmers in debt in western Massachusetts form an angry mob to forcibly prevent the courts from foreclosing on their mortgages. Local militia sent out by the governor to stop them wind up joining the mob instead. This armed group then marches on the state legislature and threatens physical violence if immediate relief is not forthcoming.

   a. What specific measures would these farmers have demanded from their state legislature before ratification of the Constitution?
   b. Under what provisions of the Constitution would such measures be illegal?
   c. What specific powers does each branch of the federal government have to stop this mob action?
   d. Why, according to James Madison, could these farmers never get the federal government to agree to their demands on a national level?

2. At the specific request of the secretary of the treasury, Congress and the president approve a series of measures designed to place the financial structure of the new nation on a sound footing. These measures include a series of taxes and tariffs to raise revenue for government operations and to pay off

the national debt, a new currency, and the creation of a national bank to oversee the country's financial structure. Within the space of a few months, it becomes apparent to a considerable number of Americans that this system has completely fallen into the hands of a small group of corrupt bankers and speculators and that this faction is in effect manipulating the country's financial structure to its benefit and to the detriment of everyone else.

a. What specific actions could be taken by the legislative branch of the federal government to stop this faction?
b. What specific actions could be taken by the executive branch of the federal government to stop this faction?
c. What specific actions could be taken by the judicial branch of the federal government to stop this faction?
d. If these branches have all been bribed into inaction, what legal recourse do the people have?

3. A European power with possessions bordering the United States refuses to recognize America's boundaries or to open her overseas empire to American trade. While Congress is in adjournment, word arrives that this power is inciting Indian attacks and secessionist movements along the American frontier.

a. What actions could the president take without calling a special session of Congress?
b. If those actions failed and the president then did decide to call Congress into special session, what actions, short of war, could that body take?
c. What would happen if the president and Congress disagreed as to proper action?
d. What steps would be taken if they agreed that war was necessary?

4. As a result of the scenario sketched out in the previous situation, the United States goes to war—over the vehement objections of a vocal minority. In response to continued antiwar statements by that minority, a panicky Congress passes a series of bills virtually outlawing internal dissent for the duration of the conflict.

a. To which branches of the federal government can dissenters turn to regain their freedoms?
b. How can those branches act?
c. If they refuse to act, can a state legislature opposed to the war take any action?
d. Do dissenters have any other legal recourse?

ALTERNATIVE ASSIGNMENTS

1. While the Constitution and the Federalist papers are written in general terms, any reader in 1787–88 would have realized that the provisions and arguments enunciated reflected concern with specific problems that had emerged under the Articles of Confederation. As an alternative assignment, identify those problems from your textbook readings and class notes, and for each one cite

the relevant passages in the Federalist papers and the constitutional provisions designed to prevent a repetition. In retrospect, did these provisions prevent a repetition of the problems as the Founding Fathers had anticipated? Why?

2. Although Hamilton and Madison collaborated on the Federalist papers and the ratification debate, they soon disagreed on interpretation of the new Constitution and became political opponents. As an alternative assignment, compare their individual Federalist papers and explain in a brief essay how these papers illustrate disagreements beneath the surface that would soon emerge.

ADDITIONAL QUESTIONS TO CONSIDER

1. All four of the "hypothetical situations" given above are based on events that actually took place between 1787 and 1800. Can you identify them? If so, compare the answers you gave to the specific questions with what actually took place and account for the differences.
2. In what ways does the actual constitutional system today differ from what was envisaged in 1787? Why have such differences emerged?
3. Read the amendments that have been added to the Constitution since 1787. Why was each one added, and what have been the repercussions of the changes emanating from each amendment?
4. Compare the Declaration of Independence with the original Constitution. What is the relationship between these two documents?

No. 10: Madison

AMONG the numerous advantages promised by a well-constructed Union, none deserves to be more accurately developed than its tendency to break and control the violence of faction. The friend of popular governments never finds himself so much alarmed for their character and fate as when he contemplates their propensity to this dangerous vice. He will not fail, therefore, to set a due value on any plan which, without violating the principles to which he is attached, provides a proper cure for it. The instability, injustice, and confusion introduced into the public councils have, in truth, been the mortal diseases under which popular governments have everywhere perished, as they continue to be the favorite and fruitful topics from which the adversaries to liberty derive their most specious declamations. The valuable improvements made by the American constitutions on the popular models, both ancient and modern, cannot certainly be too much admired; but it would be an unwarrantable partiality to contend that they have as effectually obviated the danger on this side, as was wished and expected. Complaints are everywhere heard from our most considerate and virtuous citizens, equally the friends of public and private faith and of public and personal liberty, that our governments are too unstable, that the public good is disregarded in the conflicts of rival parties, and that measures are too often decided, not according to the rules of justice and the rights of the minor party, but by the superior force of an interested and overbearing majority. However anxiously we may wish that these complaints had no foundation, the evidence of known facts will not permit us to deny that they are in some degree true. It will be found, indeed, on a candid review of our situation, that some of the distresses under which we labor have been erroneously charged on the operation of our governments; but it will be found, at the same time, that other causes will not alone account for many of our heaviest misfortunes; and, particularly, for that prevailing and increasing distrust of public engagements and alarm for private rights which are echoed from one end of the continent to the other. These must be chiefly, if not wholly, effects of the unsteadiness and injustice with which a factious spirit has tainted our public administration.

By a faction I understand a number of citizens, whether amounting to a majority or minority of the whole, who are united and actuated by some common impulse of passion, or of interest, adverse to the rights of other citizens, or to the permanent and aggregate interests of the community.

There are two methods of curing the mischiefs of faction: the one, by removing its causes; the other, by controlling its effects.

There are again two methods of removing the causes of faction: the one, by destroying the liberty which is essential to its existence; the other, by giving to every citizen the same opinions, the same passions, and the same interests.

It could never be more truly said than of the first remedy that it was worse than the disease. Liberty is to faction what air is to fire, an aliment without which it instantly expires. But it could not be a less folly to abolish liberty, which is essential to political life, because it nourishes faction than it would be to wish the annihilation of air, which is essential to animal life, because it imparts to fire its destructive agency.

The second expedient is as impracticable as the first would be unwise. As long as the reason of man continues fallible, and he is at liberty to exercise it, different opinions will be formed. As long as the connection subsists between his reason and his self-love, his opinions and his passions will have a reciprocal influence on each other; and the former will be objects to which the latter will attach themselves. The diversity in the faculties of men, from which the rights of property originate, is not less an insuperable obstacle to a uniformity of interests. The protection of these faculties is the first object of government. From the protection of different and unequal faculties of acquiring property, the possession of different degrees and kinds of property immediately results; and from the influence of these on the sentiments and views of the respective proprietors ensues a division of the society into different interests and parties.

The latent causes of faction are thus sown in the nature of man; and we see them everywhere brought into different degrees of activity, according to the different circumstances of civil society. A zeal for different opinions concerning religion, concerning government, and many other points, as well of speculation as of practice; an attachment to different leaders ambitiously contending for pre-eminence and power; or to persons of other descriptions whose fortunes have been interesting to the human passions, have, in turn, divided mankind into parties, inflamed them with mutual animosity, and rendered them much more disposed to vex and oppress each other than to co-operate for their common good. So strong is this propensity of mankind to fall into mutual animosities that where no substantial occasion presents itself the most frivolous and fanciful distinctions have been sufficient to kindle their unfriendly passions and excite their most violent conflicts. But the most common and durable source of factions has been the various and unequal distribution of property. Those who hold and those who are without property have ever formed distinct interests in society. Those who are creditors, and those who are debtors, fall under a like discrimination. A landed interest, a manufacturing interest, a mercantile interest, a moneyed interest, with many lesser interests, grow up of necessity in civilized nations, and divide them into different classes, actuated by different sentiments and views. The regulation of these various and interfering interests forms the principal task of modern legislation and involves the spirit of party and faction in the necessary and ordinary operations of government.

No man is allowed to be a judge in his own cause, because his interest would certainly bias his judgment, and, not improbably, corrupt his integrity. With equal, nay with greater reason, a body of men are unfit to be both judges and parties at the same time; yet what are many of the most important acts of legislation but so many judicial determinations, not indeed concerning the rights of single persons, but concerning the rights of large bodies of citizens? And what are the different classes of legislators but advocates and parties to the causes which they determine? Is a law proposed concerning private debts? It is a question to which the creditors are parties on one side and the debtors on the other. Justice ought to hold the balance between them. Yet the parties are, and must be, themselves the judges; and the most numerous party, or in other words, the most powerful faction must be expected to prevail. Shall domestic manufacturers be encouraged, and in what degree, by restrictions on foreign manufacturers? are questions which would be differently decided by the landed and the manufacturing classes, and probably by neither with a sole regard to justice and the public good. The apportionment of taxes on the various descriptions of property is an act which seems to require the most exact impartiality; yet there is, perhaps, no legislative act in which greater opportunity and temptation are given to a predominant party to trample on the rules of justice. Every shilling with which they overburden the inferior number is a shilling saved to their own pockets.

It is in vain to say that enlightened statesmen will be able to adjust these clashing interests and render them all subservient to the public good. Enlightened statesmen will not always be at the helm. Nor, in many cases, can such an adjustment be made at all without taking into view indirect and remote considerations, which will rarely prevail over the immediate interest which one party may find in disregarding the rights of another or the good of the whole.

The inference to which we are brought is that the *causes* of faction cannot be removed and that relief is only to be sought in the means of controlling its *effects.*

If a faction consists of less than a majority, relief is supplied by the republican principle, which enables the majority to defeat its sinister views by regular vote. It may clog the administration, it may convulse the society; but it will be unable to execute and mask its violence under the forms of the Constitution. When a majority is included in a faction, the form of popular government, on the other hand, enables it to sacrifice to its ruling passion or interest both the public good and the rights of other citizens. To secure the public good and private rights against the danger of such a faction, and at the same time to preserve the spirit and the form of popular government, is then the great object to which our inquiries are directed. Let me add that it is the great desideratum by which alone this form of government can be rescued from the opprobrium under which it has so long labored and be recommended to the esteem and adoption of mankind.

By what means is this object attainable? Evidently by one of two only. Either the existence of the same passion or interest in a majority at the same time must be prevented, or the majority, having such coexistent passion or interest, must be rendered, by their number and local situation, unable to concert and carry into effect schemes of oppression. If the impulse and the opportunity be suffered to coincide, we well know that neither moral nor religious motives can be relied on as an adequate control. They are not found to be such on the injustice and violence of individuals, and lose their efficacy in proportion to the number combined together, that is, in proportion as their efficacy becomes needful.

From this view of the subject it may be concluded that a pure democracy, by which I mean a society consisting of a small number of citizens, who assemble and administer the government in person, can admit of no cure for the mischiefs of faction. A common passion or interest will, in almost every case, be felt by a majority of the whole; a communication and concert results from the form of government itself; and there is nothing to check the inducements to sacrifice the weaker party or an obnoxious individual. Hence it is that such democracies have ever been spectacles of turbulence and contention; have ever been found incompatible with personal security or the rights of property; and have in general been as short in their lives as they have been violent in their deaths. Theoretic politicians, who have patronized this species of government, have erroneously supposed that by reducing mankind to a perfect equality in their political rights, they would at the same time be perfectly equalized and assimilated in their possessions, their opinions, and their passions.

A republic, by which I mean a government in which the scheme of representation takes place, opens a different prospect and promises the cure for which we are seeking. Let us examine the points in which it varies from pure democracy, and we shall comprehend both the nature of the cure and the efficacy which it must derive from the Union.

The two great points of difference between a democracy and a republic are: first, the delegation of the government, in the latter, to a small number of citizens elected by the rest; secondly, the greater number of citizens and greater sphere of country over which the latter may be extended.

The effect of the first difference is, on the one hand, to refine and enlarge the public views by passing them through the medium of a chosen body of citizens, whose wisdom may best discern the true interest of their country and whose patriotism and love of justice will be least likely to sacrifice it to temporary or partial considerations. Under such a regulation it may well happen that the public voice, pronounced by the representatives of the people, will be more consonant to the public good than if pronounced by the people themselves, convened for the purpose. On the other hand, the effect may be inverted. Men of factious tempers, of local prejudices, or of sinister designs, may, by intrigue, by corruption, or by other means, first obtain the suffrages, and then betray the interests of the people. The question resulting is, whether small or extensive republics are most favorable to the election of proper guardians of the public weal; and it is clearly decided in favor of the latter by two obvious considerations.

In the first place it is to be remarked that however small the republic may be the representatives must be raised to a certain number in order to guard against the cabals of a few; and that however large it may be they must be limited to a certain number in order to guard against the confusion of a multitude. Hence, the number of representatives in the two cases not being in proportion to that of the constituents, and being proportionally greatest in the small republic, it follows that if the proportion of fit characters be not less in the large than in the small republic, the former will present a greater option, and consequently a greater probability of a fit choice.

In the next place, as each representative will be chosen by a greater number of citizens in the large than in the small republic, it will be more difficult for unworthy candidates to practise with success the vicious arts by which elections are too often carried; and the suffrages of the people being more free, will be more likely to center on men who possess the most attractive merit and the most diffusive and established characters.

It must be confessed that in this, as in most other cases, there is a mean, on both sides of which inconveniencies will be found to lie. By enlarging too much the number of electors, you render the representative too little acquainted with all their local circumstances and lesser interests; as by reducing it too much, you render him unduly attached to these, and too little fit to comprehend and pursue great and national objects. The federal Constitution forms a happy combination in this respect; the great and aggregate interests being referred to the national, the local and particular to the State legislatures.

The other point of difference is the greater number of citizens and extent of territory which may be brought within the compass of republican than of democratic government; and it is this circumstance principally which renders factious combinations less to be dreaded in the former than in the latter. The smaller the society, the fewer probably will be the distinct parties and interests composing it; the fewer the distinct parties and interests, the more frequently will a majority be found of the same party; and the smaller the number of individuals composing a majority, and the smaller the compass within which they are placed, the more easily will they concert and execute their plans of oppression. Extend the sphere and you take in a greater variety of parties and interests; you make it less probable that a majority of the whole will have a common motive to invade the rights of other citizens; or if such a common motive exists, it will be more difficult for all who feel it to discover their own strength and to act in unison with each other. Besides other impediments, it may be remarked that, where there is a consciousness of unjust or dishonorable purposes, communication is always checked by distrust in proportion to the number whose concurrence is necessary.

Hence, it clearly appears that the same advantage which a republic has over a democracy in controlling the effects of faction is enjoyed by a large over a small republic—is enjoyed by the Union over the States composing it. Does this advantage consist in the substitution of representatives whose enlightened views and virtuous sentiments render them superior to local prejudices and to schemes of injustice? It will not be denied that the representation of the Union will be most likely to possess these requisite endowments. Does it consist in the greater security afforded by a greater variety of parties, against the event of any one party being able to outnumber and oppress the rest? In an equal degree does the increased variety of parties comprised within the Union increase this security. Does it, in fine, consist in the greater obstacles opposed to the concert and accomplishment of the secret wishes of an unjust and interested majority? Here again the extent of the Union gives it the most palpable advantage.

The influence of factious leaders may kindle a flame within their particular States but will be unable to spread a general conflagration through the other States. A religious sect may degenerate into a political faction in a part of the Confederacy; but the variety of sects dispersed over the entire face of it must secure the national councils against any danger from that source. A rage for paper money, for an abolition of debts, for an equal division of property, or for any other improper or wicked project, will be less apt to pervade the whole body of the Union than a particular member of it, in the same proportion as such a malady is more likely to taint a particular county or district than an entire State.

In the extent and proper structure of the Union, therefore, we behold a republican remedy for the diseases most incident to republican government. And according to the degree of pleasure and pride we feel in being republicans ought to be our zeal in cherishing the spirit and supporting the character of federalists.

PUBLIUS

No. 15: Hamilton

IN THE course of the preceding papers I have endeavored, my fellow-citizens, to place before you in a clear and convincing light the importance of Union to your political safety and happiness. I have unfolded to you a complication of dangers to which you would be exposed, should you permit that sacred knot which binds the people of America together to be severed or dissolved by ambition or by avarice, by jealousy or by misrepresentation. In the sequel of the inquiry through which I propose to accompany you, the truths intended to be inculcated will receive further confirmation from facts and arguments hitherto unnoticed. If the road over which you will still have to pass should in some places appear to you tedious or irksome, you will recollect that you are in quest of information on a subject the most momentous which can engage the attention of a free people, that the field through which you have to travel is in itself spacious, and that the difficulties of the journey have been unnecessarily increased by the mazes with which sophistry has beset the way. It will be my aim to remove the obstacles to your progress in as compendious a manner as it can be done, without sacrificing utility to dispatch.

In pursuance of the plan which I have laid down for the discussion of the subject, the point next in order to be examined is the "insufficiency of the present Confederation to the preservation of the Union." It may perhaps be asked what need there is of reasoning or proof to illustrate a position which is not either controverted or doubted, to which the understandings and feelings of all classes of men assent, and which in substance is admitted by the opponents as well as by the friends of the new Constitution. It must in truth be acknowledged that, however these may differ in other respects, they in general appear to harmonize in this sentiment at least: that there are material imperfections in our national system and that something is necessary to be done to rescue us from impending anarchy. The facts that support this opinion are no longer objects of speculation. They have forced themselves upon the sensibility of the people at large, and have at length extorted from those, whose mistaken policy has had the principal share in precipitating the extremity at which we are arrived, a reluctant confession of the reality of those defects in the scheme of our federal government which have been long pointed out and regretted by the intelligent friends of the Union.

We may indeed with propriety be said to have reached almost the last stage of national humiliation. There is scarcely anything that can wound the pride or degrade the character of an independent nation which we do not experience. Are there engagements to the performance of which we are held by every tie respectable among men? These are the subjects of constant and unblushing violation. Do we owe debts to foreigners and to our own citizens contracted in a time of imminent peril for the preservation of our political existence? These remain without any proper or satisfactory provision for their discharge. Have we valuable territories and important posts in the possession of a foreign power which, by express stipulations, ought long since to have been surrendered? These are still retained to the prejudice of our interests, not less than of our rights. Are we in a condition to resent or to repel the aggression? We have neither troops, nor treasury, nor government.* Are we even in a condition to remonstrate with dignity? The just imputations on our own faith in respect to the same treaty ought first to be removed. Are we entitled by nature and compact to a free participation in the navigation of the Mississippi? Spain excludes us from it. Is public credit an indispensable resource in time of public danger? We seem to have abandoned its cause as desperate and irretrievable. Is commerce of importance to national wealth? Ours is at the lowest point of declension. Is respectability in the eyes of foreign powers a safeguard against foreign encroachments? The imbecility of our government even forbids them to treat with us. Our ambassadors abroad are the mere pageants of mimic sovereignty. Is a violent and unnatural decrease in the value of land a symptom of national distress? The price of improved land in most parts of the country is much lower than can be accounted for by the quantity of waste land at market, and can only be fully explained by that want of private and public confidence, which are so alarmingly prevalent among all ranks and which have a direct tendency to depreciate property of every kind. Is private credit the friend and patron of industry? That most useful kind which relates to borrowing and lending is reduced within the narrowest limits, and this still more from an opinion of insecurity than from a scarcity of money. To shorten an enumeration of particulars which can afford neither pleasure

*"I mean for the Union."

nor instruction, it may in general be demanded, what indication is there of national disorder, poverty, and insignificance that could befall a community so peculiarly blessed with natural advantages as we are, which does not form a part of the dark catalogue of our public misfortunes?

This is the melancholy situation to which we have been brought by those very maxims and counsels which would now deter us from adopting the proposed Constitution; and which, not content with having conducted us to the brink of a precipice, seem resolved to plunge us into the abyss that awaits us below. Here, my countrymen, impelled by every motive that ought to influence an enlightened people, let us make a firm stand for our safety, our tranquillity, our dignity, our reputation. Let us at last break the fatal charm which has too long seduced us from the paths of felicity and prosperity.

It is true, as has been before observed, that facts too stubborn to be resisted have produced a species of general assent to the abstract proposition that there exist material defects in our national system; but the usefulness of the concession on the part of the old adversaries of federal measures is destroyed by a strenuous opposition to a remedy upon the only principles that can give it a chance of success. While they admit that the government of the United States is destitute of energy, they contend against conferring upon it those powers which are requisite to supply that energy. They seem still to aim at things repugnant and irreconcilable; at an augmentation of federal authority without a diminution of State authority; at sovereignty in the Union and complete independence in the members. They still, in fine, seem to cherish with blind devotion the political monster of an *imperium in imperio.* This renders a full display of the principal defects of the Confederation necessary in order to show that the evils we experience do not proceed from minute or partial imperfections, but from fundamental errors in the structure of the building, which cannot be amended otherwise than by an alteration in the first principles and main pillars of the fabric.

The great and radical vice in the construction of the existing Confederation is in the principle of LEGISLATION for STATES OF GOVERNMENTS, in their CORPORATE OR COLLECTIVE CAPACITIES, and as contradistinguished from the INDIVIDUALS of whom they consist. Though this principle does not run through all the powers delegated to the Union, yet it pervades and governs those on which the efficacy of the rest depends. Except as to the rule of apportionment, the United States have an indefinite discretion to make requisitions for men and money; but they have no authority to raise either by regulations extending to the individual citizens of America. The consequence of this is that though in theory their resolutions concerning those objects are laws constitutionally binding on the members of the Union, yet in practice they are mere recommendations which the States observe or disregard at their option.

It is a singular instance of the capriciousness of the human mind that after all the admonitions we have had from experience on this head, there should still be found men who object to the new Constitution for deviating from a principle which has been found the bane of the old and which is in itself evidently incompatible with the idea of GOVERNMENT; a principle, in short, which, if it is to be executed at all, must substitute the violent and sanguinary agency of the sword to the mild influence of the magistracy.

There is nothing absurd or impracticable in the idea of a league or alliance between independent nations for certain defined purposes precisely stated in a treaty regulating all the details of time, place, circumstance, and quantity, leaving nothing to future discretion, and depending for its execution on the good faith of the parties. Compacts of this kind exist among all civilized nations, subject to the usual vicissitudes of peace and war, of observance and nonobservance, as the interests or passions of the contracting powers dictate. In the early part of the present century there was an epidemical rage in Europe for this species of compacts, from which the politicians of the times fondly hoped for benefits which were never realized. With a view to establishing the equilibrium of power and the peace of that part of the world, all the resources of negotiations were exhausted, and triple and quadruple alliances were formed; but they were scarcely formed before they were broken, giving an instructive but afflicting lesson to mankind how little dependence is to be placed on treaties which have no other sanction than the obligations of good faith, and which oppose general considerations of peace and justice to the impulse of any immediate interest or passion.

If the particular States in this country are disposed to stand in a similar relation to each other, and to drop the project of a general DISCRETIONARY SUPERINTENDENCE, the scheme would indeed be pernicious and would entail upon us all the mischiefs which have been enumerated under the first head; but it would have the merit of being, at least, consistent and practicable. Abandoning all views towards a confederate government, this would bring us to a simple alliance offensive and defensive; and would place us in a situation to be alternate friends and enemies of each other, as our mutual jealousies and rivalships, nourished by the intrigues of foreign nations, should prescribe to us.

But if we are unwilling to be placed in this perilous situation; if we still will adhere to the design of a national government, or, which is the same thing, of a superintending power under the direction of a common council, we must resolve to incorporate into our plan those ingredients which may be considered as forming the characteristic difference between a league and a government; we must extend the authority of the Union to the persons of the citizens —the only proper objects of government.

Government implies the power of making laws. It is essential to the idea of a law that it be attended with a sanction; or, in other words, a penalty or punishment for disobedience. If there be no penalty annexed to disobedience, the resolutions or commands which pretend to be laws will, in fact, amount to nothing more than advice or recommendation. This penalty, whatever it may be, can only be inflicted in two ways: by the agency of the courts and ministers of justice, or by military force; by the COERCION of the magistracy, or by the COERCION of arms. The first kind can evidently apply only to men; the last kind must of necessity be employed against bodies politic, or communities, or States. It is evident that there is no process of a court by which the observance of the laws can in the last resort be enforced. Sentences may be denounced against them for violations of their duty; but these sentences can only be carried into execution by the sword. In an association where the general authority is confined to the collective bodies of the communities that compose it, every breach of the laws must involve a state of war; and military execution must become the only instrument of civil obedience. Such a state of things can certainly not deserve the name of government, nor would any prudent man choose to commit his happiness to it.

There was a time when we were told that breaches by the States of the regulations of the federal authority were not to be expected; that a sense of common interest would preside over the conduct of the respective members, and would beget a full compliance with all the constitutional requisitions of the Union. This language, at the present day, would appear as wild as a great part of what we now hear from the same quarter will be thought, when we shall have received further lessons from that best oracle of wisdom, experience. It at all times betrayed an ignorance of the true springs by which human conduct is actuated, and belied the original inducements to the establishment of civil power. Why has government been instituted at all? Because the passions of men will not conform to the dictates of reason and justice without constraint. Has it been found that bodies of men act with more rectitude or greater disinterestedness than individuals? The contrary of this has been inferred by all accurate observers of the conduct of mankind; and the inference is founded upon obvious reasons. Regard to reputation has a less active influence when the infamy of a bad action is to be divided among a number than when it is to fall singly upon one. A spirit of faction, which is apt to mingle its poison in the deliberations of all bodies of men, will often hurry the persons of whom they are composed into improprieties and excesses for which they would blush in a private capacity.

In addition to all this, there is in the nature of sovereign power an impatience of control that disposes those who are invested with the exercise of it to look with an evil eye upon all external attempts to restrain or direct its operations. From this spirit it happens that in every political association which is formed upon the principle of uniting in a common interest a number of lesser sovereignties, there will be found a kind of eccentric tendency in the subordinate or inferior orbs by the operation of which there will be a perpetual effort in each to fly off from the common center. This tendency is not difficult to be accounted for. It has its origin in the love of power. Power controlled or abridged is almost always the rival and enemy of that power by which it is controlled or abridged. This simple proposition will teach us how little reason there is to expect that the persons intrusted with the administration of the affairs of the particular members of a confederacy will at all times be ready with perfect good humor and an unbiased regard to the public weal to execute the resolutions or decrees of the general authority. The reverse of this results from the constitution of man.

If, therefore, the measures of the Confederacy cannot be executed without the intervention of the particular administrations, there will be little prospect of their being executed at all. The rulers of the respective members, whether they have a constitutional right to do it or not, will undertake to judge of the propriety of the measures themselves. They will consider the conformity of the thing proposed or required to their immediate interests or aims; the momentary conveniences or inconveniences that would attend its adoption. All this will be done; and in a spirit of interested and suspicious scrutiny, without that knowledge of national circumstances and reasons of state, which is essential to a right judgment, and with that strong predilection in favor of local objects, which can hardly fail to mislead the decision. The same process must be repeated in every member of which the body is constituted; and the execution of the plans, framed by the councils of the whole, will always fluctuate on the discretion of the ill-informed and prejudiced opinion of every part. Those who have been conversant in the proceedings of popular assemblies; who have seen how difficult it often is, when there is no exterior pressure of circumstances, to bring them to harmonious resolutions on important points, will readily conceive how impossible it must be to induce a number of such assemblies, deliberating at a distance from each other, at different times and under different impressions, long to co-operate in the same views and pursuits.

In our case the concurrence of thirteen distinct sovereign wills is requisite under the Confederation to the complete execution of every important measure that proceeds from the Union. It has happened as was to have been foreseen. The measures of the Union have not been executed; and the delinquencies of the States have step by step matured themselves to an extreme, which has, at length, arrested all the wheels of the national government and brought them to an awful stand. Congress at this time scarcely possess the means of keeping up the forms of administration, till the States can have time to agree upon a more substantial substitute for the present shadow of a federal government. Things did not come to this desperate extremity at once. The causes which have been specified produced at first only unequal and disproportionate degrees of compliance with the requisitions of the Union. The greater deficiencies of some States furnished the pretext of example and the temptation of interest to the complying, or to the least delinquent States. Why should we do more in proportion than those who are embarked with us in the same political voyage? Why should we consent to bear more than our proper share of the common burden? There were suggestions which human selfishness could not withstand, and which even speculative men, who looked forward to remote consequences, could not without hesitation combat. Each State yielding to the persuasive voice of immediate interest or convenience has successively withdrawn its support, till the frail and tottering edifice seems ready to fall upon our heads and to crush us beneath its ruins.

PUBLIUS

No. 23: Hamilton

THE necessity of a Constitution, at least equally energetic with the one proposed, to the preservation of the Union is the point at the examination of which we are now arrived.

This inquiry will naturally divide itself into three branches—the objects to be provided for by a federal government, the quantity of power necessary to the accomplishment of those objects, the persons upon whom that power ought to operate. Its distribution and organization will more properly claim our attention under the succeeding head.

The principal purposes to be answered by union are these—the common defense of the members; the preservation of the public peace, as well against internal convulsions as external attacks; the regulation of commerce with other nations and between the States; the superintendence of our intercourse, political and commercial, with foreign countries.

The authorities essential to the common defense are these: to raise armies; to build and equip fleets; to prescribe rules for the government of both; to direct their operations; to provide for their support. These powers ought to exist without limitation, *because it is impossible to foresee or to define the extent and variety of national exigencies, and the correspondent extent and variety of the means which may be necessary to satisfy them.* The circumstances that endanger the safety of nations are infinite, and for this reason no constitutional shackles can wisely be imposed on the power to which the care of it is committed. This power ought to be coextensive with all the possible combinations of such circumstances; and ought to be under the direction of the same councils which are appointed to preside over the common defense.

This is one of those truths which to a correct and unprejudiced mind carries its own evidence along with it, and may be obscured, but cannot be made plainer by argument or reasoning. It rests upon axioms as simple as they are universal; the *means* ought to be proportioned to the *end;* the persons from whose agency the attainment of any *end* is expected ought to possess the *means* by which it is to be attained.

Whether there ought to be a federal government intrusted with the care of the common defense is a question in the first instance open to discussion; but the moment it is decided in the affirmative, it will follow that that government ought to be clothed with all the powers requisite to complete execution of its trust. And unless it can be shown that the circumstances which may affect the public safety are reducible within certain determinate limits; unless the contrary of this position can be fairly and rationally disputed, it must be admitted as a necessary consequence that there can be no limitation of that authority which is to provide for the defense and protection of the community in any matter essential to its efficacy—that is, in any matter essential to the *formation, direction,* or *support* of the NATIONAL FORCES.

Defective as the present Confederation has been proved to be, this principle appears to have been fully recognized by the framers of it; though they have not made proper or adequate provision for its exercise. Congress have an unlimited discretion to make requisitions of men and money; to govern the army and navy; to direct their operations. As their requisitions are made constitutionally binding upon the States, who are in fact under the most solemn obligations to furnish the supplies required of them, the intention evidently was that the United States should command whatever resources were by them judged requisite to the "common defense and general welfare." It was presumed that a sense of their true interests, and a regard to the dictates of good faith, would be found sufficient pledges for the punctual performance of the duty of the members to the federal head.

The experiment has, however, demonstrated that this expectation was ill-founded and illusory; and the observations made under the last head will, I imagine, have sufficed to convince the impartial and discerning that there is an absolute necessity for an entire change in the first principles of the system; that if we are in earnest about giving the Union energy and duration we must abandon the vain project of legislating upon the States in their collective capacities; we must extend the laws of the federal government to the individual citizens of America; we must discard the fallacious scheme of quotas and requisitions as equally impracticable and unjust. The result from all this is that the Union ought to be invested with full power to levy troops; to build and equip fleets; and to raise the revenues which will be required for the formation and support of an army and navy in the customary and ordinary modes practiced in other governments.

If the circumstances of our country are such as to demand a compound instead of a simple, a confederate instead of a sole, government, the essential point which will remain to be adjusted will be to discriminate the OBJECTS, as far as it can be done, which shall appertain to the different provinces or departments of power; allowing to each the most ample authority for fulfilling the objects committed to its charge. Shall the Union be constituted the guardian of the common safety? Are fleets and armies and revenues necessary to this purpose? The government of the Union must be empowered to pass all laws, and to make all regulations which have relation to them. The same must be the case in respect to commerce, and to every other matter to which its jurisdiction is permitted to extend. Is the administration of justice between the citizens of the same State the proper department of the local governments? These must possess all the authorities which are connected with this object, and with every other that may be allotted to their particular cognizance and direction. Not to confer in each case a degree of power commensurate to the end would be to violate the most obvious rules of prudence and propriety, and improvidently to trust the great interests of the nation to hands which are disabled from managing them with vigor and success.

Who so likely to make suitable provisions for the public defense as that body to which the guardianship of the public safety is confided; which, as the center of information, will best understand the extent and urgency of the dangers that threaten; as the representative of the WHOLE, will feel itself most deeply interested in the preservation of every part; which, from the responsibility implied in the duty assigned to it, will be most sensibly impressed with the necessity of proper exertions; and which, by the extension of its authority throughout the States, can alone establish uniformity and concert in the plans and measures by which the common safety is to be secured? Is there not a manifest inconsistency in devolving upon the federal government the care of the general defense and leaving in the State governments the *effective* powers by which it is to be provided for? Is not a want of co-operation the infallible consequence of such a system? And will not weakness, disorder, an undue distribution of the burdens and calamities of war, an unnecessary and intolerable increase of expense, be its natural and inevitable concomitants? Have we not had unequivocal experience of its effects in the course of the revolution which we have just achieved?

Every view we may take of the subject, as candid inquirers after truth, will serve to convince us that it is both unwise and dangerous to deny the federal government an unconfined authority in respect to all those objects which are intrusted to its management. It will indeed deserve the most vigilant and careful attention of the people to see that it be modeled in such a manner as to admit of its being safely vested with the requisite powers. If any plan which has been, or may be, offered to our consideration should not, upon a dispassionate inspection, be found to answer this description, it ought to be rejected. A government, the constitution of which renders it unfit to be trusted with all the powers which a free people *ought to delegate to any government,* would be an unsafe and improper depositary of the NATIONAL INTERESTS. Wherever THESE can with propriety be confided, the co-incident powers may safely accompany them. This is the true result of all just reasoning upon the subject. And the adversaries of the plan promulgated by the convention would have given a better impression of their candor if they had confined themselves to showing that the internal structure of the proposed government was such as to render it unworthy of the confidence of the people. They ought not to have wandered into inflammatory declamations and unmeaning cavils about the extent of the powers. The POWERS are not too extensive for the OBJECTS of federal administration, or, in other words, for the management of our NATIONAL INTERESTS; nor can any satisfactory argument be framed to show that they are chargeable with such an excess. If it be true, as has been insinuated by some of the writers on the other side, that the difficulty arises from the nature of the thing, and that the extent of the country will not permit us to form a government in which such ample powers can safely be reposed, it would prove that we ought to contract our views, and resort to the expedient of separate confederacies, which will move within more practicable spheres. For the absurdity must continually stare us in the face of confiding to a government the direction of the most essential national interests, without daring to trust it to the authorities which are indispensable to their proper and efficient management. Let us not attempt to reconcile contradictions, but firmly embrace a rational alternative.

I trust, however, that the impracticability of one general system cannot be shown. I am greatly mistaken if anything of weight has yet been advanced of this tendency; and I flatter myself that the observations which have been made in the course of these papers have served to place the reverse of that position in as clear a light as any matter still in the womb of time and experience is susceptible of. This, at all events, must be evident, that the very difficulty itself, drawn from the extent of the country, is the strongest argument in favor of an energetic government; for any other can certainly never preserve the Union of so large an empire. If we embrace the tenets of those who oppose the adoption of the proposed Constitution as the standard of our political creed we cannot fail to verify the gloomy doctrines which predict the impracticability of a national system pervading the entire limits of the present Confederacy.

PUBLIUS

No. 51: Madison

TO WHAT expedient, then, shall we finally resort, for maintaining in practice the necessary partition of power among the several departments as laid down in the Constitution? The only answer that can be given is that as all these exterior provisions are found to be inadequate the defect must be supplied, by so contriving the interior structure of the government as that its several constituent parts may, by their mutual relations, be the means of keeping each other in their proper places. Without presuming to undertake a full development of this important idea I will hazard a few general observations which may perhaps place it in a clearer light, and enable us to form a more correct judgment of the principles and structure of the government planned by the convention.

In order to lay a due foundation for that separate and distinct exercise of the different powers of government, which to a certain extent is admitted on all hands to be essential to the preservation of liberty, it is evident that each department should have a will of its own; and consequently should be so constituted that the members of each should have as little agency as possible in the appointment of the members of the others. Were this principle rigorously adhered to, it would require that all the appointments for the supreme executive, legislative, and judiciary magistracies should be drawn from the same fountain of authority, the people, through channels having no communication whatever with one another. Perhaps such a plan of constructing the several departments would be less difficult in practice than it may in contemplation appear. Some difficulties, however, and some additional expense would attend the execution of it. Some deviations, therefore, from the principle must be admitted. In the constitution of the judiciary department in particular, it might be inexpedient to insist rigorously on the principle: first, because peculiar qualifications being essential in the members, the primary consideration ought to be to select that mode of choice which best secures these qualifications; second, because the permanent tenure by which the appointments are held in that department must soon destroy all sense of dependence on the authority conferring them.

It is equally evident that the members of each department should be as little dependent as possible on those of the others for the emoluments annexed to their offices. Were the executive magistrate, or the judges, not independent of the legislature in this particular, their independence in every other would be merely nominal.

But the great security against a gradual concentration of the several powers in the same department consists in giving to those who administer each department the necessary constitutional means and personal motives to resist encroachments of the others. The provision for defense must in this, as in all other cases, be made commensurate to the danger of attack. Ambition must be made to counteract ambition. The interest of the man must be connected with the constitutional rights of the place. It may be a reflection on human nature that such devices should be necessary to control the abuses of government. But what is government itself but the greatest of all reflections on human nature? If men were angels, no government would be necessary. If angels were to govern men, neither external nor internal controls on government would be necessary. In framing a government which is to be administered by men over men, the great difficulty lies in this: you must first enable the government to control the governed; and in the next place oblige it to control itself. A dependence on the people is, no doubt, the primary control on the government; but experience has taught mankind the necessity of auxiliary precautions.

This policy of supplying, by opposite and rival interests, the defect of better motives, might be traced through the whole system of human affairs, private as well as public. We see it particularly displayed in all the subordinate distributions of power, where the constant aim is to divide and arrange the several offices in such a manner as that each may be a check on the other —that the private interest of every individual may be a sentinel over the public rights. These inventions of prudence cannot be less requisite in the distribution of the supreme powers of the State.

But it is not possible to give to each department an equal power of self-defense. In republican government, the legislative authority necessarily predominates. The remedy for this inconveniency is to divide the legislature into different branches; and to render them, by different modes of election and different principles of action, as little connected with each other as the nature of their common functions and their common dependence on the society will admit. It may even be necessary to guard against dangerous encroachments by still further precautions. As the weight of the legislative authority requires that it should be thus divided, the weakness of the executive may require, on the other hand, that it should be fortified. An absolute negative on the legislature appears, at first view, to be the natural defense with which the executive magistrate should be armed. But perhaps it would be neither altogether safe nor alone sufficient. On ordinary occasions it might not be exerted with the requisite firmness, and on extraordinary occasions it might be perfidiously abused. May not this defect of an absolute negative be supplied by some qualified connection between this weaker department and the weaker branch of the stronger department, by which the latter may be led to support the constitutional rights of the former, without being too much detached from the rights of its own department?

If the principles on which these observations are founded be just, as I persuade myself they are, and they be applied as a criterion to the several State constitutions, and to the federal Constitution, it will be found that if the latter does not perfectly correspond with them, the former are infinitely less able to bear such a test.

There are, moreover, two considerations particularly applicable to the federal system of America, which place that system in a very interesting point of view.

First. In a single republic, all the power surrendered by the people is submitted to the administration of a single government; and the usurpations are guarded against by a division of the government into distinct and separate departments. In the compound republic of America, the power surrendered by the people is first divided between two distinct governments, and then the portion allotted to each subdivided among distinct and separate departments. Hence a double security arises to the rights of the people. The different governments will control each other, at the same time that each will be controlled by itself.

Second. It is of great importance in a republic not only to guard the society against the oppression of its rulers, but to guard one part of the society against the injustice of the other part. Different interests necessarily exist in different classes of citizens. If a majority be united by a common interest, the rights of the minority will be insecure. There are but two methods of providing against this evil: the one by creating a will in the community independent of the majority—that is, of the society itself; the other, by comprehending in the society so many separate descriptions of citizens as will render an unjust combination of a majority of the whole very improbable, if not impracticable. The first method prevails in all governments possessing an hereditary or self-appointed authority. This, at best, is but a precarious security; because a power independent of the society may as well espouse the unjust views of the major as the rightful interests of the minor party, and may possibly be turned against both parties. The second method will be exemplified in the federal republic of the United States. Whilst all authority in it will be derived from and dependent on the society, the society itself will be broken into so many parts, interests and classes of citizens, that the rights of individuals, or of the minority, will be in little danger from interested combinations of the majority. In a free government the security for civil rights must be the same as that for religious rights. It consists in the one case in the multiplicity of interests, and in the other in the multiplicity of sects. The degree of security in both cases will depend on the number of interests and sects; and this may be presumed to depend on the extent of country and number of people comprehended under the same government. This view of the subject must particularly recommend a proper federal system to all the sincere and considerate friends of republican government, since it shows that in exact proportion as the territory of the Union may be formed into more circumscribed Confederacies, or States, oppressive combinations of a majority will be facilitated; the best security, under the republican forms, for the rights of every class of citizen, will be diminished; and consequently the stability and independence of some member of the government, the only other security, must be proportionally increased. Justice is the end of government. It is the end of civil society. It ever has been and ever will be pursued until it be obtained, or until liberty be lost in the pursuit. In a society under the forms of which the stronger faction can readily unite and oppress the weaker, anarchy may as truly be said to reign as in a state of nature, where the weaker individual is not secured against the violence of the stronger; and as, in the latter state, even the stronger individuals are prompted, by the uncertainty of their condition, to submit to a government which may protect the weak as well as themselves; so, in the former state, will the more powerful factions or parties be gradually induced, by a like motive, to wish for a government which will protect all parties, the weaker as well as the more powerful. It can be little doubted that if the State of Rhode Island was separated from the Confederacy and left to itself, the insecurity of rights under the popular form of government within such narrow limits would be displayed by such reiterated oppressions of factious majorities that some power altogether independent of the people would soon be called for by the voice of the very factions whose misrule had proved the necessity of it. In the extended republic of the United States, and among the great variety of interests, parties, and sects which it embraces, a coalition of a majority of the whole society could seldom take place on any other principles than those of justice and the general good; whilst there being thus less danger to a minor from the will of a major party, there must be less pretext, also, to provide for the security of the former, by introducing into the government a will not dependent on the latter, or, in other words, a will independent of the society itself. It is no less certain than it is important, notwithstanding the contrary opinions which have been entertained, that the larger the society, provided it lie within a practicable sphere, the more duly capable it will be of self-government. And happily for the *republican cause,* the practicable sphere may be carried to a very great extent by a judicious modification and mixture of the *federal principle.*

PUBLIUS

5

THOMAS JEFFERSON AND THE PROBLEMS OF INTERPRETATION

INTERPRETIVE ESSAYS FROM OUTLINING TO REVISION

In February 1799, John Fries, a self-styled captain and traveling auctioneer, led a small band of Pennsylvania farmers in a protest against a recently levied federal property tax. He and his followers drove the federal tax collectors out of Bucks County and freed a number of prisoners in Bethlehem. The federal government responded to this local disturbance with alacrity and force; President John Adams ordered U.S. troops out to restore order and apprehend Fries. Federalist supporters of the president applauded this show of force, while some Republicans muttered darkly about tyranny and military usurpation.

Even a minor event like "Fries's Rebellion" revealed how deeply divided the new nation was at the end of its first decade. Two powerful political factions—a development unanticipated by the Founding Fathers—faced one another with growing mistrust and fear. The Federalists, led by John Adams and Alexander Hamilton, had put forth a series of measures—the best known of which were the Alien and Sedition Laws—designed to harass and silence their Republican opposition. The Republicans, for whom James Madison and Thomas Jefferson were principal spokesmen, had responded with the Kentucky and Virginia Resolutions, which asserted the right of an individual state to judge the constitutionality of federal laws. The crisis was sufficiently intense that one informed observer, the British minister, believed that the "whole system of American government [was] tottering at its foundations."

In this crisis of 1799–1800, the fragile balance between authority and liberty that the Founding Fathers had hoped to achieve might have been fractured on any of a number of issues. The fracture did not take place for a number of reasons. Neither Federalists nor Republicans resorted to force. President Adams, having broken with a faction of his party that advocated war with France, sought peace instead. And finally, Thomas Jefferson survived an electoral tie with Aaron Burr and, as a candidate of an opposition party, was elected to the presidency to displace an existing government in what he later called the "Revolution of 1800."

Historians differ about how "revolutionary" Jefferson's election actually was, but few would quarrel with its importance. The Jeffersonians had survived a national crisis, had peacefully achieved power, and proved able to govern the nation. For this feat alone, Thomas Jefferson deserves the accolades of grateful national historians. Yet Jefferson is remembered for much more; he remains one of the most fascinating and controversial figures of American history.

To his admirers, Jefferson's achievements mark him not only as a leading actor on the national political stage but also as one of the most talented and accomplished individuals of the nation's past. He was a planter, agricultural expert, scientist, inventor, philosopher, architect, political theorist, writer, political leader, and statesman. Prior to 1800, he had already served as governor of Virginia, a representative to the Continental Congress, and minister to France. He had written the Declaration of Independence, the progressive Virginia state constitution, and his well-known *Notes on the State of Virginia.* Following ratification of the federal Constitution, he became the nation's first secretary of state. With his close friend and collaborator James Madison, he also led the Democratic-Republican opposition to the Federalists. He was elected to the vice-presidency in 1796 and finally, as we have seen, to the presidency in 1800.

For the next eight years, Jefferson not only governed the nation effectively but also helped to soothe the violent partisan passions of the preceding decade. Almost simultaneously he succeeded in doubling the size of what he called our "empire of liberty" through the purchase of the Louisiana Territory. During a well-deserved but active retirement, Jefferson designed the Virginia state capitol at Richmond, founded the University of Virginia, and served as mentor to his successors of the Virginia dynasty, James Madison and James Monroe. Jeffersonian ideas so pervaded the national politics that James Monroe, his protege, was reelected to the presidency in 1820 without organized opposition. Later generations revered Jefferson as the great apostle of reason, liberty, democracy, limited government, education, and human rights. President John F. Kennedy captured the veneration with which Jefferson is regarded when he told a group of Nobel Prize winners dining at the White House that they represented the greatest array of talent assembled there since Thomas Jefferson had dined alone.[1]

To his critics at the time, however, the real Thomas Jefferson was less awe-inspiring. Behind the myths, they charged, was an intellectually thin, venal, cowardly hypocrite who, in his intellectual endeavors, was more a fuzzy-headed dabbler than a deep or original thinker. His actions, they said, violated nearly every principle he held dear. The great defender of human freedom, he owned slaves and was accused of siring some with a slave mistress. A believer in agrarian ideals, he pursued policies to foster manufacturing. An advocate of limited government, he used extraordinary executive power both in acquiring Louisiana and in attempting to enforce the embargo of 1807 against the British. A proponent of civil liberties, he used his prestige as president in political vendettas against Supreme Court Justice Samuel Chase and his own vice-president, Aaron Burr.

While most historians have praised Jefferson's ideas and accomplishments, others have found evidence to support the charges of his political opponents. For example, in his *Jefferson and Civil Liberties,* published in 1963, Leonard Levy pointed out that

> . . . Jefferson at one time or another supported loyalty oaths; countenanced internment camps for political suspects; drafted a bill of attainder; urged prosecutions for seditious libel; trampled on the Fourth Amendment; condoned military despotism; used the Army to enforce laws in time of peace; censored reading; chose professors for their political opinions; and endorsed the doctrine that the means, however odious, were justified by the ends.[2]

More recently, novelist Gore Vidal has taken up the vendetta argument and portrayed Jefferson as a despicable hypocrite for his treatment of Aaron Burr. And psychohistorian Fawn Brodie accepts the authenticity of the slave mistress allegations in her portrait of a neurotic Jefferson driven far more by irrational fears and desires than by the reason he so highly prized.[3]

HISTORICAL INTERPRETATION

All these judgments of Jefferson, as you should recognize, are statements of *opinion* or *interpretation.* They are not statements of fact. It is important for you to realize that interpretations can be analyzed, changed, and contradicted. Indeed, historians do this all the time. They often reach *different*

[1]The standard Jefferson biographies are Dumas Malone's definitive *Jefferson and His Times,* 6 vols. (Boston: Little, Brown, 1948–1981) and Merrill Peterson's *Thomas Jefferson and the New Nation* (London and New York: Oxford University Press, 1970).

[2]Leonard W. Levy, *Jefferson and Civil Liberties: The Darker Side* (Boston: Harvard University Press, 1963), p. 3.

[3]Gore Vidal, *Burr* (New York: Random House, 1973); Fawn Brodie, *Thomas Jefferson: An Intimate History* (New York: Norton, 1974).

conclusions based on their evaluation of the *same* evidence, because history involves more than the discovery of past facts. Historians must put those facts together into a coherent pattern, assess their interrelationship, and reach some conclusions. These tasks are always speculative, seldom easy, and never foolproof; mistakes can be made. Moreover, every historian is a product of a particular time and tends to interpret the past in light of his or her experiences. Good historians are aware of this tendency and know that history thus teaches much about present beliefs and their origins as well as about the past. In the final analysis, history is a subjective, interpretive discipline.

Does this mean, then, that the facts of history are fair game and can be used or abused in any way that partisans in the present choose? Absolutely not. As we emphasized in the preceding chapter, historical events can be properly understood only when analyzed in the context of their time. Moreover, all events in history are linked in a complex cause-and-effect relationship that can only be comprehended when events are placed in their proper order. Thus, an understanding of historical time, or *chronology,* is fundamental to any interpretive analysis that seeks context, causation, or meaning in history.

To illustrate something of the complexity of this cause-and-effect relationship and the importance of chronology, let us look briefly at the Kentucky Resolutions of 1798. In these resolutions, Jefferson argued that the Alien and Sedition Acts threatened the liberties of the citizens of the United States. This clearly suggests that the Alien and Sedition Acts caused the Kentucky Resolutions, a verdict accepted by most historians. Yet the Federalists could and did respond that the Alien and Sedition Acts were themselves a justified response to the XYZ Affair and the quasi-war with France, which they believed to be the result of Jeffersonian opposition to their policies. Moreover, Jefferson saw the Kentucky Resolutions as a useful statement of principles for his presidential campaign. These points argue a more complex relationship of events in the 1790s than the simple statement that the Alien and Sedition Acts caused the Kentucky Resolutions.

It is also true that historical events often have repercussions far beyond their own time. In 1948, for example, the *William and Mary Quarterly,* an important journal of early American history published in Williamsburg, Virginia, printed an article on the Kentucky and Virginia Resolutions arguing that Jefferson and Madison intended these resolutions "*primarily* as a defense, practical and spirited, of civil liberties." The editors of the journal saw fit to introduce this article with a remarkable "Editor's Note." That note labeled the recent use of the resolutions by Virginia's states rights advocates as a barrier against federal efforts to protect the civil rights of black Virginians a misuse and abuse of history.[4] One hundred and fifty years after the event and in a context dramatically

[4]Adrienne Koch and Harry Ammon, "The Virginia and Kentucky Resolutions: An Episode in Jefferson's and Madison's Defense of Civil Liberties," *William and Mary Quarterly* 3rd ser., V (1948), 145–176.

altered over time, the Kentucky and Virginia Resolutions of 1798 thus continued to have important consequences, and good historical analysis provided a valuable corrective for an abuse of history.

The best way to appreciate the value of historical analysis and interpretation is to complete some serious historical writing yourself. So far your writing has been limited to questions, summaries, and brief explanations. You now have an opportunity to attempt a real essay and grapple with the problems of interpretation.

The writing of this essay will require the use of skills you have already learned as well as the acquisition of some new ones. First, you need to define an interpretive thesis for your paper, a process related to the questioning process discussed in Chapters 1 and 2. Do you, as a result of your reading and lectures, have questions about Jefferson? Jot some of them down and see if you can use them to define an essay topic that will enable you to comment on how historians have interpreted Jefferson. Do your questions, for example, relate to some limited aspect of Jefferson's career where one of the interpretive issues seems especially clear or interesting? If so, use these questions to define a topic for an interpretive essay on Jefferson. A partial list of such interpretive topic statements is provided in the assignment section of this chapter. Use these statements as a guide to devise one of your own or, if you prefer, choose one of them as your own.

After defining and/or selecting a topic statement, you should research your topic in the library, as explained in Chapter 1, and summarize all the readings you select according to the method of summarization described in Chapter 3. You should then examine the historical *context* in which Jefferson's activities took place, as described in Chapter 4, as well as the chronology and interrelationship of key events and the repercussions of these activities. After this, you should be able to reach your own tentative conclusions on the basis of the evidence you have examined.

As with most historical problems, the evidence you uncover will not lead to a simple, single conclusion. And in forming your interpretation, you cannot simply cite the evidence that tends to support your conclusions while ignoring the rest of the information. Your interpretation, and your paper, must somehow take into account *all* the evidence you have uncovered and synthesize this data into a coherent framework.

OUTLINING AND REVISION

The primary method of synthesizing and organizing historical material in preparation for writing a paper is to create an *outline*. An outline is a useful tool to help clarify your thoughts and aid you in organizing the evidence you have collected. For many students, making an outline is of value for *all* writing exercises—including essay examination questions.

Your first step in creating an outline is to write a *thesis statement*. This statement will provide you, in sentence form, with the basic point you wish to make and will serve as a guide for your outline and subsequent paper. For an interpretive essay, your thesis statement could be merely a restatement in positive or negative terms of your interpretive topic sentence, or it might be a more complex statement that illustrates a degree of agreement combined with a degree of disagreement regarding that sentence.

Your second step is to organize your information in outline form. Some students find less formal outlines or lists more useful than what we suggest below; others prefer to write a very rough draft before outlining and then proceed to more polished versions. If one of these methods works for you, by all means use it in the future. Only experience will make clear which form is most appropriate for you, however, and in this essay you should use a formal outline if only to experiment with it.

In formal outlines, Roman numerals (I) and capital letters (A) are used for major points and concepts; arabic numerals (1) and lowercase letters (a) are used for subordinate, minor points. You can use an indefinite number of subheadings, depending upon the complexity of the subject, but you should seldom, if ever, carry subheadings beyond five or six levels. However many you use, headings and subheadings should be consistent. Do not, for example, make capital letter "A" a major issue and then make letter "B" a minor, related event; the less important event should be a numerical subheading under "A." You should also try not to phrase "A" as a complete sentence, "B" as a clause or phrase, and "C" as a single noun; any of these forms is acceptable, but whichever one is chosen should be used consistently. Furthermore, every heading should have at least two citations; in other words, if you have an "A" there should also be a "B," and if you have a 1 there should also be a 2.

The first Roman numeral for any essay should indicate the outline of your introduction; the last Roman numeral should contain the outline of your conclusion. Roman numerals and subheadings in between should organize your major points and evidence in a logical, consistent, and coherent manner. For examples and more detailed information, consult one of the writer's guides listed in Chapter 2.

After you complete an outline, you are ready to begin writing. But do not assume that your first draft is what you should hand in. Most writers, no matter how skilled, find that they go through numerous drafts before their written work accurately reflects their thoughts. Indeed, many writers can clarify their thoughts *only* by examining and editing early drafts of their work; revising enables them to recognize weaknesses in logic and presentation, to alter their interpretations accordingly, and to strengthen their prose. In reading your first draft, for example, you may very well discover not merely grammatical and spelling errors but also illogical conclusions; such problems may call for additional thought or research that would lead to changes in your thesis. These problems with logic did not emerge earlier because you had not yet spelled out in detail what you thought. Once you did, previously unnoticed flaws in your generalizations become apparent. Correction of such problems may very well require a new outline and draft. (In this regard it is advisable to let some time pass before you read and revise your first draft, so that you can clear your mind and rethink your conclusions.)

Redrafting should continue until you are convinced that your most recent version is logical, readable, and an accurate reflection of your final thoughts. You should then make sure to *proofread* your paper prior to submission. Constantly remember that your readers can understand only what you present to them on paper, not what is going on inside your head. Moreover, as previously implied, an illogical or sloppy paper often reflects illogical, incomplete, or sloppy thinking. If you are uncertain after the first or after numerous drafts as to how a reader would react to your paper, ask a friend or classmate to read, summarize, and comment on it. The summary should reflect accurately what you were trying to say, and the comments should note whether or not the paper is clearly argued, written, and presented.

ASSIGNMENTS

1. Either select one of the statements below or devise one of your own as the basis for writing an interpretive essay.

   a. Jefferson's differences with Hamilton during the 1790s were as much the result of differing sectional interests as they were due to philosophical or constitutional disagreements.
   b. As president of the United States, Jefferson succeeded largely because he adapted Federalist methods to Republican ends.
   c. Although he sometimes appeared inconsistent, Jefferson, in his public career, revealed an unswerving loyalty to a few major principles.
   d. Questions of race relations (Indians and/or blacks) trapped Jefferson in a conflict between principle and reality that he was never able to resolve.
   e. A passion for liberty often blinded Jefferson to the economic and political realities of international affairs.

2. Complete the appropriate research for your essay as explained in this chapter.
3. Compose an outline of your paper with thesis statement.
4. Compose the first draft of a two- to three-page (500- to 750-word) essay from this outline. Revise it as you see fit.
5. On the direction of your professor, either meet with him or her, a teaching assistant, or another member of the class to receive commentary and criticism on your outline and draft.
6. Revise your essay again and produce a final copy that includes bibliography and footnotes. Submit this along with your original outline and first draft as instructed.
7. As an alternative assignment, your professor may request a critical review of a book about Thomas Jefferson. Such a review is as appropriate an exercise as an interpretive essay for the skills discussed in this chapter.

BOOK REVIEWS

A *book review* bears little relationship to the book reports you completed in high school. Rather than summarizing the contents of the work under study, you are expected to describe briefly those contents and then to proceed with a *critical* analysis of the book and its thesis. Such an analysis involves answering a series of questions about the book. What, for example, are the author's subject, purpose, theme, and qualifications? Is the treatment comprehensive and convincing? Are the sources used appropriate and adequate? Do they include original primary research or only secondary material? What is the method of organization and the style of writing? What biases are evident? What contribution does the book make? What other conclusions can be and have been reached by different authors? Which conclusions seem most valid to you and why? Do you have an original one of your own?

While you may find that using the interpretive statements listed above enables you to make some judgments about the book under review, answering all of the questions will require a detailed knowledge of the author, the subject, and differing viewpoints. Since few undergraduates possess such knowledge, they are often advised to research and read previous scholarly reviews of the book as well as works containing different interpretations. You may also wish to examine some examples of this type of book review. Most historical journals contain very brief critical reviews, but you should also examine the more extensive reviews contained in journals such as *Reviews in American History* and the *New York Review of Books.*

If your professor chooses this alternative assignment or if you are given discretion and decide to write a book review, choose a book according to the instructions given in class and follow the directions for outlining and drafting described for the interpretive essay.

ADDITIONAL QUESTIONS TO CONSIDER

1. Be prepared to defend your conclusions orally in class, and do so if instructed by your professor.
2. Try to defend the opposite conclusion to the one you have reached.
3. Why do you consider your conclusions the correct ones?
4. How and why will different people reach different conclusions about the same historical issue after examining the same evidence?

6

CHANGING MATERIAL SOCIETY

USING STATISTICS AND GRAPHS

Rip Van Winkle, so the story goes, was an amiable fellow who was fond of idle gossip and storytelling with his friends at the local tavern. One day his wife, weary with nagging Rip to provide for himself and his family, ordered him to go hunting to obtain some meat for the family dinner table. Rip dutifully trudged off to the woods and, after a bowling and drinking session that he may have imagined, laid down to take a nap. When he awakened after a nap of twenty years, which seemed but overnight to him, he returned to the sleepy little village that had been his home. There, he found rows of houses he had never seen before, while his own house stood "empty, forlorn and apparently abandoned." Everything had changed.

The story of Rip Van Winkle, originally published by Washington Irving in 1819, proved enormously popular in the middle of the nineteenth century. Not only did Irving's *Sketch Book,* in which Rip first appeared, sell well, but the story was also adapted for a popular theatrical production that opened in Washington, D.C., in 1829. Moreover, the legend of Rip Van Winkle was featured in the works of popular artists like John Quidor and Albertus D. O. Browere.

Historian Douglas T. Miller in *The Birth of Modern America* has suggested that the enduring popularity of Irving's creation can be partly explained by the fact that it reflected an American reality; everything *had* changed. Most historians would agree that you cannot begin to understand

American history in the period 1820–1860 without some grasp of the dimensions of change in that society.

This change can be illustrated in a number of ways. One would be to imagine an average American born in one of the original thirteen states in 1790, who was granted her biblical life span of three score and ten (i.e., seventy years). In 1860 she could look back on a lifetime that had included momentous changes. The number of states, for example, had increased from 13 to 34, while the population had jumped from 4 million to 13 million. The land area occupied by U.S. citizens had increased from just under 900,000 square miles in 1790 to almost 3 million square miles in 1860. Moreover, the transportation revolution, the rise of manufacturing, and related factors discussed in your text had had a dramatic impact on the personal lives of many Americans. To cite just one example, in 1790, more than 90 percent of the labor force in the United States was employed in agriculture; by 1850, that proportion had decreased to 55 percent.

Other evidence could be presented here, but the basic point has been made; using numbers is a powerful way of expressing the dimensions of change that occurred between 1820 and 1860. Since history is a discipline that is concerned with change over time, historians often use numbers to illustrate, refine, or prove their arguments. This is not new. Statistics and graphs have long been used for analysis in economic and social history. Recently, however, increasing sophistication in the computer sciences has led to a significant expansion in the kind and number of historical problems that can be statistically analyzed. Thus, now more than ever, some knowledge of statistical principles and the way historians use tables and graphs is a vital skill for the student of history.

PERCENTAGES

The first prerequisite for any valid statistical analysis is knowledge of basic arithmetic terms and concepts. Most basic is *percentage* calculation. This section assumes that you know what a percentage is and how to calculate one. To refresh your memory, examine the figures and calculations given below.

Year	Value of all U.S. exports	Value of cotton exports
1840	$112,000,000	$ 64,000,000
1860	$316,000,000	$192,000,000

To determine the percentage of all U.S. exports consisting of cotton in either year, divide the value of cotton exports by the value of all exports and multiply by 100. For 1840, the figures would be as follows:

$$\frac{\$\ 64{,}000{,}000}{\$112{,}000{,}000} \times 100 = 57.1\%$$

For 1860, the equation would be:

$$\frac{\$192{,}000{,}000}{\$316{,}000{,}000} \times 100 = ?$$

The percentage of cotton in all U.S. exports would therefore have risen from 57.1 percent in 1840 to ______ percent in 1860.

Suppose you were interested in the *percentage increase* of cotton exports during these years. To calculate that percentage increase, take the quantities exported in both years (as listed below), subtract the 1840 figure from the 1860 figure, divide your answer by the 1840 figure, and multiply by 100.

Year	Quantity exported
1840	744,000,000 pounds
1860	1,768,000,000 pounds

$$\begin{array}{r} 1{,}768{,}000{,}000 \\ -\ \ 744{,}000{,}000 \\ \hline 1{,}024{,}000{,}000 \end{array}$$ is the increase in the number of pounds exported

$$\frac{1{,}024{,}000{,}000}{744{,}000{,}000} \times 100 = 137\%$$ is the percentage increase

Cotton exports on the eve of the Civil War had thus increased by 137 percent *over* the level of 1840. If you calculate the percentage increase from 128 million pounds in 1820 to the 1,768 million pounds of 1860, the answer of ______ percent reflects an astonishing increase during this forty-year period.

The outbreak of war in 1861 produced a precipitous decline in cotton exports, from 1,768 million pounds in 1860 to 308 million pounds in 1861. Can you calculate that percentage *decrease?* If your answer is over 100 percent, you have miscalculated; remember, nothing can be anything more than all gone.

AVERAGES

Everyone knows what "average" is, but few people realize that there are different types of averages. The *arithmetic* average is called the *mean,* while the central case is called the *median.* Quite often, these two are drastically different. Suppose, for example, that there are 11 plantations in a particular area, and that the slaves on these plantations number 18, 21, 56, 19, 29, 14, 23, 15, 41, 12, and 16. The *arithmetic* average or *mean* number is determined by totaling the number of slaves on all the plantations (264) and dividing that figure by the number of plantations (11). 264 divided by 11 is 24. Is 24, then, "typical" of the 11 plantations? Realize that none of the plantations has this number of slaves. To determine the *median,* rank the plantations from lowest to highest number of slaves and choose the number of slaves in the central case: 12, 14, 15, 16, 18, 19, 21, 23, 29, 41, 56. Here the median is the sixth case, or 19. Half the plantations have more than 19 slaves and half have fewer than 19 slaves. If the number of cases is an even number, then the two central cases are added together and divided by 2, and the result is the median.

Misuse of mean and median can lead to some startling distortions, and you should always examine carefully any news item or document that uses the word "average" so that you know which average the writer is employing. Means, for example, are very sensitive to extreme values. If multibillionaire Bunker Hunt sat down to dinner with six Vermont farmers, the mean income of the seven diners would be rather large (one extreme case and six moderate-to-low income cases). The median income, however, would be much lower and in this case more representative of the group.

Table 6.1 lists the number of bales of cotton produced by and the number of slaves working on 15 imaginary plantations. Determine the mean and median values of cotton production (in bales) on these plantations and the mean and median number of slaves. Then determine another "average": the *per capita* production of the slaves on these plantations.

GRAPHS

Statistics are often organized on a graph to show relationships and/or trends in a simple form. Historians like to use the *time-series* graph for

TABLE 6.1 Cotton Production of Selected Plantations in 1859

Plantation	Cotton Production (in bales)	Slaves
1	80	24
2	118	56
3	21	13
4	98	45
5	153	62
6	8	7
7	275	91
8	81	29
9	274	78
10	33	18
11	79	30
12	106	57
13	47	26
14	114	43
15	54	22

these purposes. This type of graph has measurements of time on one axis and measurements of the factor being analyzed on the other. Each set of coordinates is properly marked with a dot, and the dots are then connected to form a continuous line. A graph can be a valuable analytical tool as well as a way of effectively presenting information, as the following graph from a standard U.S. history text shows.

ASSIGNMENTS

1. Your instructor may ask you to hand in your calculations and results on cotton exports and plantation averages; if not, he or she can provide you with the correct answers.
2. Using the information about the total presidential vote presented in Table 6.2, prepare your own time-series graph for the presidential elections from 1824 to 1860.
3. Calculate the percentage increase in voters (the same formula as for cotton exports) for each of these elections. Which election shows the highest percentage increase? Using the total population graph as well as the presidential vote table, see if this increase can be accounted for by population growth alone (you can calculate the percentage of voters relative to the entire population in the election of 1840 as a guide here). If population growth does not account for the percentage increase in the vote, what other factors can you suggest that would have contributed to this increase?

FIGURE 6.1 Total Population 1790–1850

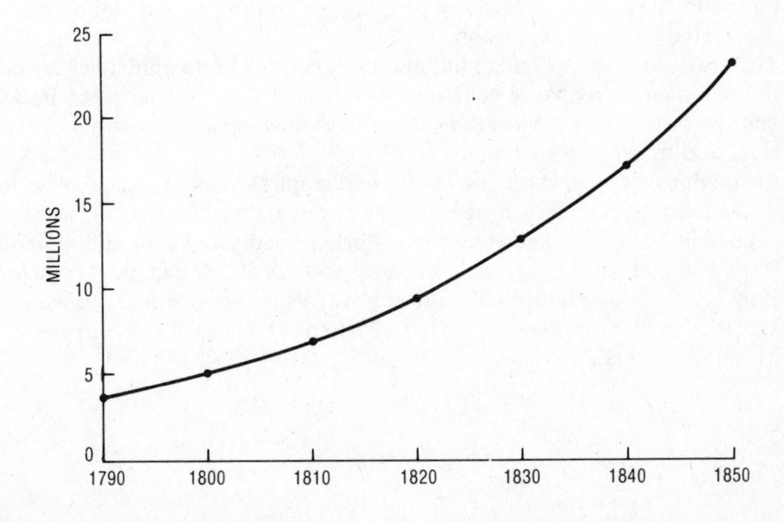

From Rebecca Brooks Gruver, *An American History,* 3rd ed. (Reading, Mass.: Addison-Wesley, 1981), p. 288. Reprinted by permission of Alfred A. Knopf, Inc.

TABLE 6.2 Total Popular Vote in Presidential Elections 1824–1860

Election	Total Votes Cast
1824	356,038
1828	1,156,328
1832	1,250,799
1836	1,479,799
1840	2,403,719
1844	2,698,611
1848	2,871,906
1852	3,143,679
1856	4,053,396
1860	4,680,193

ADDITIONAL QUESTIONS TO CONSIDER

1. Election statistics can be deceiving. Winners often seek to make them so by declaring a mandate where none really exists. To illustrate this, carefully analyze the election of 1844 by reviewing what your text says about this election and then examining the popular and electoral votes for candidates James K. Polk, Henry Clay, and James G. Birney (this information can probably be found in the appendix of your text if not within the appropriate chapter). By electoral votes, Polk's victory seems secure enough. Yet, as the popular vote shows, more voters cast their ballots for Clay and Birney than for Polk. Is it possible that Birney, with no electoral votes and just over 60,000 popular votes, actually determined the election? Using the *Guide to U.S. Elections* (Washington, D.C.: Congressional Quarterly, 1975), try to discover statistically how Clay might have won this election. Use the evidence you amass to compose a brief essay or oral presentation on popular support for aggressive national expansion.
2. The era 1820–1860 presents multiple opportunities to do statistical research. Develop some graphs of your own to illustrate the relationships between improvements in transportation, economic development, westward expansion, and increasing sectionalism.
3. As previously noted, statistics, tables, and graphs are often deceptive. Indeed, your ability to complete correctly large segments of this assignment has depended more on your knowledge of historical events and your ability to place statistical evidence in historical perspective than on the numbers themselves. Why are these numbers so often deceptive? What are the limits to the use of statistics, tables, and graphs? What questions should you ask whenever you use such evidence?

7

WESTWARD EXPANSION AND INDIAN REMOVAL

THE USE OF MAPS IN HISTORY

In 1828 and again in 1840, American voters elected feared Indian fighters to the presidency. Interestingly, Andrew Jackson and William Henry Harrison were also the first two presidents who might be said to represent the interests of those new territories that had not been part of the original thirteen states. Of course, Jackson was born in South Carolina and Harrison in Virginia, but it was as territorial governors, Indian fighters, and military heroes that they earned national prominence. And the years of their presidential terms (1828 to 1844) marked the climax of a movement to relocate those native Americans called "Indians" to territories west of the Mississippi.

The War of 1812 and the Peace of Ghent probably sealed the fate of Indians living within the territorial boundaries of the United States. It has been argued about the War of 1812 that the United States "lost the war but won the peace"; the Indians, however, lost both the war and the peace. Military defeats during the war destroyed the possibility of a northern and southern confederation that might have afforded the prospect of a united Indian movement. The terms of the peace cost the Indians the possibility of continuing European support, without which they were unable to resist the encroachment of white settlers.

The war also brought Andrew Jackson, the "hero of New Orleans," to national attention. In 1828, Jackson came to the presidency determined to reverse those Jeffersonian policies that were designed to encourage the gradual integration of the Indian into American society. Jackson proposed a bolder and simpler solution: insist that civilized Indians become citizens of the individual states and give up tribal rights and responsibilities, and compel those Indians who chose not to be citizens to migrate to lands west of the Mississippi. To this end, Congress in 1830 passed the Indian Removal Act, which authorized the president to negotiate treaties for the removal of Indian tribes still living east of the Mississippi. In arguing for this measure, which passed by five votes, Jackson asked rhetorically:

> What good man would prefer a country covered with forests and ranged by a few thousand savages to our extensive Republic, studded with cities, towns, and prosperous farms embellished with all the improvements which art can devise or industry execute, occupied by more than 12,000,000 happy people and filled with all the blessings of liberty, civilization, and religion?

Jackson's remarks embodied assumptions about the superiority of republican institutions that fueled much of the United States's dynamic expansion in the first half of the nineteenth century. Indians became victims of this expansionist thrust. During Jackson's presidency alone, the United States forcibly relocated 46,000 Indians, of whom 4,000 died. The benefits for white settlers were obvious: the United States had acquired approximately 100 million acres of Indian land. The costs to the national government were substantial as well: the long and bitter war against the Seminoles, who refused to leave their home in central Florida, cost the lives of 2,000 officers and soldiers and over 40 million taxpayer dollars. Moreover, Indian removal troubled the nation's conscience. One veteran recorded in his memoirs, "I fought through the Civil War and have seen men shot to pieces and slaughtered by the thousands, but the Cherokee removal was the cruelest work I ever knew." Nevertheless, Jackson and his followers carried the day and, by 1844—except for rural, isolated pockets chiefly in New York, Michigan, and Florida—the "cruelest work" had been completed and the Indians had been removed.

As Map 7.1 indicates, the study of Indian removal specifically and westward expansion generally provides an excellent opportunity to explore the importance of maps and some basic concepts in geography for the study of history. Maps, globes, and atlases are basic organizing devices that portray, conceptually, the space in which historical events take place. Your ability to read and understand maps will enhance your understanding of history.

As you look at Map 7.1, you will discover a number of conventions common to most historical maps. The first of these is *scale,* which defines the number of miles represented by inches of map space. On this particular map, 1 inch is equivalent to 200 miles. You could therefore use a ruler to calculate the distance that the Cherokee who left New Echota had to travel

MAP 7.1

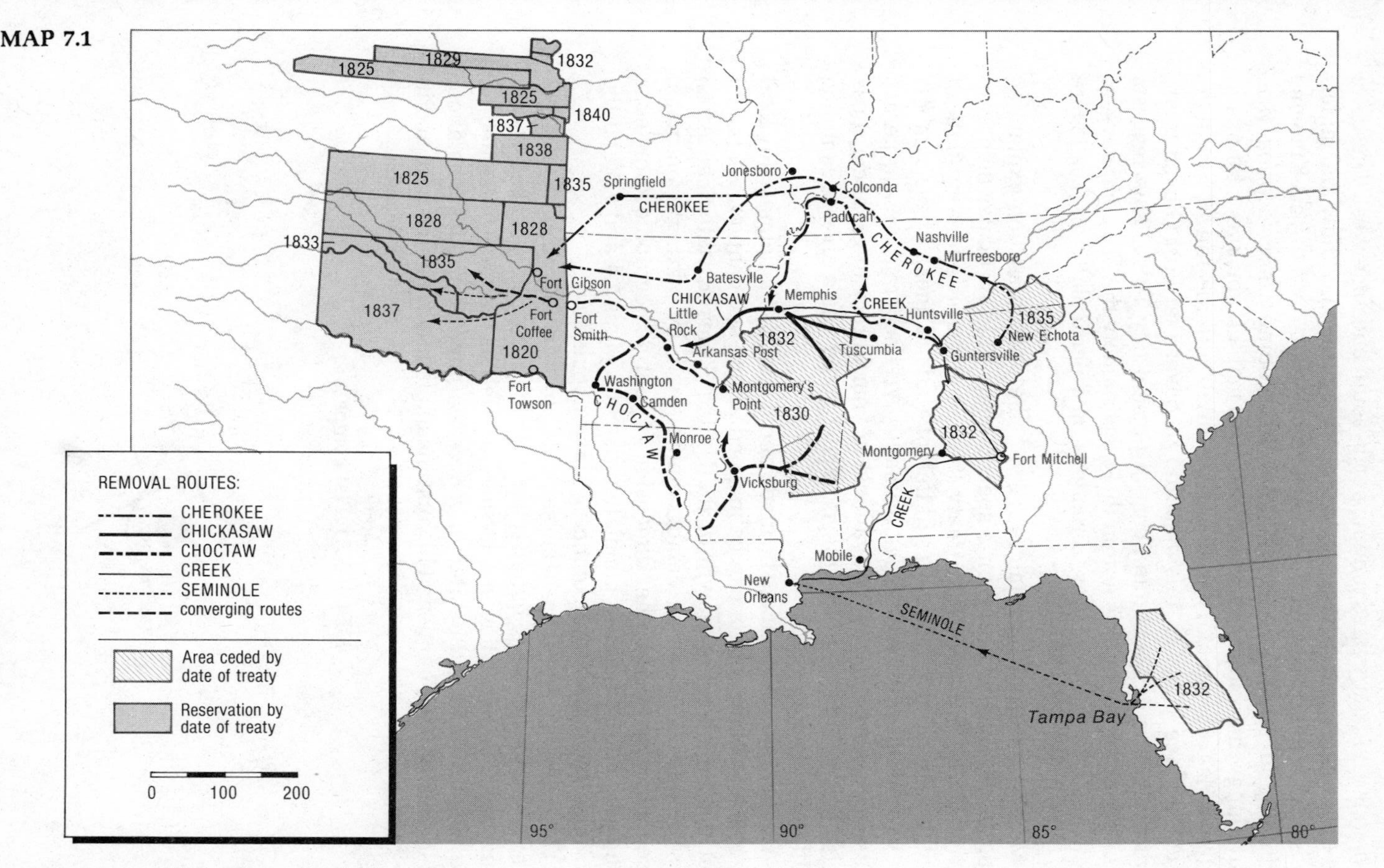

Reprinted by permission from *The American Heritage Pictorial Atlas of United States History* (New York: American Heritage, 1966).

to reach their destination just outside Fort Gibson. You will also notice that this map is divided by lines running north–south and east–west. These are lines of *longitude* and *latitude*, respectively. You should know and understand these terms; any good dictionary will explain them to you. Knowing longitude and latitude is critical to understanding *place location* (i.e., determining where something should go on a map). If you knew, for example, that Tulsa, Oklahoma, was located at 36° 10′ latitude and 96° longitude, you could place Tulsa on this map and discover that Fort Gibson is approximately 45 miles south and east of present day Tulsa. This suggests one map convention that is not on this map, namely the *flat compass*—or directional arrows—that show directions on a particular map (see Figure 7.1).

Most maps usually contain a *legend,* the printed section explaining the particular symbols used on a specific map. This particular map indicates areas ceded by date of treaty (hatching), reservations by date of treaty (gray), and removal routes (different kinds of lines). These symbols vary widely with different types of maps. We encourage you to peruse some of the historical atlases available in your library to get some sense of this variety. Your textbook, too, is likely to offer you a diverse sampling of different kinds of maps.

Another point that should be made about maps is that almost any kind of social or economic data can be mapped. In the last chapter, we talked about the demographic growth of the United States in statistical terms; Maps 7.2 and 7.3 illustrate demographic growth by putting it on maps. These maps also add another dimension to your demographic knowledge by showing you changes in population density. Maps 7.4 and 7.5 add the geographic location of an expanding slave population.

These maps have also been selected to provide you with a larger context for understanding Indian removal in the 1830s. By using knowledge gleaned from your reading and lectures as well as material presented on these maps, you should be able to generate a number of questions about why Indian removal happened beyond the explanation offered here and in your textbook.

FIGURE 7.1 Flat compass

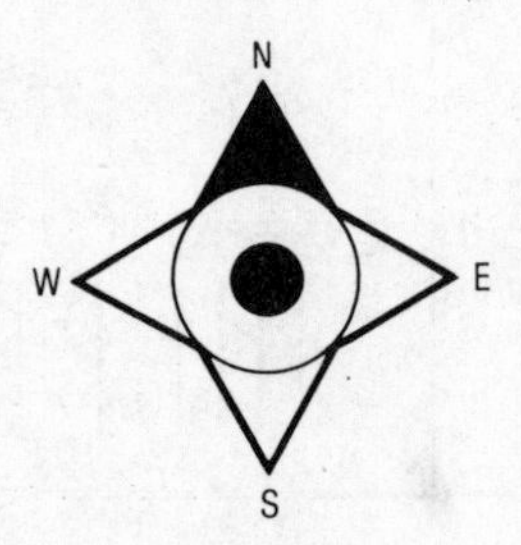

MAP 7.2

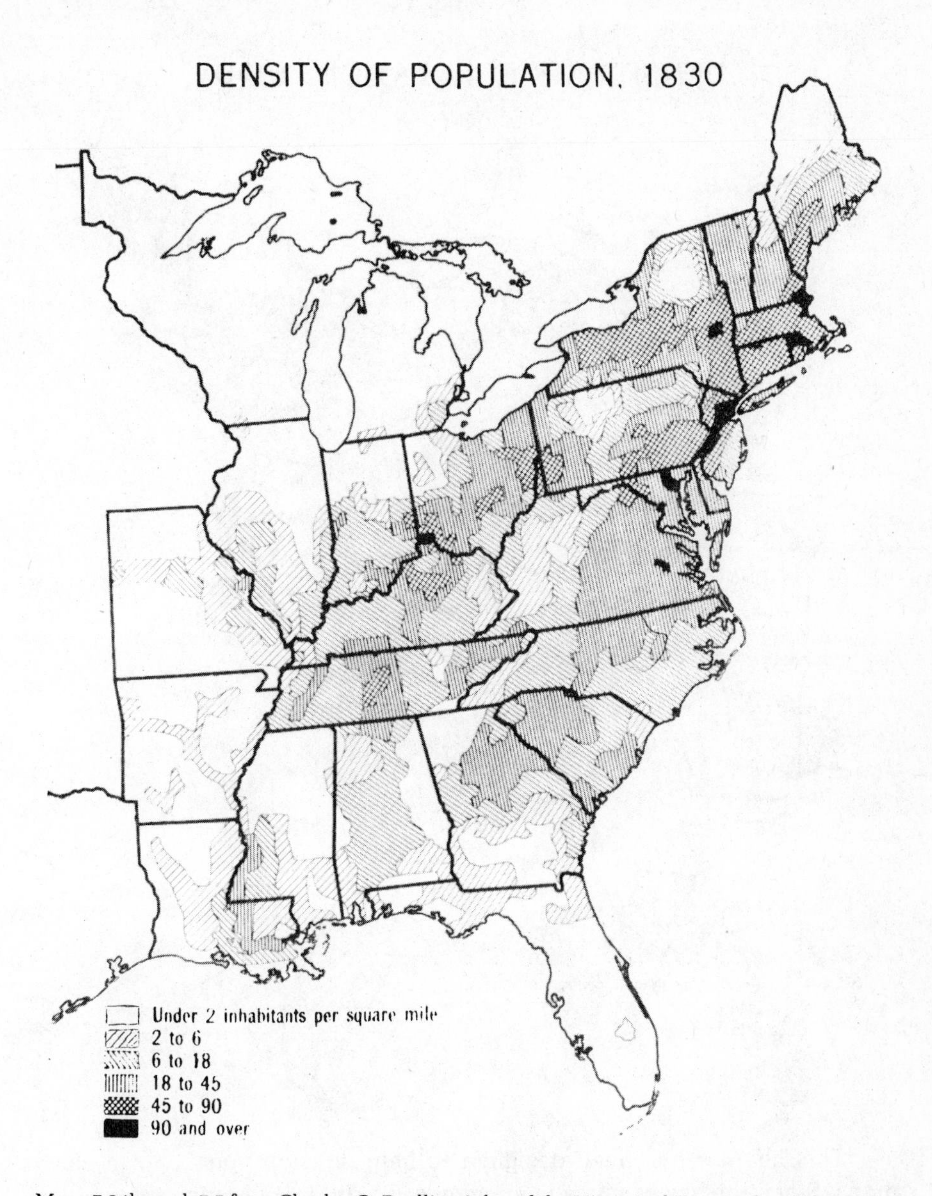

Maps 7.2 through 7.5 from Charles O. Paullin, *Atlas of the Historical Geography of the United States* (Washington, D.C., and New York: Carnegie Institute and American Geographical Society, 1932), plates 67 and 76. Reprinted by permission.

MAP 7.3

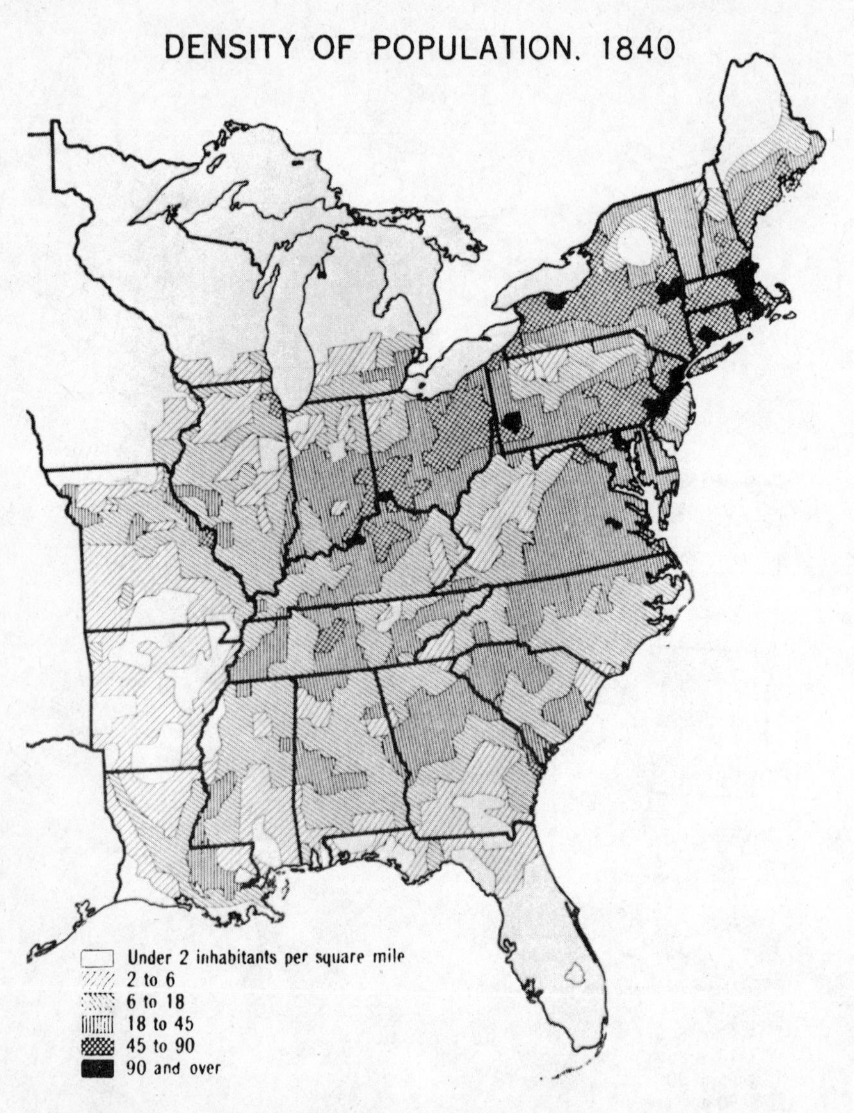

This chapter has been designed to help develop your skill in using maps. Since the use of maps is an acquired skill, this chapter should also help you make more effective use of the maps in your textbook. Many of you will find that preparing your own maps is a most effective study aid; we have therefore included a blank outline map of the United States for that purpose (inexpensive outline maps should also be available for purchase at your college bookstore). Some suggestions about the kinds of

MAP 7.4

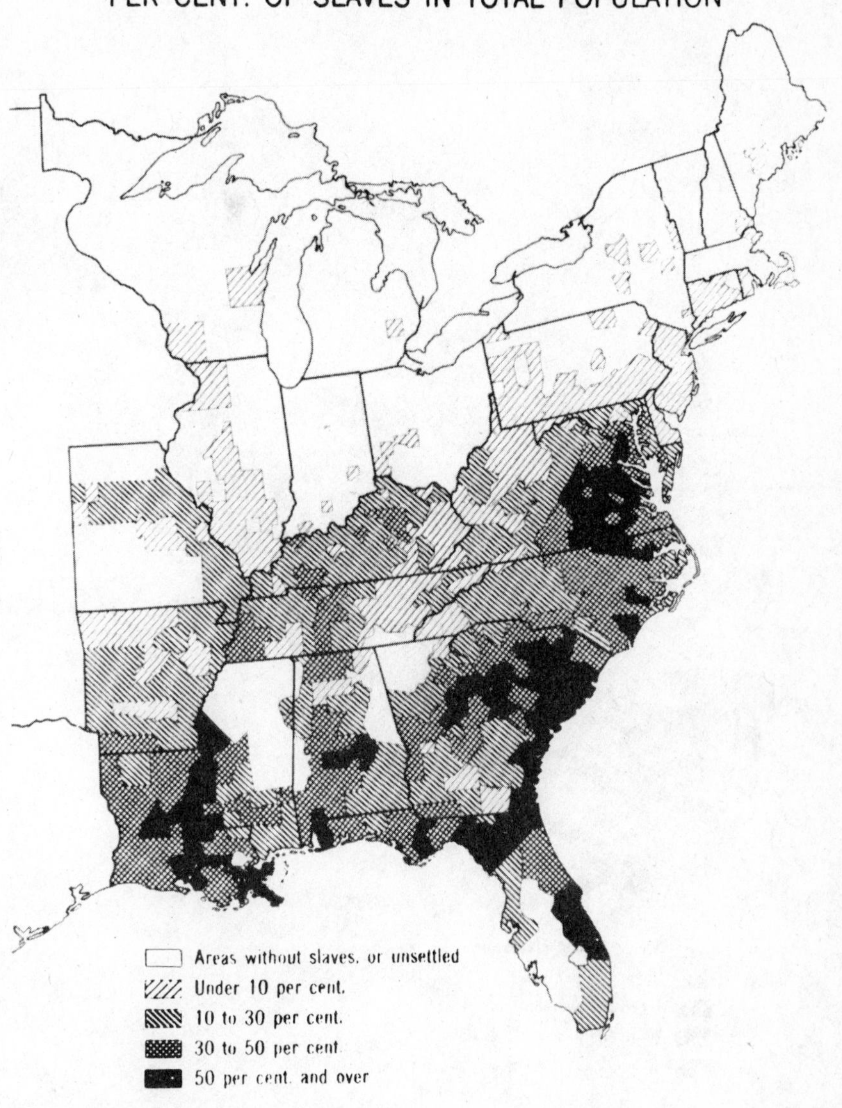
SLAVES, 1830
PER CENT. OF SLAVES IN TOTAL POPULATION
Areas without slaves, or unsettled
Under 10 per cent.
10 to 30 per cent.
30 to 50 per cent.
50 per cent. and over

MAP 7.5

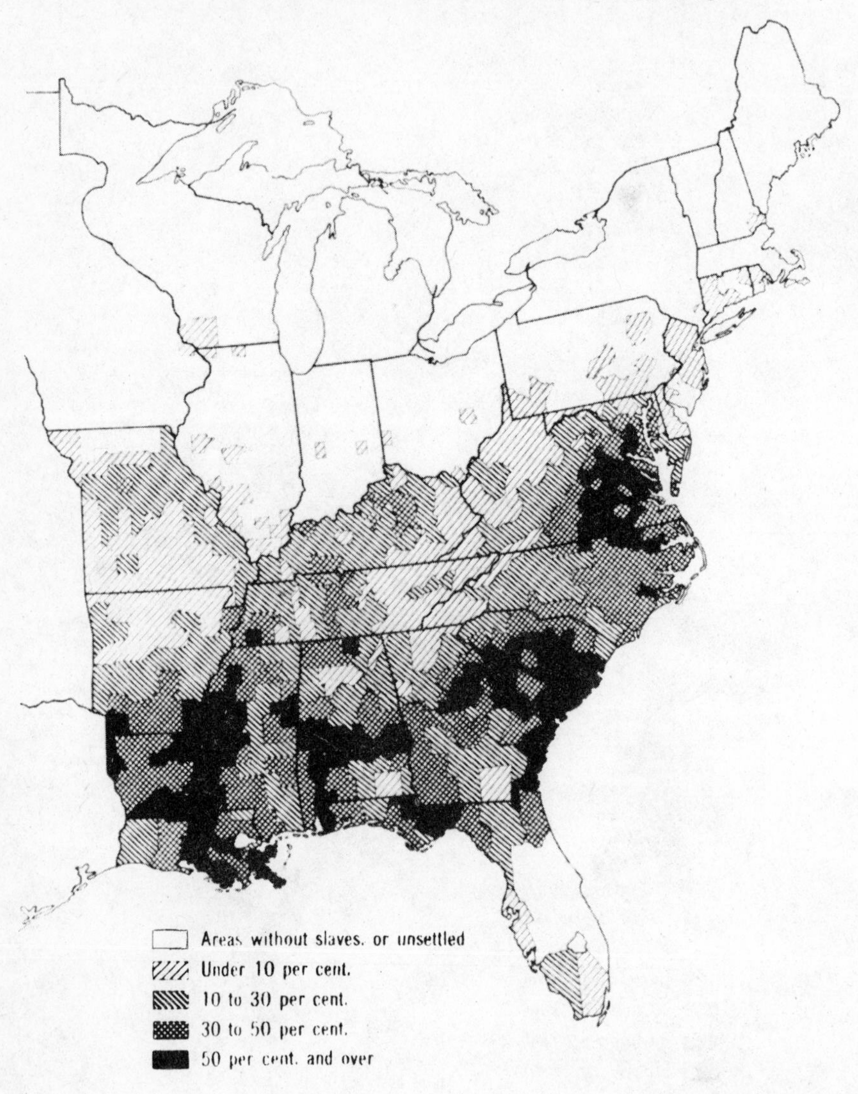
SLAVES, 1840
PER CENT. OF SLAVES IN TOTAL POPULATION
Areas without slaves, or unsettled
Under 10 per cent.
10 to 30 per cent.
30 to 50 per cent.
50 per cent. and over

maps you might want to make are included in the section "Additional Questions to Consider," below.

ASSIGNMENTS

1. Carefully examine the maps included in this chapter and prepare a list of at least three questions for future research based on the possible relationship between factors included on these maps and Indian removal. You might, for example, wish to raise questions regarding the relationship between Indian removal and an expanding white population, the expansion of slavery, or the fact that most of the removed Indian populations lived in the southern states.
2. As an alternative assignment, suggest at least three ways in which the evidence provided on these maps would support, refute, or refine the hypothesis that Indian removal was largely the product of expansionist energies related to a dynamic cotton economy based on slave labor. What additional kinds of maps would you like to examine for additional information related to this hypothesis?

ADDITIONAL QUESTIONS TO CONSIDER

1. The territorial expansion of the United States during the eighteenth and nineteenth centuries was a dual process whereby the government first acquired vast chunks of territory from another nation and then negotiated treaties of cession with the Indians who actually lived in the territory. Can you indicate the dual nature of this process on a map? How?
2. Would a map showing new states entering the union, along with their date of entry and their slave or free status, be useful in understanding the growing national conflict over slavery? If so, how could such a map be used?
3. How could a map showing major transportation developments between 1820 and 1860 be used to interpret the population density data contained on Maps 7.2 and 7.3?
4. What are the limits of maps? What are some of the ways in which they cannot be used?

MAP 7.6

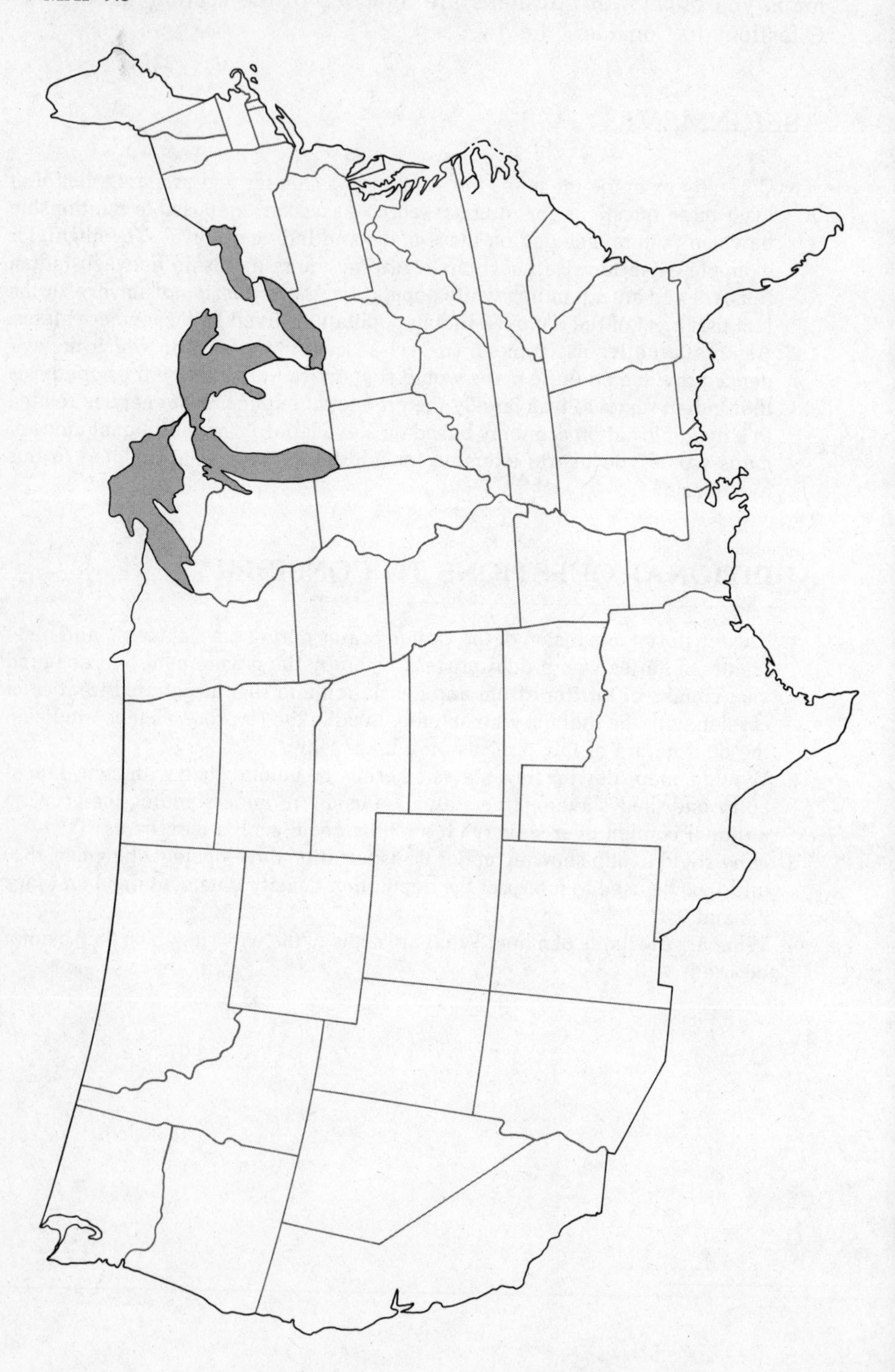

8

MATERIAL CULTURE IN ANTEBELLUM AMERICA

HYPOTHESIS FORMATION AND THE USE OF HISTORICAL ARTIFACTS

On April 13, 1844, according to the *New York Sun,* eight aeronauts successfully completed a transatlantic flight in Mr. Monck Mason's flying machine. The story, of course, was a hoax perpetrated by Edgar Allan Poe, but thousands reportedly believed the tale. Their acceptance testified to the dramatic impact that technological change had had on the lives of many Americans in the first half of the nineteenth century. Henry Adams, in fact, dated the passing of the old order precisely to May 1844, for in that month the Boston and Albany Railroad opened, the first regular transatlantic steamers arrived in Boston, and Washington, D.C., received word via telegraph that Henry Clay and James K. Polk had been nominated for the presidency. While few Americans were as exact as Adams, they were conscious that they lived in what Edward Everett called "an age of improvement," a new technological age characterized by industrialization.

In an age of satellite communications and space exploration, it is difficult to comprehend how dramatic were the changes introduced by the telegraph, the steam locomotive, and other innovations of the early nineteenth century. One way is to realize that the railroad was the first real improvement in the rate of overland travel since the invention of the wheel. Ralph Waldo Emerson, who took his first railroad ride in England in 1833, commented that "The very permanence of matter seems compromised and oaks, fields, hills, hitherto esteemed symbols of stability do absolutely dance by you." Emerson concluded in his essay "The Young American," published in 1844, that as a result of the telegraph and railroad, "distance is annihilated."

Technology would play a decisive role in the emergence of an independent American culture. While some Americans were uneasy about it (Henry David Thoreau flatly asserted in *Walden* that "We do not ride on the railroad; it rides on us"), most embraced technological change and industrialization as critical developments for the nation's future. Moses Brown, whom you may remember (Chapter 3) as a neutral regarding America's *political* revolution, was an ardent partisan in the country's *industrial* revolution. Indeed, the young nation teemed with schemes and dreams of progress and improvement. Sculptor Horatio Greenough commented sardonically, "Go ahead is the order of the day. The whole continent presents a scene of scrabbling and roars with greedy hurry." But "go ahead" transformed American life. Food, clothing, shelter, transportation, work—indeed, all aspects of American material culture were altered by industrialization.

Material culture consists of artifacts—such as quilts, pottery, chairs, paintings, tools, machines, and houses—that constitute a large percentage of the environment in which we live. Common sense suggests that these "things" reveal something of the ways in which we live and think. Archeologists, searching for the history of preliterate societies, have long recognized the importance of studying the remains of human material culture. Recently, historians of literate societies have also begun to look at the built environment and other made objects as sources of important historical evidence. In material culture, they reason, one can see the story of our physical environment and our manipulation of it. Historians of material culture recognize that our physical environment is shaped, changed, and modified by culturally determined behavior and that the careful study of material remains can provide important insights into the social and cultural patterns of literate societies, like that of Jacksonian America.

The study of material culture is also an invaluable vehicle for getting at history "from the bottom up." Objects designed and produced by ordinary men and women often provide information about or even communication from individuals who did not leave us any formal or informal written material. Furthermore, the study of the environment in which people lived can refine, challenge, and even revise existing historical interpretations based upon more conventional written sources.

Historical examination of material evidence (as, indeed, of all kinds of evidence) involves the formation of *hypotheses.* Hypothesis formation is just a more sophisticated kind of question asking. Yet hypotheses are not merely questions, nor are they conclusions or interpretations. A hypothesis is a tentative theory or supposition designed both to explain certain existing facts and to guide the researcher in the investigation of other facts. Without hypotheses, making sense out of any evidence would be extremely difficult. This is the central point about hypotheses: they should help you to make sense of the evidence.

For example, one hypothesis that historians currently find useful for understanding the Jacksonian era is the theory of modernization. The term "modernization" is used to refer to, and includes, a series of changes that took place between 1790 and 1840. These changes when viewed together produced a markedly different American society. They included intensive economic growth, the rise of cities, the diminution of family size, the rise of distinct social classes, the expansion of primary education, increased democratization in the political process, and the appearance of domesticity in family life.[1]

Many of these changes can be illustrated by working with a particular type of material culture from this era: the architectural designs of Andrew Jackson Downing. Downing was one of the leading landscape architects and architectural critics of his era. His designs were heavily influenced by what he saw in mid-nineteenth-century American society, and those designs, in turn, influenced the tastes of Americans at that time. His book *The Architecture of Country Houses* went to nine printings and sold over 16,000 copies by the end of the Civil War.

Reprinted at the end of this chapter are excerpts and designs from the 1850 edition of *The Architecture of Country Houses.* In this work and others, Downing put forth his belief that "much of the character of every man can be read in his house," and his hope that attractive homes with carefully landscaped grounds might counter what he saw as growing disorder and corruption in the United States. Whether or not this hope was shared by many Americans, they did appreciate and use Downing's designs. His ideas thus became a key component of America's nineteenth-century material culture and one that can show you much about that culture.

ASSIGNMENTS

1. Study the preface and designs from Downing's *The Architecture of Country Houses,* reproduced below. Develop two plausible hypotheses about how Downing's ideas and designs reflect the values of his age and/or how the living arrangements reproduced here provide evidence to challenge, support, refine, or revise the modernization hypothesis for Jacksonian America.
2. Sources taken from material culture have limitations, like any other historical sources. Briefly describe one bias or shortcoming inherent in any hypothesis about Jacksonian society that originates with Downing's designs.

[1]Richard D. Brown, *Modernization: The Transformation of American Life* (New York: Hill and Wang, 1976), passim.

ADDITIONAL QUESTIONS TO CONSIDER

1. Read the first chapter of Henry David Thoreau's *Walden,* especially the section called "Shelter." How do Thoreau's ideas differ from the ideas expressed by Downing? Does reading Thoreau suggest changes you would like to make in your hypotheses? If so, what changes?
2. Go to the library (or your local historical society or museum) and examine other artifacts from the United States during this era. Reproduce one or more of these objects by photocopying, tracing, or sketching, and be prepared to discuss in class what this evidence can tell you about Jacksonian America.

PREFACE

There are three excellent reasons why my countrymen should have good houses.

The first is, because a good house (and by this I mean a fitting, tasteful, and significant dwelling) is a powerful means of civilization. A nation, whose rural population is content to live in mean huts and miserable hovels, is certain to be behind its neighbors in education, the arts, and all that makes up the external signs of progress. With the perception of proportion, symmetry, order, and beauty, awakens the desire for possession, and with them comes that refinement of manners which distinguishes a civilized from a coarse and brutal people. So long as men are forced to dwell in log huts and follow a hunter's life, we must not be surprised at lynch law and the use of the bowie knife. But, when smiling lawns and tasteful cottages begin to embellish a country, we know that order and culture are established. And, as the first incentive towards this change is awakened in the minds of most men by the perception of beauty and superiority in external objects, it must follow that the interest manifested in the Rural Architecture of a country like this, has much to do with the progress of its civilization.

The second reason is, because the *individual home* has a great social value for a people. Whatever new systems may be needed for the regeneration of an old and enfeebled nation, we are persuaded that, in America, not only is the distinct family the best social form, but those elementary forces which give rise to the highest genius and the finest character may, for the most part, be traced back to the farm-house and the rural cottage. It is the solitude and freedom of the family home in the country which constantly preserves the purity of the nation, and invigorates its intellectual powers. The battle of life, carried on in cities, gives a sharper edge to the weapon of character, but its temper is, for the most part, fixed amid those communings with nature and the family, where individuality takes its most natural and strongest development.

The third reason is, because there is a moral influence in a country home —when, among an educated, truthful, and refined people, it is an echo of their character—which is more powerful than any mere oral teachings of virtue and morality. That family, whose religion lies away from its threshold, will show but slender results from the best teachings, compared with another where the family hearth is made a central point of the Beautiful and the Good. And much of that feverish unrest and want of balance between the desire and the fulfilment of life, is calmed and adjusted by the pursuit of tastes which result in making a little world of the family home, where truthfulness, beauty, and order have the largest dominion.

The mere sentiment of home, with its thousand associations, has, like a strong anchor, saved many a man from shipwreck in the storms of life. How much the moral influence of that sentiment may be increased, by making the home all that it should be, and how much an attachment is strengthened by every external sign of beauty that awakens love in the young, are so well understood, that they need no demonstration here. All to which the heart can attach itself in youth, and the memory linger fondly over in riper years, contributes largely to our stock of happiness, and to the elevation of the moral character. For this reason, the condition of the family home—in this country where every man may have a home—should be raised, till it shall symbolize the best character and pursuits, and the dearest affections and enjoyments of social life.

After the volumes I have previously written on this subject, it is needless for me to add more on the purpose of this work. But it is, perhaps, proper that I should say, that it is rather intended to develop the growing taste of the people, than as a scientific work on art. Rural Architecture is, indeed, so much more a sentiment, and so less a science, than Civil Architecture, that the majority of persons will always build for themselves, and, unconsciously, throw something of their own character into their dwellings. To do this well and gracefully, and not awkwardly and clumsily, is always found more difficult than is supposed. I have, therefore, written this volume, in the hope that it may be of some little assistance to the popular taste. For the same reason, I have endeavored to explain the whole subject in so familiar a manner, as to interest all classes of readers who can find any thing interesting in the beauty, convenience, or fitness of a house in the country.

A. J. D[OWNING]
Newburgh, on the Hudson.
June, 1850.

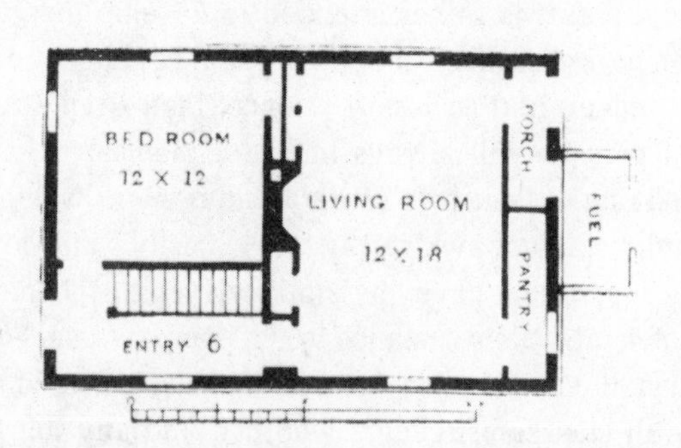

PRINCIPAL FLOOR

FIGURE 8.1 Downing design for a laborer's cottage.

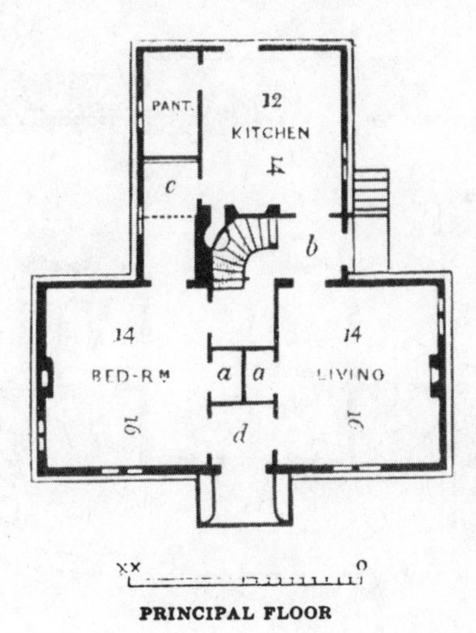

FIGURE 8.2 Downing design for a symmetrical bracketed cottage.

Small Classical Villa.]

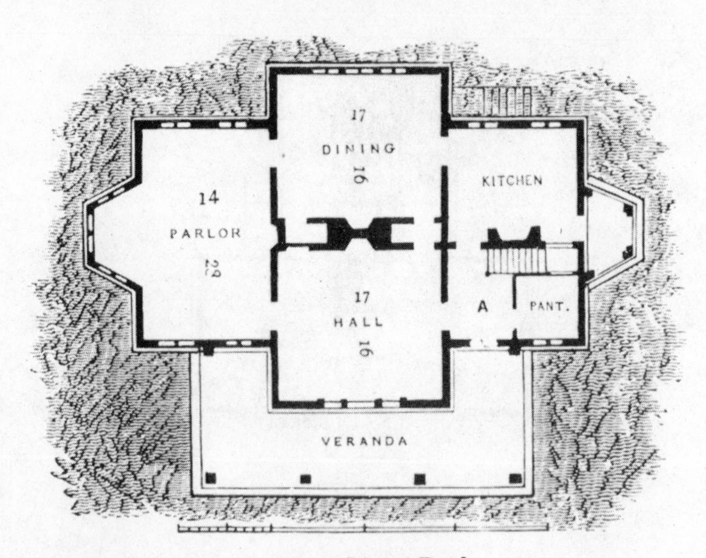

Principal Floor.]

FIGURE 8.3 Downing design for a villa or country house.

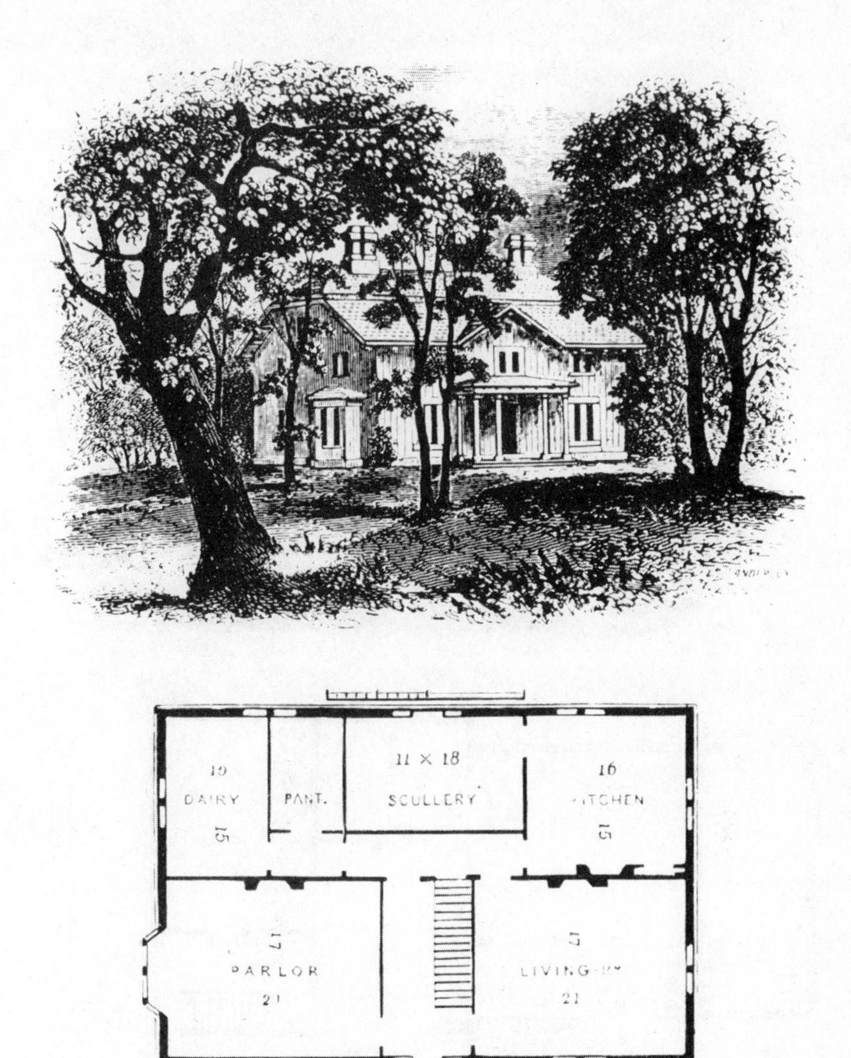

PRINCIPAL FLOOR

FIGURE 8.4 Downing design for a bracketed farmhouse of wood.

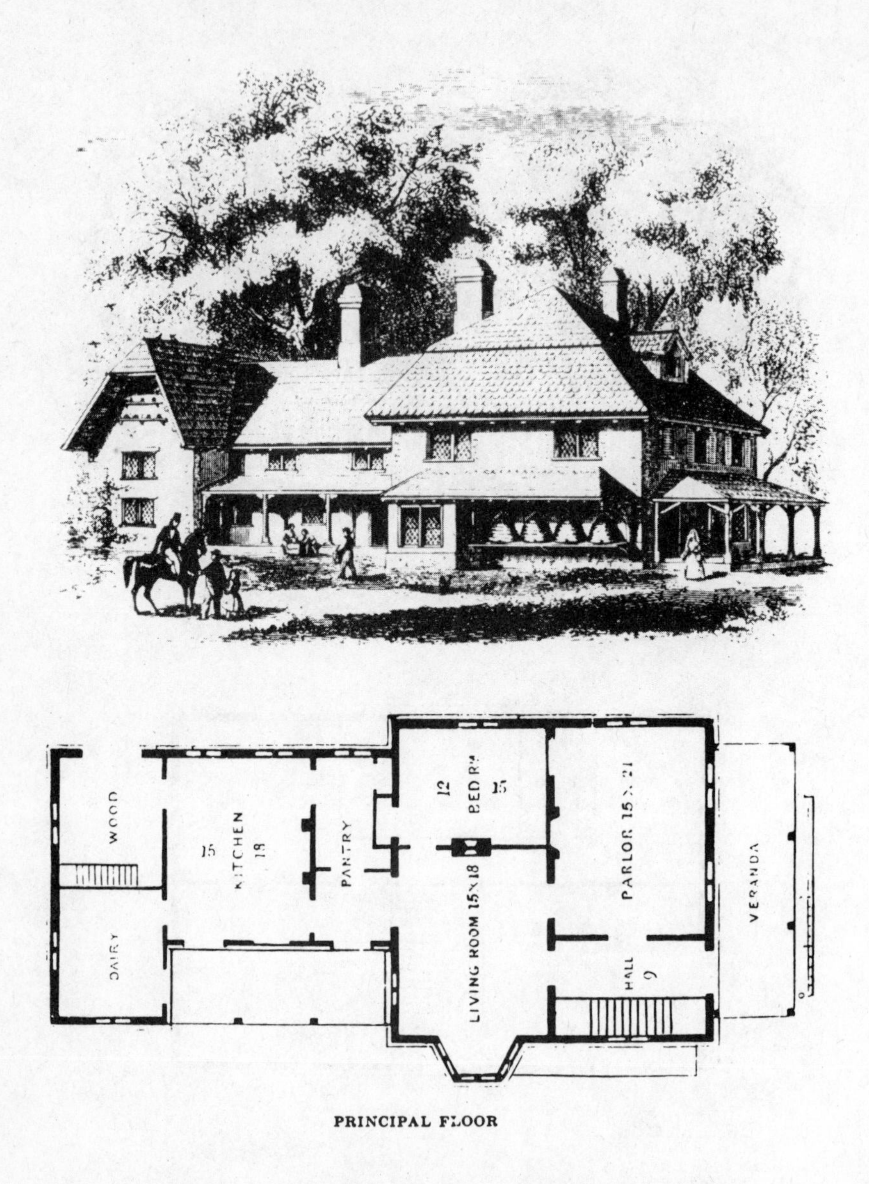

FIGURE 8.5 Downing design for a northern farm house.

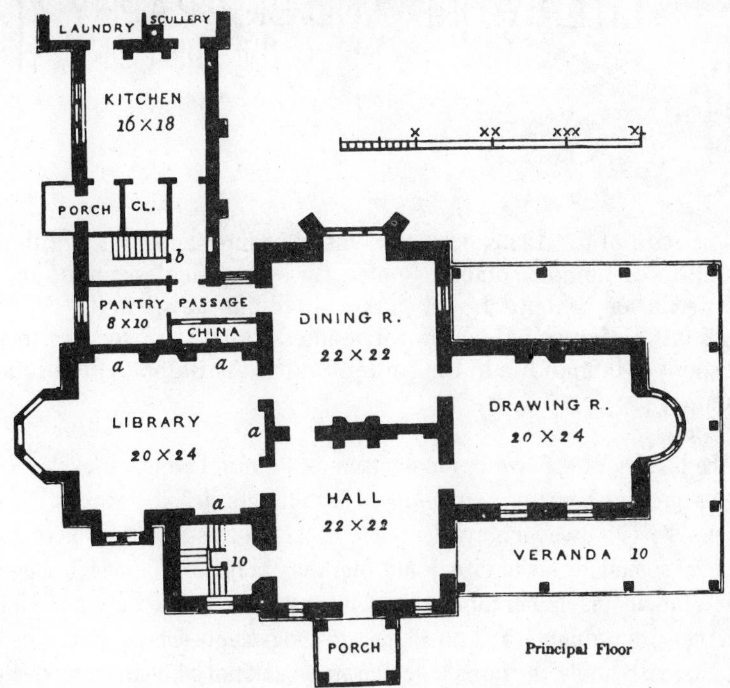

FIGURE 8.6 Downing design for a lake or river villa.

9

THE PROBLEM OF SLAVERY

LITERATURE AND BIOGRAPHY IN HISTORY

The reform era of the 1830s and '40s was characterized by its faith in the perfectibility of human society. Fueled by evangelical sermons on such biblical texts as "Behold I will make all things new" and "With God nothing shall be impossible," reform seemed to many observers to touch every aspect of human life in the United States. As Ralph Waldo Emerson remarked,

> In the history of the world, the doctrine of Reform had never such scope as at the present hour. . . . Lutherans, Herrnhutters, Jesuits, Monks, Quakers, Knox, Wesley, Swedenborg, Bentham, in their accusations of society, all respected something—church or state, literature or history, domestic usages, the market town, the dinner table, coined money. But now all these and all things else hear the trumpet and must rush to judgement—Christianity, the laws, commerce, schools, the farm, the laboratory; and not a kingdom, town statute, rite, calling, man or woman but is threatened by the new spirit.

A simple list of the areas in American life that were touched by reform in this period justifies Emerson's observation; everything from war and slavery to alcoholism and diet were targets of reformers.

Two of the most important of these reform movements were antislavery and women's rights. In a symbolic sense these two came together on February 21, 1838, when the genteel Angelina Grimké of South Carolina gave an address to the Massachusetts legislature; her topic, as she told the packed house, was "the great and solemn subject of slavery." In a society that believed the only proper place for a woman was in the home and which, accordingly, denied women the right to vote, the right to hold office, and, if married, the right to legal control over property, earnings, or, indeed, children, Angelina Grimké's determination to make the voice of women heard on the subject of slavery was a revolutionary act. Her address was fervent and forceful; she asserted the right of women to have political influence, and concluded with these words:

> I stand before you as a southerner, exiled from the land of my birth by the sound of the lash and the piteous cry of the slave. . . . I stand before you as a moral being and as a moral being I feel that I owe it to the suffering slave and to the deluded masters, to my country and to the world to do all that I can to overturn a system of complicated crimes, built upon the broken hearts and prostrate bodies of my countrymen in chains and cemented by the blood, sweat, and tears of my sisters in bonds.

As a reformer and as a woman of her time, Angelina Grimké, like her sister Sarah, was exceptional. Ordinarily, men and women lead their lives with little sense of being participants in history—people who have the power to change society's destiny. And it is true that much history, mostly unwritten, is a quiet story of births, loves, and deaths, dominated by daily joys and sorrows, and characterized by the endless struggle of people to find meaning in their own lives. Yet there are times when a profound and troublesome issue arises to change irrevocably the shape of human lives. Slavery was such an issue for the Grimké sisters and for tens of thousands of others in the United States during the thirty years preceding the Civil War.

Slavery was brought to national attention by a relatively small group of reformers—the abolitionists. These individuals took upon themselves the difficult and unpopular role of agitators and outspoken critics of a society that, in their eyes, had acquiesced too easily in an unmitigated evil. In their zeal to rid the country of slavery, they were often accused of self-righteousness, irresponsibility, and fanaticism, and they wound up alienating a large number of Americans. Simultaneously, however, they starkly exposed the gap between American ideals and practice and the hypocrisy involved in refusing to take a stand on the issue. This may help to explain the pain and anguish many Americans experienced in coming to grips with the practice of slavery as well as the profound effect of this issue on the many individuals who never formally identified themselves with the abolitionist cause.

Those who were greatly affected by slavery and/or who became abolitionists included a large number of women. Earlier than many men, these women faced the necessity of taking a stand and acting accordingly. They were inspired by their personal experiences, by their antislavery ministers, by the reform movement in general, and by mores that gave them primary responsibility for the moral values and standards within the society. All these factors resulted in radical political activity by women, which was unprecedented in American history.

Women living in the South experienced the evils of slavery firsthand, and many of them learned to fear and despise the institution as much as their northern counterparts. For these women, however, antislavery activity meant exile to the North. While some, like the Grimké sisters, took this path, others remained at home and reserved their sentiments for the privacy of their own diaries. In many ways those diaries—and the anguish they expressed—reveal more about the evils of slavery than the abolitionist propaganda that poured out of the North.

The slavery issue, then, was greatly influenced by the impact it had on the lives of individual women, and those women who did contribute, either directly or indirectly, to the antislavery cause became the appropriate subjects for an important kind of historical study—biography.

Biography is a highly popular form of history that studies individual lives. In the process, it often illuminates not only specific people and situations but also an entire society. Society is, after all, composed of separate individuals who share common beliefs and experiences; in turn, the study of any one of these individuals involves the study of the environment within which the subject lived.

Biographies can thus reveal the beliefs and general patterns of experience of an entire society as seen through the life of one of its members. According to some writers in the relatively new and highly publicized field of psychohistory, biographies can also reveal the subconscious motivations that ruled both individuals and their societies. Recent studies of Andrew Jackson, for example, have presented his beliefs, actions, popularity, and neuroses as symbolic of the consciousness of an entire era.

At the end of this chapter you will find biographical sketches and excerpts from the writings of two women whose lives were greatly affected by the institution of slavery and whose reactions were typical of other women in their situations. Harriet Beecher Stowe was a northern abolitionist whose novel *Uncle Tom's Cabin* became one of the most influential works of fiction in American history. Mary Chesnut was a southerner whose diary reveals much of the quieter antagonism that many southern women felt for the institution of slavery.

Unlike most of the documents previously included in this volume, the excerpts you will be reading in this chapter are literary. Both Mrs. Stowe and Mrs. Chesnut were artists who wrote self-consciously, with a potential audience in mind; their writings consequently raise some interesting questions about the relationship between society, literature, and history.

Literature is one of the most interesting primary sources the historian can use. It is also one of the most confusing, however, for the artist and her work stand in a unique, complex, and sometimes uncomfortable position relative to the rest of society. For example, Harriet Beecher Stowe obviously wrote *Uncle Tom's Cabin* to change society. Yet her ideas were clearly a reflection of that society. Moreover, she needed to make money from the sale of her work. What conclusions, then, can one properly draw about this specific novel, and literature in general, as a primary source and its role in history? In a different vein, the fact that Mary Chesnut wrote in a locked diary would lead one to the conclusion that she did not consider her words to be literary and did not desire wide circulation. Yet her actions, most notably her efforts to revise the diary for publication between 1865 and 1883, illustrate a clear knowledge of her literary talents and a desire to share them with the public at large. How can one reconcile this conflicting evidence? In light of the major revisions Chesnut completed, how valid is the diary as a primary source? Think about these facts and questions as you proceed through this chapter and be prepared to discuss your conclusions as explained in the "Additional Questions" section.

ASSIGNMENTS

1. Read the biographical sketches of Harriet Beecher Stowe and Mary Chesnut provided below, as well as the excerpts from their works.
2. Choose a third individual from this era whose life was affected by slavery and who left some sort of documentary evidence (i.e., book, pamphlet, memoir, diary, speech, painting) of the fact.
3. Using the library skills discussed in Chapter 1, research that individual's life and duplicate the documentary evidence.
4. Write a 2- to 3-page (500- to 750-word) biographical sketch of the individual. Organize your material and emphasize relevant factors in such a way that the sketch serves as an *introduction to the document.* You can use the two sketches provided as guides in this regard, but make sure you include footnotes and bibliography as well as the duplication.

ADDITIONAL QUESTIONS TO CONSIDER

1. What did your biographical research teach you about U.S. history during this era? In general terms, what would you consider to be the strengths and weaknesses of the biographical approach to history? Why is it such a popular form of historical writing?
2. What themes does Harriet Beecher Stowe develop in the excerpt you have read from *Uncle Tom's Cabin?* From this excerpt, try to explain whether the novel reflected or determined societal values, or both, and why its impact was so great.
3. The sketch of Harriet Beecher Stowe contains some psychohistory. What psychological interpretations is the author suggesting?
4. In light of the fact that Mary Chesnut drastically revised her Civil War diary

over a period of two decades, what are the strengths and weaknesses of the published version as a primary source? In this regard, historian C. Vann Woodward has concluded in his recent Pulitzer prize-winning edition of the diary that "The integrity of the author's experience and perception is maintained in this transformation, but not the literal record of events expected of the diarist." Consequently, the "enduring value" of the diary lies not in the historical information it provides but "in the life and reality with which it endows people and events and with which it evokes the chaos and complexity of a society at war."[1] From the excerpts you have read, do you agree? Why?

5. In general, what are the strengths and weaknesses of literature as a primary source for historical study?
6. The effect of slavery on women's lives was obviously important, varied, and complex. Using the specifics you have gathered from this chapter, your text, and your research, try to list and account for these effects.

HARRIET BEECHER STOWE

Harriet Beecher Stowe was as well known as any American woman of the nineteenth century. Her fame rests largely on her antislavery novel *Uncle Tom's Cabin,* which was one of the most influential books in all of American history. It sold over 300,000 copies in the first year after publication and soon thereafter became the first novel to sell a million copies. By 1861, sales had reached the unprecedented figure of 2.5 million. When President Lincoln met Mrs. Stowe during the Civil War, he is said to have remarked, "So this is the little lady who wrote the book that made this great war."

Harriet Beecher was born in Litchfield, Connecticut, in 1811, the seventh child and fourth daughter of the well-known Congregational minister Lyman Beecher. When Harriet was four her mother died, and although Lyman Beecher remarried, Harriet never took to her stepmother. Instead, she consistently turned to her busy father for spiritual guidance and to her younger brother Henry Ward (b. 1813) for acceptance and play. A shy, undersized child, Harriet studied deeply in an effort to find the way to her own salvation.

As a family, the Beechers firmly believed in their Christian duty to serve mankind. When Catharine, the oldest sister, determined that the feminine counterpart to the Christian minister was a redeemed woman devoted to her "natural" vocations of teaching, nursing, and motherhood, it looked as though Harriet might devote herself to teaching under Catharine's supervision.

Two events would change Harriet Beecher's life. The first was her father's acceptance, in 1832, of the presidency of Lane Theological Seminary. The second was her marriage, four years later, at the age of twenty-five, to a professor of biblical literature at Lane named Calvin Ellis Stowe.

Lane was located in Cincinnati, Ohio, a brawling, thriving river town

[1]C. Vann Woodward, ed., *Mary Chesnut's Civil War* (New Haven, Conn.: Yale University Press, 1981), pp. xxv, xxvii.

full of pork packinghouses, pig-filled streets, and riverfront bars. More important for Harriet, Cincinnati was across the river from slavery, and a constant stream of escaped blacks sought haven in the free city and state. White public opinion was divided on the slavery issue, and Cincinnati became a center for the ensuing debate. In 1835, this debate centered on Lane when a brilliant and confident student leader, Theodore Weld—against the wishes of Beecher and the Lane trustees—persuaded most of the faculty and student body to espouse radical abolitionism, resign from the seminary, and move in a body to found Oberlin as a college devoted to abolitionism. Harriet's life was inalterably shaped by these experiences with slavery and abolitionism in Ohio.

Equally important to Harriet's future were the difficulties she experienced during the early years of her marriage. She had little money; bore five children within seven years; had to support her husband's mother, who lived with the young couple; and was also burdened by Calvin's personal problems. He often berated himself for his numerous weaknesses—his lustfulness and fondness for brandy—as well as his failure as a fundraiser and the fact that he did not "know how" to be intimate.

Despite these problems, the Stowes worked hard at their marriage. Their letters show each of them struggling to articulate their dissatisfactions and seeking the reasons that they felt less contented than they thought they should be. To bring in more money, Harriet turned to writing; in 1843, she had her first modest literary success, a published collection of short stories entitled *The Mayflower.* Calvin strongly supported these literary endeavors, saying in a letter that "God has written it in His book that you must be a literary woman and who are we that we should contend against God?"

Harriet's devotion to literature did little to spare her further anguish during the 1840s. The birth of her fifth child in 1843, after a very difficult pregnancy, left both mother and daughter extremely weak and ill. In desperation, Harriet visited a fashionable "water cure" establishment at Brattleboro, Vermont, in the spring of 1846. The ensuing ten-month regimen of icy baths, water sprays, and long walks left her feeling much better, and she was able to return to her family in Cincinnati. Soon thereafter, however, her husband went to Vermont for a fifteen-month water cure of his own, leaving Harriet with their five children and pregnant for the sixth time. And during his absence in the summer of 1849, Cincinnati suffered a devastating outbreak of cholera.

At its peak, the epidemic claimed a thousand lives a week. The demoralized city became choked with fumes from coal, which people burned as a disinfectant, and was filled with upright citizens doing their best to stay drunk all the time. Harriet wrote Calvin not to come home to such a dangerous environment. As a result, she was alone when her sixth child began to have convulsions at the end of the summer. Within four days the child was dead. Harriet herself began to suffer from cramps and convulsions, and the doctors assumed that she too would soon die. But her seventy-year old father helped to pull her through with prayer, brandy, and an all-night vigil.

Harriet later remembered that summer as the most difficult time of her life. Her despair was tempered somewhat by news of an offer to Calvin to teach at his alma mater, Bowdoin College, but his new salary remained inadequate for the growing needs of their family. Harriet, therefore, continued to write while she also remodeled their new home in Brunswick, did all the cooking, read to her children two hours each night, and gave birth to her seventh child.

With all these activities, Harriet still found time to stay abreast of the slavery debate that continued to trouble the nation. She read the works of antislavery authors like Lydia Marie Child, studied the autobiographies of former slaves like Frederick Douglass, followed the careers of her preacher-abolitionist brothers Edward and Henry Ward, and wrote letters excoriating the recently passed Fugitive Slave Act. One Sunday, after she had taken communion, she had what she would later call "almost a tangible vision"—the death of an exemplary slave and Christian who would become Uncle Tom. ("How do you know there's any Christ, Tom? You never saw the Lord." "Felt him in my soul, Mas'r.—feel Him now!") She returned home from church, wrote down her vision, and *Uncle Tom's Cabin* was born.

Harriet wrote the novel at night, in installments, after the children had gone to bed. By the time the final installments appeared in the *National Era* magazine, both she and her publishers realized that she had created a national sensation. "How she is shaking the world with her Uncle Tom's Cabin!" the poet Henry Wadsworth Longfellow commented. "At one step she has reached the top of the stair case up which the rest of us climb on our knees year after year."

In a dramatic and readable form, *Uncle Tom's Cabin* captured and revealed—as no abolitionist tract had been able to do—the threat that slavery posed to individual, national, and Christian ideals. Much of the strength of the book is derived from Harriet's insistence that every person in the United States must understand this and cease treating slavery as simply a southern problem. Slavery proved as corrupting to northerners in the novel, from Cousin Ophelia of Vermont to the transplanted Yankee plantation owner and archvillain Simon Legree, as it was damaging to their southern counterparts. It is against Ophelia that Topsy's anguished cry, "She can't bar me 'cause I'm a nigger—she'd's soon have a toad touch her!" is directed.

Another strength of the book lay in its portrayal of slavery's destructive impact on home and family. The odyssey of the black characters, from plantation to plantation, reveals a progressive dehumanization for white and black alike. Equally distressing to readers was Stowe's portrayal of slavery as destructive to all Christian values and her implicit indictment of the passive, hypocritical Christianity that spoke of establishing the "benevolent empire" in the United States while allowing slavery to continue to exist. Uncle Tom is rewarded for his religious faith with separation from his family, exile, torture, imprisonment, and death. To an evangelical Christian nation convinced of its own perfectibility, the impact of this message was shattering.

Harriet Beecher Stowe enjoyed the fruits of the popularity that her best-seller brought to her. The summer after the book was published, Calvin accepted a position as professor of sacred theology at Andover Theological Seminary while she sat down to respond to her critics. That response was published as a collection, called the *Key to Uncle Tom's Cabin,* which tried to document the accuracy of her depiction of slavery. In 1856, she made another contribution to the antislavery cause with *Dred,* a novel portraying a small band of black outlaws, in North Carolina's dismal swamp, who organize a holy war to seek justice for black people. Critics dismissed the book, but her public bought and read it with enthusiasm.

Calvin Stowe retired from teaching in 1864; the family then moved to Hartford, Connecticut. There he slipped into the role of scholarly invalid while Harriet wrote a book each year to support herself, her husband, and her often impecunious children. Today none of these later works is read much except by certain scholars, but she worked seriously and prodigiously at her craft.

Calvin died in 1886, and around 1890 Harriet's mind began to fail. She was remembered by one of her neighbors, Mark Twain, as a harmless, vague, cheerful old lady who picked flowers in his garden and delighted in sneaking up behind people and frightening them with a war whoop. At church services, she would occasionally disturb the congregation by weeping loudly and convulsively. She died on July 1, 1896.

The excerpt reproduced below is taken from the latter part of *Uncle Tom's Cabin.* Tom has by this time fallen into the hands of the evil Simon Legree who, in attempting to break his faith and spirit, will eventually beat Tom to death. While not as vivid as the famous Lisa escape episode, this scene is considered by many to be one of the most moving and revealing in the entire novel.

"THE QUADROON'S STORY" FROM UNCLE TOM'S CABIN

> "And behold the tears of such as are oppressed; and on the side of their oppressors there was power. Wherefore I praised the dead that are already dead more than the living that are yet alive." (Eccl. 4:1)

It was late at night, and Tom lay groaning and bleeding alone, in an old forsaken room of the gin-house, among pieces of broken machinery, piles of damaged cotton, and other rubbish which had there accumulated.

The night was damp and close, and the thick air swarmed with myriads of mosquitos, which increased the restless torture of his wounds; whilst a burning thirst—a torture beyond all others—filled up the uttermost measure of physical anguish.

"O, good Lord! Do look down,—give me the victory!—give me the victory over all!" prayed poor Tom, in his anguish.

A footstep entered the room, behind him, and the light of a lantern flashed on his eyes.

"Who's there! O, for the Lord's massy, please give me some water!"

The woman Cassy—for it was she—set down the lantern, and, pouring water from a bottle, raised his head, and gave him drink. Another and another cup were drained, with feverish eagerness.

"Drink all ye want," she said; "I knew how it would be. It isn't the first time I've been out in the night, carrying water to such as you."

"Thank you, Missis," said Tom, when he had done drinking.

"Don't call me Missis! I'm a miserable slave, like yourself,—a lower one than you can ever be!" said she, bitterly; "but now," said she, going to the door, and dragging in a small paillasse, over which she had spread linen cloths wet with cold water, "try, my poor fellow, to roll yourself on to this."

Stiff with wounds and bruises, Tom was a long time in accomplishing this movement; but, when done, he felt a sensible relief from the cooling application to his wounds.

The woman, who long practice with the victims of brutality had made familiar with many healing arts, went on to make many applications to Tom's wounds, by means of which he was somewhat relieved.

"Now," said the woman, when she had raised his head on a roll of damaged cotton, which served for a pillow, "there's the best I can do for you."

Tom thanked her; and the woman, sitting down on the floor, drew up her knees, and embracing them with her arms, looked fixedly before her, with a bitter and painful expression of countenance. Her bonnet fell back, and long wavy streams of black hair fell around her singular and melancholy face.

"It's no use, my poor fellow!" she broke out, at last, "it's of no use, this you've been trying to do. You were a brave fellow,—you had the right on your side; but it's all in vain, and out of the question, for you to struggle. You are in the devil's hands;—he is the strongest, and you must give up!"

Give up! and, had not human weakness and physical agony whispered that, before? Tom started; for the bitter woman, with her wild eyes and melancholy voice, seemed to him an embodiment of the temptation with which he had been wrestling.

"O Lord! O Lord!" he groaned, "how can I give up?"

"There's no use calling on the Lord,—he never hears," said the woman, steadily; "there isn't any God, I believe; or, if there is, he's taken sides against us. All goes against us, heaven and earth. Everything is pushing us into hell. Why shouldn't we go?"

Tom closed his eyes, and shuddered at the dark, atheistic words.

"You see," said the woman, *"you* don't know anything about it;—I do. I've been on this place five years, body and soul, under this man's foot; and I hate him as I do the devil! Here you are, on a lone plantation, ten miles from any other, in the swamps; not a white person here who could testify, if you were burned alive,—if you were scalded, cut into inch-pieces, set up for the dogs to tear, or hung up and whipped to death. There's no law here, of God or man, that can do you, or any one of us, the least good; and, this man! there's no earthly thing he's too good to do. I could make any one's hair rise, and their teeth chatter, if I should only tell what I've seen and been knowing to, here, —and there's no resisting! Did I *want* to live with him? Wasn't I a woman delicately bred; and he—God in heaven; what was he, and is he? And yet, I've lived with him, these five years, and cursed every moment of my life,—night and day! And now, he's got a new one,—a young thing, only fifteen, and she brought up, she says, piously. Her good mistress taught her to read the Bible; and she's brought her Bible here—to hell with her!"—and the woman laughed a wild and doleful laugh, that rang, with a strange, supernatural sound, through the old ruined shed.

Tom folded his hands; all was darkness and horror.

"O Jesus! Lord Jesus! have you quite forgot us poor critturs?" burst forth, at last;—"help, Lord, I perish!"

The woman sternly continued:

"And what are these miserable low dogs you work with, that you should suffer on their account? Every one of them would turn against you, the first time they got a chance. They are all of 'em as low and cruel to each other as they can be; there's no use in your suffering to keep from hurting them."

"Poor critturs!" said Tom,—"what made 'em cruel?—and, if I give out, I shall get used to 't, and grow, little by little just like 'em! No, no, Missis! I've lost everything,—wife, children, and home, and a kind Mas'r,—and he would have set me free, if he'd only lived a week longer; I've lost everything in *this* world, and it's clean gone, forever,—and now I *can't* lose Heaven, too' no, I can't get to be wicked, besides all!"

"But it can't be that the Lord will lay sin to our account," said the woman; "he won't charge it to us, when we're forced to it; he'll charge it to them that drove us to it."

"Yes," said Tom; "but that won't keep us from growing wicked. If I get to be as hardhearted as that ar Sambo, and as wicked, it won't make much odds to me how I come so' it's the *bein'* so,—that ar's I'm a dreadin'."

The woman fixed a wild and startled look on Tom, as if a new thought had struck her; and then, heavily groaning, said,

"Oh God a' mercy! you speak the truth! O—O—O—!"—and, with groans, she fell on the floor, like one crushed and writhing under the extremity of mental anguish.

There was a silence, a while, in which the breathing of both parties could be heard, when Tom faintly said, "O, please, Missis!"

The woman suddenly rose up, with her face composed to its usual stern, melancholy expression.

"Please, Missis, I saw 'em throw my coat in that ar' corner, and in my coat-pocket is my Bible;—if Missis would please get it for me."

Cassy went and got it. Tom opened, at once, to a heavily marked passage, much worn, of the last scenes in the life of Him by whose stripes we are healed.

"If Missis would only be so good as read as that ar',—it's better than water."

Cassy took the book, with a dry, proud air, and looked over the passage. She then read aloud, in a soft voice, and with a beauty of intonation that was peculiar, that touching account of anguish and of glory. Often, as she read, her voice faltered, and sometimes failed her altogether, when she would stop, with an air of frigid composure, till she had mastered herself. When she came to the touching words, "Father forgive them, for they know not what they do," she threw down the book, and burying her face in the heavy masses of her hair, she sobbed aloud, with a convulsive violence.

Tom was weeping, also, and occasionally uttering a smothered ejaculation.

"If we only could keep up to that ar'!" said Tom;—"it seemed to come so natural to him, and we have to fight so hard for't! O Lord, help us! O blessed Lord Jesus, do help us!"

"Missis," said Tom, after a while, "I can see that, some how, you're quite 'bove me in everything; but there's one thing Missis might learn even from poor Tom. Ye said the Lord took sides against us, because he lets us be 'bused and knocked round; but ye see what come on his own Son,—the blessed Lord of Glory,—wan't he allays poor? and have we, any of us, yet come so low as he come? The Lord han't forgot us,—I'm sartin' o' that ar'. If we suffer with him, we shall also reign, Scripture says; but, if we deny Him, he also will deny us. Didn't they all suffer?—the Lord and all his? It tells how they was stoned and sawn asunder, and wandered about in sheep-skins and goat-skins, and was destitute, afflicted, tormented. Sufferin' an't no reason to make us think the Lord's turned agin us; but jest the contrary, if only we hold on to him, and doesn't give up to sin."

"But why does he put us where we can't help but sin?" said the woman.

"I think we *can* help it," said Tom.

"You'll see," said Cassy; "what'll you do? To-morrow they'll be at you again. I know 'em; I've seen all their doings; I can't bear to think of all they'll bring you to;—and they'll make you give out, at last!"

"Lord Jesus!" said Tom, "you *will* take care of my soul? O Lord, do!—don't let me give out!"

"O dear!" said Cassy; "I've heard all this crying and praying before; and yet, they've been broken down, and brought under. There's Emmeline, she's trying to hold on, and you're trying,—but what use? You must give up, or be killed by inches."

"Well, then I *will* die!" said Tom. "Spin it out as long as they can, they can't help my dying some time!—and, after that, they can't do no more. I'm clar, I'm set! I know the Lord'll help me, and bring me through."

The woman did not answer; she sat with her black eyes intently fixed on the floor.

"May be it's the way," she murmured to herself; "but those that *have* given up, there's no hope for them!—none! We live in filth, and grow loathsome, till we loathe outselves! And we long to die, and we don't dare to kill ourselves.—No hope! no hope! no hope!—this girl now,—just as old as I was!

"You see me now," she said, speaking to Tom very rapidly; "see what I am! Well, I was brought up in luxury; the first I remember is, playing about, when I was a child, in splendid parlors;—when I was kept dressed up like a doll, and company and visitors used to praise me. There was a garden opening from the saloon windows; and there I used to play hide-and-go-seek; under the orange-trees, with my brothers and sisters. I went to a convent, and there I learned music, French and embroidery, and what not; and when I was fourteen, I came out to my father's funeral. He died very suddenly, and when the property came to be settled, they found that there was scarcely enough to cover the debts; and when the creditors took an inventory of the property, I was set down in it. My mother was a slave woman, and my father had always meant to set me free; but he had not done it, and so I was set down in the list. I'd always known who I was, but never thought much about it. Nobody ever expected that a strong, healthy man is a going to die. My father was a well man only four hours before he died;—it was one of the first cholera cases in New Orleans. The day after the funeral, my father's wife took her children, and went up to her father's plantation. I thought they treated me strangely, but didn't know. There was a young lawyer who they left to settle the business; and he came every day, and was about the house, and spoke very politely to me. He brought with him, one day, a young man, who I thought the handsomest I had ever seen. I shall never forget that evening. I walked with him in the garden. I was lonesome and full of sorrow, and he was so kind and gentle to me; and he told me that he had seen me before I went to the convent, and that he had loved me a great while, and that he would be my friend and protector;—in short, though he didn't tell me, he had paid two thousand dollars for me, and I was his property—I became his willingly, for I loved him. Loved!" said the woman, stopping. "O, how I *did* love that man! How I love him now,—and always shall, while I breathe! He was so beautiful, so high, so noble! He put me into a beautiful house, with servants, horses, and carriages, and furniture, and dresses. Everything that money could buy, he gave me; but I didn't set any value on all that,—I only cared for him. I loved him better than my God and my own soul; and, if I tried, I couldn't do any other way from what he wanted me to.

"I wanted only one thing—I did want him to *marry* me. I thought, if he loved me as he said he did, and if I was what he seemed to think I was he would be willing to marry me and set me free. But he convinced me that it would be impossible; and he told me that, if we were only faithful to each other, it was marriage before God. If that is true, wasn't I that man's wife? Wasn't I faithful? For seven years, didn't I study every look and motion, and only live and breathe to please him? He had the yellow fever, and for twenty days and nights I watched with him. I alone,—and gave him all his medicine, and did everything for him; and then he called me his good angel, and said I'd saved his life. We had two beautiful children. The first was a boy, and we called him Henry. He was the image of his father,—he had such beautiful eyes, such a forehead, and his hair hung all in curls around it; and he had all his father's spirit, and his talent, too. Little Elise, he said, looked like me. He used to tell me that I was the most beautiful woman in Louisiana, he was so proud of me and the children. He used to love to have me dress them up, and take them and me about in an open carriage, and hear the remarks that people would make on us; and he used to fill my ears constantly with the fine things that were said in praise of me and the children. O, those were happy days! I thought I was as happy as any one could be; but then there came evil times. He had a cousin come to New Orleans, who was his particular friend,—he thought all the world of him;—but, for the first time I saw him, I couldn't tell why, I dreaded him; for I felt sure he was going to bring misery on us. He got Henry to going out with him; and often he wouldn't come home nights till two or three o'clock. I did not dare say a word; for Henry was so high-spirited, I was afraid to. He got him to the gaming'houses; and he was one of the sort that, when he once got a going there, there was no holding back. And then he introduced him to another lady, and I saw soon that his heart was gone from me. He never told me, but I saw it,—I knew it, day after day,—I felt my heart breaking, but I could not say a word! At this, the wretch offered to buy me and the children of Henry, to clear off his gambling debts, which stood in the way of his marrying as he wished;—and *he sold us.* He told me, one day, that he had business in the country, and should be gone two or three weeks. He spoke kinder than usual, and said he should come back; but it didn't deceive me. I knew that the time had come; I was just like one turned into stone; I couldn't speak, nor shed a tear. He kissed me and kissed the children, a good many times, and went out. I saw him get on his horse, and I watched him till he was quite out of sight; and then I fell down, and fainted.

"Then *he* came, the cursed wretch! he came to take possession. He told me that he had bought me and my children; and showed me the papers. I cursed him before God, and told him I'd die sooner than live with him.

"Just as you please,' said he; 'but, if you don't behave reasonably, I'll sell both the children, where you shall never see them again.' He told me that he always had meant to have me, from the first time he saw me; and that he had drawn Henry on, and got him in debt, on purpose to make him willing to sell me. That he got him in love with another woman; and that I might know, after all that, that he should not give up for a few airs and tears, and things of that sort.

"I gave up, for my hands were tied. He had my children;—whenever I resisted his will anywhere, he would talk about selling them, and he made me as submissive as he desired. O, what a life it was! to live with my heart breaking, every day,—to keep on, on, on, loving, when it was only misery; and to be bound, body and soul, to one I hated. I used to love to read to Henry, to play to him, to waltz with him, and sing to him; but everything I did for this one was a perfect drag,—yet I was afraid to refuse anything. He was very imperious, and harsh to the children. Elise was a timid little thing; but Henry was bold and high-spirited, like his father, and he had never been brought under, in the least, by any one. He was always finding fault, and quarreling with him; and I used to live in daily fear and dread. I tried to make the child respectful;—I tried to keep them apart, for I held on to those children like death; but it did no good. *He sold both those children.* He took me to ride, one day, and when I came home, they were nowhere to be found! He told me he had sold them; he showed me the money, the price of their blood. Then it seemed as if all good forsook me. I raved and cursed,—cursed God and man; and, for a while, I believe, he really was afraid of me. But he didn't give up so. He told me that my children were sold, but whether I ever saw their faces again, depended on him; and that, if I wasn't quiet, they should smart for it. Well, you can do anything with a woman, when you've got her children. He made me submit; he made me peaceable; he flattered me with hopes that, perhaps, he would buy them back; and so things went on, a week or two. One day, I was out walking, and passed by the calaboose; I saw a crowd about the gate, and heard a child's voice,—and suddenly my Henry broke away from two or three men who were holding him, and ran, screaming, and caught my dress. They came up to him, swearing dreadfully; and one man, whose face I shall never forget, told him that he wouldn't get away so; that he was going with him into the calaboose, and he'd get a lesson there he'd never forget. I tried to beg and plead,—they only laughed; the poor boy screamed and looked into my face, and held on to me, until, in tearing him off, they tore the skirt of my dress half away; and they carried him in, screaming, 'Mother! mother! mother!' There was one man stood there seemed to pity me. I offered him all the money I had, if he'd only interfere. He shook his head, and said that the boy had been impudent and disobedient, ever since he bought him; that he was going to break him in, once for all. I turned and ran; and every step of the way, I thought that I heard him scream. I got into the house; ran, all out of breath, to the parlor, where I found Butler. I told him, and begged him to go and interfere. He only laughed, and told me the boy had got his deserts. He'd got to be broken in,—the sooner the better; 'what did I expect?' he asked.

"It seemed to me something in my head snapped, at that moment. I felt dizzy and furious. I remember seeing a great sharp bowie-knife on the table; I remember something about catching it, and flying upon him; and then all grew dark, and I didn't know any more—not for days and days.

"When I came to myself, I was in a nice room,—but not mine. An old black woman tended me; and a doctor came to see me, and there was a great deal of care taken of me. After a while, I found that he had gone away, and left me at this house to be sold; and that's why they took such pains with me.

"I didn't mean to get well, and hoped I shouldn't; but, in spite of me, the fever went off, and I grew healthy, and finally got up. Then, they made me dress up, every day; and gentlemen used to come in and stand and smoke their cigars, and look at me, and ask questions, and debate my price. I was so gloomy and silent, that none of them wanted me. They threatened to whip me, if I wasn't gayer, and didn't take some pains to make myself agreeable. At length, one day, came a gentleman named Stuart. He seemed to have some feeling for me; he saw that something dreadful was on my heart, and he came to see me alone, a great many times, and finally persuaded me to tell him. He bought me, at last, and promised to do all he could to find and buy back my children. He went to the hotel where my Henry was; they told him he had been sold to a planter up on Pearl river; that was the last that I ever heard. Then he found where my daughter was; an old woman was keeping her. He offered an immense sum for her, but they would not sell her. Butler found out that it was for me he wanted her; and he sent me word that I should never have her. Captain Stuart was very kind to me; he had a splendid plantation, and took me to it. In the course of a year, I had a son born. O, that child!—how I loved it! How just like my poor Henry the little thing looked! But I had made up my mind,—yes, I had. I would never again let a child live up! I took the little fellow in my arms, when he was two weeks old, and kissed him, and cried over him; and then I gave him laudanum, and held him close to my bosom, while he slept to death. How I mourned and cried over it! and who ever dreamed that it was anything but a mistake, that had made me give it the laudanum? but it's one of the few things that I'm glad of, now. I am not sorry, to this day; he, at least, is out of pain. What better than death could I give him, poor child! After a while, the cholera came and Captain Stuart died; everybody died that wanted to live,—and I,—I, though I went down to death's door,—*I lived!* Then I was sold, and passed from hand to hand till I grew faded and wrinkled, and I had a fever; and then this wretch bought me, and brought me here,—and here I am!"

The woman stopped. She had hurried on through her story, with a wild, passionate utterance; sometimes seeming to address it to Tom, and sometimes speaking as in a soliloquy. So vehement and overpowering was the force with which she spoke, that, for a season, Tom was beguiled even from the pain of his wounds, and, raising himself on one elbow, watched her as she paced restlessly up and down, her long black hair swaying heavily about her, as she moved.

"You tell me," she said, after a pause, "that there is a God,—a God that looks down and sees all these things. May be it's so. The sisters in the convent used to tell me a day of judgment, when everything is coming to light;—won't there be vengeance, then!

"They think it's nothing, what we suffer,—nothing, what our children suffer! It's all a small matter; yet I've walked the streets when it seemed as if I had misery enough in my one heart to sink the city. I've wished the houses would fall on me, or the stones sink under me. Yes! and, in the judgment day, I will stand up before God, a witness against those that have ruined me and my children, body and soul!

"When I was a girl, I thought I was religious; I used to love God and prayer. Now, I'm a lost soul, pursued by devils that torment me day and night; they keep pushing me on and on—and I'll do it, too, some of these days!" she said, clenching her hand, while an insane light glanced in her heavy black eyes. "I'll send him where he belongs,—a short way, too,—one of these nights, if they burn me alive for it!" A wild, long laugh, rang through the deserted room, and ended in an hysteric sob; she threw herself on the floor, in convulsive sobbings and struggles.

In a few moments, the frenzy fit seemed to pass off; she rose slowly, and seemed to collect herself.

"Can I do anything more for you, my poor fellow?" she said, approaching where Tom lay; "shall I give you some more water?"

There was a graceful and compassionate sweetness in her voice and manner, as she said this, that formed a strange contrast with the former wildness.

Tom drank the water and looked earnestly and pitifully into her face.

"O, Missis, I wish you'd go to him that can give you living waters!"

"Go to him! Where is he? Who is he?" said Cassy.

"Him that you read of to me,—the Lord."

"I used to see the picture of him, over the altar, when I was a girl," said Cassy, her dark eyes fixing themselves in an expression of mournful reverie; but, *he isn't here!* there's nothing here, but sin and long, long, long despair! O!" She laid her hand on her breast and drew in her breath, as if to lift a heavy weight.

Tom looked as if he would speak again; but she cut him short, with a decided gesture.

"Don't talk, my poor fellow. Try to sleep, if you can." And, placing water in his reach, and making whatever little arrangements for his comfort she could, Cassy left the shed.

MARY CHESNUT

In contrast to Harriet Beecher Stowe, Mary Chesnut spent her entire life in the South and never received public renown outside her local circle of friends and acquaintances. Nevertheless, she too was a talented literary woman. Her diary, never published in her lifetime, is one of the most extraordinary documents of the Civil War. Historians agree that it offers an unmatched, candid view of the war from the vantage point of an intelligent and well-educated southern woman.

Born in 1823, Mary was the oldest child of Stephen Decatur Miller and Mary Boykin Miller. Of Scotch-Irish Presbyterian ancestry, both parental families had lived in South Carolina for generations. Stephen had risen in the world out of a small farming background to become a highly successful lawyer and politician. From 1828 to 1830 he had been governor of South Carolina and from 1831 to 1833 served briefly in the U.S. Senate.

As a young girl, Mary actively followed her father's political career, and by all accounts lived a happy childhood in her home town of Stateburgh, South Carolina. She was sent to boarding school in Charleston at age twelve, after her parents moved to Mississippi, and received a remarkable education. People whom she met later in life often thought that she had been educated in Europe.

A superb education was not all that Mary gained in Charleston. At age thirteen, she met her future husband there, a law student named James Chesnut, Jr. Disapproving of the growing relationship, her father ordered her back to Mississippi, but he allowed her to return to Charleston the following fall.

Mary's father suddenly died that spring, thereby ending her carefree girlhood. Chesnut's courtship continued, however, and in 1840 Mary Miller and James Chesnut were married. The union grew into a rich and deep relationship that, despite her childlessness, formed the center of Mary's life.

The record of Mary's life for the next several years is meager. Her husband pursued his business and political interests while she supervised the domestic routine and kept a scant daily journal. In 1859, however, they moved to Washington while James served briefly in the U.S. Senate. Here they became acquainted with political leaders from all over the South, and Mary greatly enjoyed the social life available at the nation's capital. Her rooms became a center for visiting young women from South Carolina and Virginia, and their gaiety and chatter enhanced her appreciation of the rounds of dinners and balls enjoyed by Washington society.

When South Carolina seceded from the Union, Mary began to expand her daily journal into a full-scale diary. She liked to write, was convinced that she was a witness to history in the making, and wanted to "at some future day afford facts about these times [to] prove useful to more important people." The value of Mary's diary was further enhanced by the fact that she consistently occupied excellent observation posts. She accompanied her husband on his travels as a delegate to the Provisional Congress of the Confederate States, as an aide to General Beauregard, as a liaison between Richmond and Columbia, and finally as commander of the South Carolina reserves. She knew most of the South's civil and military leaders and had constant access to fresh and firsthand information. Her diary recorded the crowded scene and fast tempo of wartime Richmond and was filled with deft, incisive portraits of southerners both great and small.

Mary devoted herself to the war effort in many ways. She opened her house to the point of overflow in an attempt to offer young southern men a respite from the grim realities of war. With other women, she also knitted, made shirts for soldiers and sandbags for coastal defense, and collected medical supplies for the southern hospitals. Although she was intensely loyal to the southern cause, she was not blind to the weaknesses of the Confederacy. She deplored its factionalism and political rivalries and mistrusted its glorification of southern military virtues, which led to too easy and incorrect assumptions about victory.

Mary's diary also condemned slavery on numerous occasions. These condemnations sprang from her sense of social justice and from her experience of life in the South. She was particularly disturbed by the problem of miscegenation. Slavery afforded southern men unlimited opportunities to exercise their lust on black women. Mary's diary frequently cried out against the degradation this fact imposed on the slave women and their families as well as on the wives and daughters of the planter class. In one instance, at the close of the war, Mary recorded with implicit approval her husband's report of what some southerners were saying regarding the ruin of the planters: "They will have no Negroes now to lord it over. They can swell and peacock about and tyrannize now over only a small parcel of women and children, those only who are their very own family."

At war's end, the Chesnuts returned to Camden, South Carolina, where James tried to restore their disrupted plantations. Both continued to play an active role in state and local politics. In 1865, they worked together to draft dozens of letters of opposition to the passage of South Carolina's Black

Code, regulating the behavior of the newly freed blacks. Mrs. Chesnut also kept busy in a number of other ways: she organized a local book club, went into the butter business (with a faithful former maid), researched and wrote a biographical sketch of her husband, and worked steadily on revising her diary for publication. She never completed these revisions but did ensure that the diaries would not be destroyed by specifically bequeathing them to a younger friend, Isabella Martin, who, seventeen years after Mary's death, helped prepare the first edition for publication.

In 1872–1873, Mrs. Chesnut supervised the building of her last home, Sarsfield, a family property on the outskirts of Camden. There Mary and James enjoyed a quiet country existence until his death in 1885. Mary never fully recovered from her husband's death; she died in 1886 and was buried next to him in King's Hill Cemetery in Camden.

The diary excerpts reproduced below are taken from the (1949) published edition, *A Diary from Dixie,* edited by Ben Ames Wilson, which in turn was the last version Mary Chesnut revised before her death. While dealing with many themes and issues, these excerpts concentrate on the famous story of Mrs. Witherspoon.

FROM MARY CHESNUT'S DIARY

[September 19, 1861]—A painful piece of news came to us yesterday. Our cousin, Mrs. Witherspoon of Society Hill, was found dead in her bed. She was quite well the night before. Killed, people say, by family troubles; by contentions, wrangling, ill blood among those nearest and dearest to her. She was a proud and high-strung woman, of a warm and tender heart, truth and uprightness itself. Few persons have ever been more loved and looked up to. A very handsome old lady, of fine presence, dignified and commanding. "Killed by family troubles!" . . .

September 21st.—Last night when the mail came in, I was seated near the lamp. Mr. Chesnut, lying on a sofa at a little distance, called out to me: "Look at my letters and tell me whom they are from?" I began to read one of them aloud. It was from Mary Witherspoon, and I broke down; horror and amazement was too much for me. Poor cousin Betsey Witherspoon was murdered! She did not die peacefully in her bed, as we supposed, but was murdered by her own people, her Negroes. I remember when Dr. Keith was murdered by his Negroes, Mr. Miles met me and told me the dreadful story. "Very awkward indeed, this sort of thing. There goes Keith in the House always declaiming about the 'Benificent Institution'—How now?" Horrible beyond words! Her household Negroes were so insolent, so pampered, and insubordinate. She lived alone. She knew, she said, that none of her children would have the patience she had with these people who had been indulged and spoiled by her until they were like spoiled children, simply intolerable. Mr. Chesnut and David Williams have gone over at once. . . .

September 24th.—The men who went to Society Hill (the Witherspoon home) have come home again with nothing very definite. William and Cousin Betsey's old maid, Rhody, are in jail; strong suspicion but as yet no proof of their guilt. The neighborhood is in a ferment. Evans and Wallace say these Negroes ought to be burnt. Lynching proposed! But it is all idle talk. They will be tried as the law directs, and not otherwise. John Witherspoon will not allow anything wrong or violent to be done. He has a detective there from Charleston.

Hitherto I have never thought of being afraid of Negroes. I had never injured any of them; why should they want to hurt me? Two thirds of my religion consists in trying to be good to Negroes, because they are so in our power, and it would be so easy to be the other thing. Somehow today I feel that the ground is cut away from under my feet. Why should they treat me any better than they have done Cousin Betsey Witherspoon?

Kate and I sat up late and talked it all over. Mrs. Witherspoon was a saint on this earth, and this is her reward. Kate's maid Betsey came in—a strong-built, mulatto woman—dragging in a mattress. "Missis, I have brought my bed to sleep in your room while Mars' David is at Society Hill. You ought not to stay in a room by yourself these times." She went off for more bed gear. "For the life of me," said Kate gravely, "I cannot make up my mind. Does she mean to take care of me, or to murder me?" I do not think Betsey heard, but when she came back she said: "Missis, as I have a soul to be saved, I will keep you safe. I will guard you." We know Betsey well, but has she soul enough to swear by? She is a great stout, jolly, irresponsible, unreliable, pleasant-tempered, bad-behaved woman, with ever so many good points. Among others, she is so clever she can do anything, and she never loses her temper; but she has no moral sense whatever.

That night, Kate came into my room. She could not sleep. The thought of those black hands strangling and smothering Mrs. Witherspoon's grey head under the counterpane haunted her; we sat up and talked the long night through. . . .

Went over just now to have a talk with that optimist, my mother-in-law. Blessed are the pure in mind, for they shall see God. Her mind certainly is free from evil thoughts. Someone says, the most unhappy person is the one who has bad thoughts. She ought to be happy. She thinks no evil. And yet, she is the cleverest woman I know. She began to ask me something of Charlotte Temple (I call her this to keep back her true name). "Has she ever had any more children:" "She has one more." "Is she married?" "No." "Is she a bad girl, really?" "Yes." "Oh! Don't say that. Poor thing! Maybe after all she is not really bad, only to be pitied!" I gave it up. I felt like a fool. Here was one thing I had made sure of as a fixed fact. In this world, an unmarried girl with two children was, necessarily, not a good woman. If that can be waved aside, I give up, in utter confusion of mind. Ever since she came here sixty or seventy years ago, as a bride from Philadelphia, Mrs. Chesnut has been trying to make it up to the Negroes for being slaves. Seventeen ninety-six, I think, was the year of her marriage. Today someone asked her about it, when she was describing Mrs. Washington's drawingroom to us. Through her friendship for Nelly Custis, and living very near, and stiff, stern old Martha Washington not liking to have her coach horses taken out for trifles, and Mrs. Cox letting Nelly Custis and Mary Cox have the carriage at their pleasure, Mrs. Chesnut was a great deal thrown with the Washington household. Now she eloquently related for the hundredth time all this. "How came you to leave that pleasant Philadelphia and all its comforts for this half civilized Up-Country and all the horrors of slavery?" "Did you not know that my father owned slaves in Philadelphia? In his will he left me several of them." In the Quaker City, and in the lifetime of a living woman now present, there were slave holders. It is hard to believe. Time works its wonders like enchantment. So quickly we forget.

Grandma is so awfully clever, and you can't make her think any harm of anybody. She is a resolute optimist. A caller, speaking of "Charlotte Temple," said it was better for the world to call a fallen woman by her proper name. It might be unchristian and nasty; but it was better, just as it was better for the world to hang a murderer, however unpleasant for the individual. She said she did not believe in seduced women. They knew the consequences. To smile amiably, and with a lovely face and a sweet voice to call evil good, would hardly do for everybody to try, if there was to be any distinction made between right and wrong.

Mrs. Chesnut has a greediness of books such as I never saw in anyone else. Reading is the real occupation and solace of her life. In the soft luxurious life she leads, she denies herself nothing that she wants. In her well-regulated character she could not want anything that she ought not to have. Economy is one of her cherished virtues, and strange to say she never buys a book, or has been known to take a magazine or periodical; she has them all. They gravitate toward her, they flow into her room. Everybody is proud to send, or lend, any book they have compassed by any means, fair or foul. Other members of the family who care nothing whatever for them buy the books and she reads them.

She spends hours every day cutting out baby clothes for the Negro babies. This department is under her supervision. She puts little bundles of things to be made in everybody's work basket and calls it her sewing society. She is always ready with an ample wardrobe for every newcomer. Then the mothers bring their children for her to prescribe and look after whenever they are ailing. She is not at all nervous. She takes a baby and lances its gums quite coolly and scientifically. She dresses all hurts, bandages all wounds. These people are simply devoted to her, proving they can be grateful enough when you give them anything to be grateful for. Two women always sleep in her room in case she should be ill, or need any attention during the night; and two others sleep in the next room—to relieve guard, so to speak. When it is cold, she changes her night clothes. Before these women give her the second dress, they iron every garment to make sure that it is warm and dry enough. For this purpose, smoothing irons are always before the fire, and the fire is never allowed to go down while it is cool enough for the family to remain at Mulberry. During the summer at Sandy Hill it is exactly the same, except that then she gets up and changes everything because it is so warm! It amounts to this, these old people find it hard to invent ways of passing the time, and they have such a quantity of idle Negroes about them that some occupation for them must be found. In the meantime, her standing employment is reading, and her husband is driving out with a pair of spanking thoroughbred bays, which have been trained to trot as slowly as a trot can be managed. . . .

[October 7] And now comes back on us that bloody story that haunts me night and day, Mrs. Witherspoon's murder. The man William, who was the master spirit of the gang, once ran away and was brought back from somewhere west; and then his master and himself had a reconciliation and the master henceforth made a pet of him. The night preceding the murder, John Witherspoon went over to his mother's to tell her of some of William's and Rhody's misdeeds. While their mistress was away from home, they had given a ball fifteen miles away from Society Hill. To that place, they had taken their mistress's china, silver, house linen, etc. After his conversation with his mother, as he rode out of the gate, he shook his whip at William and said: "Tomorrow I mean to come here and give every one of you a thrashing." That night Mrs. Witherspoon was talking it all over with her grandson, a half-grown boy who lived with her and slept indeed in a room opening into hers. "I do not intend John to punish these Negroes. It is too late to begin discipline now. I have indulged them past bearing. They all say I ought to have tried to control them, that it is all my fault." Mrs. Edwards, who was a sister of Mrs. Witherspoon, sometime ago was found dead in her bed. It is thought this suggested their plan of action to the Negroes. What more likely than she should die as her sister had done! When John went off, William said: "Listen to me and there will be no punishment here tomorrow." They made their plan, and then all of them went to sleep, William remaining awake to stir up the others at the proper hour.

What first attracted the attention of the family to the truth about her death was the appearance of black and blue spots about the face and neck of the body of their mother. Then someone, in moving the candle from the table at her bedside, found blood upon their fingers. Looking at the candlestick, they saw the print of a bloody hand which had held it. There was an empty bed in the entry, temporarily there for some purpose, and as they were preparing to lay out, someone took up the counterpane from his bed to throw over her. On the under side of it, again, bloody fingers. Now they were fairly aroused. Rhody was helping Mary Witherspoon, a little apart from the rest. Mary cried: "I wish they would not say such horrid things. Poor soul, she died in peace with all the world. It is bad enough to find her dead, but nobody ever touched a hair of her head. To think any mortal could murder her. Never! I will not believe it!" To Mary's amazement, Rhody drew near her and, looking strangely in her eyes, she said: "Miss Mary, you stick to dat!" Mary thrilled all over with suspicion and dread.

There was a trunk in Mrs. Witherspoon's closet where she kept money and a complete outfit ready for traveling at any moment; among other things, some new and very fine night gowns. One of her daughters noticed that her mother must have opened that trunk, for she was wearing one of those night gowns. They then looked into the closet and found the trunk unlocked and all the gold gone. The daughters knew the number of gold pieces she always kept under lock and key in that trunk. Now they began to scent mischief and foul play in earnest, and they sent for the detective.

The detective dropped in from the skies quite unexpectedly. He saw that one of the young understrappers of the gang looked frightened and uncomfortable. This one he fastened upon, and got up quite an intimacy with him; and finally, he told this boy that he knew all about it, that William had confessed privately to him to save himself and hang the others. But he said he had taken a fancy to this boy, and if he would confess everything, he would take him as State's evidence instead of William. The young man fell in the trap laid for him and told every particular from beginning to end. Then they were all put in jail, the youth who had confessed among them, as he did not wish them to know of his treachery to them.

This was his story. After John went away that night, Rhody and William made a great fuss. They were furious at Mars' John threatening them after all these years. William said: "Mars' John more than apt to do what he say he will do, but you all follow what I say and he'll have something else to think of beside stealing and breaking glass and china. If old Master was alive now, what would he say to talk of whipping us!" Rhody always kept the key to the house to let herself in every morning, so they arranged to go in at twelve, and then William watched and the others slept the sleep of the righteous. Before that however, they had a "real fine supper and a heap of laughing at the way dey'd all look tomorrow." They smothered her with a counterpane from a bed in the entry. They had no trouble the first time, because they found her asleep and "done it all 'fore she waked." But after Rhody took her keys and went into the trunk and got a clean night gown—for they had spoiled the one she had on—and fixed everything, candle, medicine and all, she came to! Then she begged them hard for life. She asked them what she had ever done that they should want to kill her? She promised them before God never to tell on them.

Nobody should ever know! But Rhody stopped her mouth with the counterpane, and William held her head and hands down, and the others two sat on her legs. Rhody had a thrifty mind and wished to save the sheets and night gown, so she did not destroy them. They were found behind her mantelpiece. There the money was also, all in the hole made among the bricks behind the wooden mantelpiece. A grandson of Rhody's slept in her house. Him she locked up in his room. She did not want him to know anything of this fearful night.

That innocent old lady and her grey hair moved them not a jot. Fancy how we feel. I am sure I will never sleep again without this nightmare of horror haunting me.

Mrs. Chesnut, who is their good angel, is and has always been afraid of Negroes. In her mind, the San Domingo stories were indelibly printed on her mind. She shows her dread now by treating every one as if they were a black Prince Albert or Queen Victoria. We were beginning to forget Mrs. Cunningham, the only other woman we ever heard of who was murdered by her Negroes. Poor cousin Betsey was goodness itself. After years of freedom and indulgence and tender kindness, it was an awful mistake to threaten them like children. It was only threats. Everybody knew she would never do anything. Mr. Cunningham had been an old bachelor, and the Negroes had it all their own way till he married. Then they hated her. They took her from her room, just over one in which her son-in-law and her daughter slept. They smothered her, dressed her, and carried her out—all without the slightest noise—and hung her by the neck to an apple tree, as if she had committed suicide. If they want to kill us, they can do it when they please, they are noiseless as panthers. They were discovered because, dressing her in the dark, her tippet was put on hindpart before, and she was supposed to have walked out and hung herself in a pair of brand new shoes whose soles obviously had never touched the ground.

We ought to be grateful that anyone of us is alive, but nobody is afraid of their own Negroes. I find everyone, like myself, ready to trust their own yard. I would go down on the plantation tomorrow and stay there even if there were no white person in twenty miles. My Molly and all the rest I believe would keep me as safe as I should be in the Tower of London.

Romeo was the Negro who first confessed to the detective; then Rhody, after she found they had discovered the money and sheets where she had hidden them. William and Silvie still deny all complicity in the plot or the execution of it.

John Williams has a bride! Has she not married South at a fine time? She is terrified, and who can blame her? It will be a miracle if she don't bolt altogether. The very name of Society Hill is enough to scare the life out of anyone. To expect the bride to come back, simply because her husband was here, and with details of that black tragedy ringing in her ears; indeed it was too much. I dare say she would as soon take up her abode in Sodom or Gomorrah.

It was Rhody who pointed out the blood on the counterpane. They suppose she saw it, knew they would see it, and did it to avert suspicion from herself. . . .

October 18th.—Mrs. Witherspoon's death has clearly driven us all wild. Mrs. Chesnut, although she talks admirably well and is a wonderfully clever woman, bored me by incessantly dwelling upon the transcendant virtues of her colored household, in full hearing of the innumerable Negro women who literally swarm over this house. She takes her meals in her own rooms, but today came in while we were at dinner. "I warn you, don't touch that soup! It is bitter. There is something wrong about it!" The family answered her pleasantly, but continued calmly to eat their soup. The men who waited at table looked on without change of face. Kate whispered: "It is cousin Betsey's fate. She is watching every trifle, and is terrified." My husband gave his mother his arm, and she went quietly back to her room. Afterwards Kate said to me: "She is afraid they will poison us. . . ."

10

THE CAUSES OF THE CIVIL WAR

INTERPRETATION AND HISTORIOGRAPHY

Americans have always been fascinated, even obsessed by the Civil War. From the end of the conflict to the present, they have devoted an enormous amount of time and energy to efforts aimed at remembering, understanding, memorializing, and even canonizing the event. The result has been a flood of books, articles, essays, paintings, statues, monuments, and clichés, which combine myth and reality into an almost sacred vision of the past.

Numerous factors account for this fascination. The Civil War has been labeled by some as the first example of "total" war, and it remains the bloodiest conflict by far in all of American history. It was also the only American war that was fratricidal in nature, literally pitting brother against brother and father against son. Furthermore, it was the culmination of a host of major controversies that had dominated previous American history—slave vs. free labor, state vs. national power, industrial vs. agrarian economies and societies, to name but a few—and while it settled by force one of these controversies forever, it bequeathed the others as legacies to future generations of Americans. It also bequeathed the numerous wounds associated with those controversies and with the war itself, wounds that are still far from totally healed.

While the Civil War is thus an emotional and pivotal event in America's past, it is simultaneously an event under whose shadow Americans still live; in fact, they have often returned to it in an attempt to find a usable past to help with present-day problems. Most revealing in this regard was the Civil Rights Movement of the early 1960s, which used the imagery of the Civil War in its efforts to deal with one of that conflict's most disturbing unsettled legacies—race relations. It is no accident, for example, that Dr. Martin Luther King, Jr., chose to deliver his extraordinary "I Have a Dream" speech at the site of one of the most famous and awe-inspiring symbols of that conflict—the Lincoln Memorial in Washington, D.C. Nor is it accidental that his white opponents in the South attempted to stop him with the same constitutional argument that their antebellum ancestors had used—states rights.

As the above example illustrates, different Americans have drawn drastically different lessons from the Civil War and they perceive it very differently. The same is true of historians. Although the war itself ended over a century ago, the questions of why it took place and what it means remain major battlegrounds for historians today.

Such disagreements divide historians on most other important past events as well. As this volume has previously emphasized, history is much more than simply what happened in the past. It is, or should be, a means of trying to understand why events took place, what those events meant during their time, and what those events mean today. And while historians can usually agree on what happened, they just as often disagree sharply when answering the other questions. The disagreements are basically matters of interpretation, and their analysis is part of *historiography*—the study of the writing and writers of history.

As previously noted in Chapter 5, every historian and every individual views the past from a unique perspective in time and place, and those perspectives are constantly shifting with events and values. As a result, each generation and each region has approached the questions of why events took place, what they meant, and what they mean in the present from the unique vantage point of its own era and location.

On no issue in American history is this fact more apparent than on that of the Civil War. Ever since this conflict ended, scholars have been debating its causes and arriving at conflicting interpretations that clearly reflect the values of their era and region. Listed at the end of this chapter are several statements, along with author and year, from some of the major schools of historical thought on the causes of the Civil War; these are followed by a brief historiographical essay that may help you to understand the various arguments as well as the concept of historiography. As that essay notes, each interpretation has weaknesses. And while some today are clearly more convincing than others, they should not be analyzed simply on the basis of "right" vs. "wrong." Rather, one should try to understand why each interpretation emerged at a specific time, what its strengths and weaknesses are, and which interpretation individually or in combination with others best accounts for the *totality* of the historical event, both during its time and today.

Only one person is truly capable of answering this question—you. In this chapter, you are to determine for yourself which interpretations of the causes of the Civil War seem to be the most valid. Your assignment—the major one in this volume—is to write your own history by presenting your interpretation of this major and highly debated event.

Obviously, you cannot resolve all the deep historical problems associated with the Civil War and with historical interpretations in general. Nor can you possibly incorporate all the events, ideas, and personalities leading up to this cataclysmic event in a short paper. But this volume should have provided you with sufficient information and skills to analyze and verbalize what you have in fact already done, perhaps without realizing it. As noted above (and in the preface), we all interpret the past in light of the present, and we act on the basis of this knowledge or lack thereof. Consciously or not, you walked into this course with your own "interpretation" of the Civil War. Your studies over the semester may have reinforced that interpretation or changed it. It is now time to express your conclusions.

ASSIGNMENTS

1. You should begin by determining exactly why you think the Civil War took place. Listed below are several statements from some of the major schools of historical thought; there is also a brief historiographical essay that may help you to understand the various arguments. You may choose any one of the major interpretations or any combination or synthesis of them, or you may propose an original interpretation of your own. You should then justify it in writing (i.e., explain the interpretation you chose and your reasons for thinking it the most satisfactory).
2. After this explanation, give an example of its practical application by choosing a major event, person, or idea from antebellum U.S. history that you deem central to an understanding of the coming of the Civil War; using your interpretations, explain (a) what (or who) this event, person, or idea was; (b) how and why it was of central importance to the coming of the Civil War; and (c) what it meant within the context of its time.
3. As an alternative to selecting an event, person, or idea, use statistics, maps, or items of material culture as described and explained in the preceding chapters to explain and develop your interpretation of the causes of the Civil War.

Your total essay should be three to five double-spaced, typewritten pages in length and should not exceed 1,500 words. You should use all relevant material and skills learned in this volume and complete additional research in the library if you wish or if so instructed by your professor. Your essay should be carefully outlined, revised, edited, and corrected as needed. Use proper footnote and bibliographic form and proofread your paper before submission. Remember that only you can be certain your essay says exactly what you want it to say and that its arguments are clear.

ADDITIONAL QUESTIONS TO CONSIDER

1. Be prepared to defend your interpretations orally in class and, where applicable, to describe the historical context, in the period after the Civil War, in which this interpretation gained popularity. What specific events in that period led Americans to accept such an interpretation?
2. Try to analyze the beliefs and events that have had the greatest impact on you as an individual and as a member of a generation of Americans. What role did these beliefs and events play in your choice of interpretations?
3. What interpretation of the causes of the Civil War did you hold when this course began? How does this interpretation compare to the interpretations you chose for your essay? How do you account for the differences or lack thereof?

MAJOR INTERPRETATIONS OF THE CAUSES OF THE CIVIL WAR

There is a risk of referring any historic event to a single cause . . .[But] of the American Civil War it may be safely asserted that there was a single cause, slavery.

JAMES FORD RHODES, 1913

The conflict, on this question of slavery, in the Federal Councils, from the beginning, was not a contest between the advocates or opponents of that peculiar institution, but a contest . . . between the supporters of a strictly Federative Government, on the one side, and a thoroughly National one, on the other. . . . It was a strife between the principles of Federation . . . and Centralism. . . .

ALEXANDER H. STEPHENS, 1868

[The] Civil War was nothing less than a conflict between two different systems of economic production; and with the victory at the Presidential polls in 1860 of the higher order, the young industrial capitalism of the North and Middle West, a counterrevolutionary movement was launched by the defenders of the lower order, the slave lords of the South.

LOUIS M. HACKER, 1935

. . . the Civil War had one basic cause: sectionalism. . . . Our national state was built, not upon the foundations of a homogeneous land and people, but upon geographical sections inhabited severally by provincial, self-conscious, self-righteous, aggressive, and ambitious populations of varying origins and diverse social and economic systems; and the passage of time and the cumulative effect of history have accentuated these sectional patterns.

FRANK L. OWSLEY, 1941

The main root of the conflict . . . was the problem of slavery *with its complementary problem of race adjustment;* the main source of the tragedy was the refusal of either section to face these conjoined problems squarely and pay the heavy costs of a peaceful settlement.

ALLAN NEVINS, 1947

Let one take all the factors traditionally presented . . . and it will be seen that only by a kind of false display could any of these issues, or all of them together, be said to have caused the war if one omits the elements of emotional unreason and overbold leadership. If one word or phrase were selected to account for the war, that word would not be slavery, or economic grievance, or states rights, or diverse civilizations. It would have to be such a word as fanaticism, misunderstanding, misrepresentation, or perhaps politics. . . .

JAMES G. RANDALL, 1947

A society closed in the defense of evil institutions . . . forces upon everyone, both those living at the time and those writing about it later, the necessity for a moral judgment; and the moral judgment in such cases becomes an indispensable factor in the historical understanding. . . . It was the moral issue of slavery, for example, that gave the struggles over slavery in the territories or over enforcement of the fugitive slave laws their significance. These issues . . . were not in themselves basic. But they were the available issues; they were almost the only points within the existing constitutional framework where the moral conflict could be faced. . . .

ARTHUR SCHLESINGER, JR., 1949

. . . *right* and *rights* had become the symbols or carriers of all those interests and values [which divided North and South]. . . . [A]s symbols they carried an emotional force and moral power in themselves that was far greater than the sum total of all the material issues involved.

AVERY CRAVEN, 1950

> . . . Simply because Americans by the middle of the nineteenth century suffered from an excess of liberty, they were increasingly unable to arrive at reasoned, independent judgments upon the problems which faced their society. The permanent revolution that was America had freed its citizens from the bonds of prescription and custom but had left them leaderless. . . . Huddling together in their loneliness, they sought only to escape their freedom. . . . Hysterical fears and paranoid suspicions marked . . . [a] shift of Americans to "other-directedness." Never was there a field so fertile before the propagandist, the agitator, the extremist.
>
> DAVID DONALD, 1960

> The period from 1820 to 1860 witnessed a progressive extension of limits, an overleaping of boundaries of every kind. . . . The American people, like the American individual, seemed to be free from the burdens of the past and free to shape their own character. The one problem their ingenuity could not resolve was Negro slavery. . . . Paradoxically, the South increasingly came to regard Negro slavery as the necessary base on which freedom must rest. From the North a commitment to slavery's ultimate extinction was the test of freedom. Each section detected a fatal change in the other, a betrayal of the principles and mission of the Founding Fathers. Each section feared that the other had become transformed into a despotic and conspiratorial power. . . .
>
> DAVID BRION DAVIS, 1977

SOME COMMENTS ON HISTORIANS AND THE COMING OF THE CIVIL WAR

You may have thought that the question as to why the Civil War took place would be an odd area for historical disagreement. More than most events in history, the Civil War would seem to have been the result of one issue —slavery. The North opposed it; the South defended it; and the result was, in William Seward's famous phrase, an "irrepressible conflict." However, most historians do not wholly accept this interpretation of the onset of the Civil War. In fact, a number of them have maintained that slavery was a minor issue in the coming of the war and that any attempt to make the "peculiar institution" the focal point fails to come to grips with a host of other disturbing facts.

For example, disagreement between North and South over slavery had existed for almost a hundred years without leading to either disunion or armed conflict. In fact, earlier confrontations—in 1820 and 1850, for example—had led to compromise, which, for a time at least, appeared to strengthen the Union. Moreover, despite the efforts of a well-organized, articulate minority, no major northern spokesman had called for the abolition of slavery before the war began. Abraham Lincoln, even after his election to the presidency, had been willing to guarantee the continued existence of slavery in the South. During the early years of the war, he consistently portrayed the conflict as one over union, rebellion, and law and order—not slavery. It was not until 1862 that Lincoln agreed to emancipation as a Union war aim, and then largely because it would be an effective war measure. Similarly, in the South, no major spokesman ever argued for the extension of slavery to the North.

In fact, much of the controversy that divided North and South was not over slavery itself as it existed in the South but rather over its extension into the territories of the United States. Some historians are convinced that these areas were incapable of supporting slavery anyway, because there was not enough good land for growing cotton. At the height of the North–South controversy over "Bleeding Kansas," for example, that territory contained a grand total of two slaves.

Faced with these arguments, many historians, sometimes called "revisionists," have rejected slavery as the major cause of the Civil War and have sought other explanations for what eventually happened. Some, returning to a major theme of antebellum southern politicians, have concluded that the most important issue dividing North and South was the very nature of the social compact at the heart of the American union. Southerners had long maintained that the national government was a creation of the states and, therefore, subordinate to them and possessing very limited powers. Northerners had consistently maintained that the national government was a union of the people, not the states, and that it therefore possessed strong implied powers over the states. These historians thus see the debate over the extension of slavery as but one example of a continuing North–South debate over the powers of the federal government. And in this interpretation, the South emerges as the defender of states' rights against centralized power.

A problem with this interpretation is that the doctrine of states' rights has been used by each section of the country whenever it has found its interests challenged by the central government. While the question of states' rights is certainly a fundamental constitutional issue, the constant shifts of North and South suggest that it was most frequently used merely as a device to protect specific sectional interests.

What were those interests? Looking at them in broad perspective, some historians have seen slavery as part of a larger southern interest—an agrarian economy pitted against a diametrically opposed economic system of industrial and commercial capitalism in the North. These two systems did, in fact, have sharply conflicting needs; slave vs. free labor was by no means the only conflict between them. Taxation, tariffs, and railroads as well as monetary and land policies also aggravated sectional division. Furthermore, all these questions required federal action. Since the "three-fifths" slavery clause of the Constitution was the basis of southern agrarian power within the federal government, disagreements over economic interests became a struggle between competing economic systems for control of the federal government.

Yet economic differences had existed since colonial times and had not previously led to civil war. Actually, many Americans had considered the agricultural economy of the South and the industrial-commercial economy of the North to be complementary rather than competitive. The result had been the creation of the Union and a long history of compromise. Why, then, was economic conflict thought to be irreconcilable in the 1850s?

Some historians maintain that the two economic systems were in themselves only part of what, by the 1850s, had become two unique cultures. The South did not simply possess an agrarian *economy* (the North was overwhelmingly agricultural too). Rather, the South was a unique agrarian *society,* with political, economic, social, and intellectual values to match. It was rural, deliberate, paternalistic, and hierarchical. Within it, slavery, by the 1850s, had a social as well as an economic function: it served to keep blacks in a subordinate position. The North did not have to deal with the question of keeping numerous blacks subservient, or with any of the other values associated with an agrarian culture, for it had developed a bustling, capitalist, urban value structure that was accepted by its farmers as well as its employers and workers. Long before secession, therefore, two very different "nations" had come into existence.

On the other hand, the similarities between North and South in the 1850s far outweighed the differences. An explanation of the Civil War in terms of an aristocratic, agrarian, "cavalier" society in the South as opposed to a bustling, capitalist "Yankee" society in the North may make for interesting literature and movies, but it flies in the face of historical fact. Contrary to this cultural mythology, the South was not settled by rural aristocrats and the North by an urban middle class. Furthermore, the North was as racist as the South. In point of fact, northerners and southerners both considered themselves Americans; despite their racism, both drew pride from their definition of the United States as the nation of individual liberty.

Ironically, however, many individuals within the two sections saw their opponents engaged in a conspiracy against their liberty; this perception, according to some historians, is the basis for the Civil War. Despite the fact that no major northern spokesman argued for the abolition of slavery in the South, many southerners believed that the hidden aim of the North was to destroy slavery and to institute black rule in the South. Northerners similarly believed that despite the lack of open statements, slaveholders were engaged in a conspiracy to spread slavery to the North and thereby to control the entire Union.

Careful historical examination has shown that no such conspiracies ever existed. But, many people believed that they existed, and beliefs about what is happening can be much more important than what is actually happening. People act according to their *perceptions* of reality, not in accordance with reality itself, and some historians argue that those perceptions led each side—threatened by an illusionary plot—to go to war in defense of its rights.

Why could no one see through these illusions? According to another school of historical thought, the blame lies with fanatical, irresponsible agitators, and blundering, incompetent politicians. These individuals, in the North and in the South, blinded people to reality and, for a host of motives, fanned the flames of irrational fears.

Here again, however, one must ask why the country had changed to such an extent as to replace the Founding Fathers and their immediate successors with a group of irresponsible rabble-rousers and fools. One must also ask why the American people would believe and follow these individuals and whether their perceptions could have been all that foolish. All societies live by sets of beliefs that appear to later generations as illusions. In their time, however, these views have extraordinary power and validity; to label their believers as fools is to use historical hindsight to distort the past unfairly.

Recognizing this fact, many recent historians have concentrated on examining the general beliefs, or ideology, that led Americans to their various perceptions and thus to civil war, and they have concluded that the basic problem lay in the belief system itself. Americans in the early nineteenth century believed that there should be no barriers to stop individuals from attempting to achieve their own perfection in a democratic society of equal rights and individual liberty. The problem was that southerners and northerners had, by the 1850s, defined their freedom in terms that were often diametrically opposed. The southerner's fundamental *right* to his property, including slaves, collided with the northerner's *right* to compete in a "free market" and with his concept of the *rights* of all human beings. Equally damaging, the nation, devoted to individual liberty, lacked a social or institutional framework adequate to deal with ideological excesses that could drag its people into civil war.

Acceptance of this approach leads to some interesting conclusions. If one argues that ideology and perceptions of reality are paramount, then all the previously discussed interpretations retain their validity. Even if there were no conspiracies, no truly irreconcilable differences in economies or cultures, no basic disagreement over the nature of the Union, and no chance of slavery establishing itself in the territories, Americans, North and South, believed otherwise because of their ideology—and the beliefs and ideology together created a new reality.

Furthermore, ideology and perceptions are themselves the products of all the general factors previously cited and dismissed as causes of the war: economics, culture, politics and political theory, moral values. Thus, deep down, were southerners not correct in seeing abolition as the eventual goal of the North and federal power to outlaw slavery in the territories as simply the first stage in this long-range program? On the other side, did not the southern defense of slavery as a "positive good" logically imply its eventual extension over the entire country? And was Abraham Lincoln, therefore, being simplistic and wrong, or, in actuality, very perceptive, when he phrased the basic issue in terms of the fact that the nation could not continue to exist half slave and half free? As he wrote to a southern senator in 1860, "You think slavery is right and ought to be extended, while we think it is wrong and ought to be restricted. That I suppose is the rub. It is certainly the only substantial difference between us."

ABOUT THE AUTHORS

Mark A. Stoler was born in New York City in 1945. He received his B.A. from the City College of New York in 1966, and his M.A. and Ph.D. in history from the University of Wisconsin in 1967 and 1971. Specializing in U.S. diplomatic and military history, he has authored *The Politics of the Second Front* (Greenwood, 1977) and a series of articles dealing with World War II strategy, diplomacy, and historiography, the Vietnam war, and the teaching of U.S. history. He has been a member of the History Department at the University of Vermont since 1970, and in 1984 he received the University's Outstanding Faculty award. He has also been a lecturer at the University of Wisconsin—Milwaukee, a visiting professor in the Strategy Department of the Naval War College in Newport, Rhode Island, and a Fulbright lecturer at the University of Haifa in Israel.

Marshall True has degrees from Bates College (B.A.) and the University of Virginia (M.A., Ph.D.) and has been teaching American history for twenty years. A specialist in the cultural and social history of the nineteenth century, Professor True recently edited and compiled, with William A. Doyle, *Vermont and the New Nation,* a collection of documents illustrating the national context of Vermont's founding. He also edits the journal *Vermont History* and is working on a biography of nineteenth-century scholar and soldier Ethan Allen Hitchcock. At the University of Vermont since 1967, Marshall True lives in East Fairfield with Charon True, an attorney, and is the father of four children: daughters Julia and Katherine, and twin sons Adam and Steven.

A NOTE ON THE TYPE

The text of this book was composed in Melior, a typeface designed by Hermann Zapf and issued in 1952. Born in Nürnberg, Germany, in 1918, Zapf has been a strong influence in printing since 1939. Melior, like Times Roman, another popular twentieth-century typeface, was created specifically for use in newspaper composition.

Instructor's Manual to Accompany

EXPLORATIONS IN AMERICAN HISTORY
A SKILLS APPROACH

Volume I: To 1865

Alfred A. Knopf  New York

CONTENTS

TO THE INSTRUCTOR

Explorations in American History introduces students to the skills associated with historical study. It is designed to be used in conjunction with a U.S. history textbook and/or whatever other historical material you may choose to assign. The chapters are arranged chronologically, and each skill is linked to a specific era or issue in U.S. history. Each chapter consists of an explanation of the era/issue and the skill(s) under study, a series of written assignments, and a series of additional questions to consider for class discussion. Supplemental material related to the skill(s) under study is often included. While the chapters and assignments are interrelated and increase in complexity, they are sufficiently independent that you can select the ones most appropriate for your class.

This guide both summarizes the contents of *Explorations in American History* and explains its assignments and the options available to you on a chapter-by-chapter basis. It also provides you with answers to the exercises in the volume, sample answer sheets that you may reproduce or modify for class use, and suggestions for conducting class discussions. While all this material is based on our experiences with the volume in class, we have rewritten it and provided numerous alternatives to suit the needs of any introductory U.S. history survey. In light of those numerous alternatives, we strongly recommend that you read this guide in conjunction with *Explorations in American History* before assigning any chapters to your class.

In our own classes, the students meet twice each week for lectures and then break into small groups once a week for discussions and to hand in specific assignments. This method is most suitable for large classes at institutions where graduate teaching assistants are available to help staff the small groups. The volume can also be used, however, with small classes in which you would lead the discussions, either as a separate section or in conjunction with your lecture(s).

Along with the options for assignments and discussions presented in this guide are numerous options for grading. We generally have the written assignments in *Explorations in American History* count for 50 percent of the final grade, with examinations counting for the other 50 percent. Most of the assignments used are graded on a four- or five-point pass/fail basis, but selected assignments involving the writing of three- to five-page essays or research papers are graded on a A-F scale for ten to fifteen points each so that the total for all assignments is fifty points. Numerous other methods are possible. You may choose, for example, to make successful completion of the chapters you assign nongraded but required work, with failing assignments to be redone. You may also choose to grade first as well as final drafts of the papers, or simply to assign the reading of each chapter without any written work. You could also have students grade/evaluate either their own or a classmate's paper. Should you choose to make all or some of the written work required, the point value of each assignment will of course depend on your grading system and the number of chapters you assign. Since one purpose of this volume is to help students learn how to write as well as read history, we strongly recommend using as many of the written assignments as possible.

EXPLORATION AND COLONIZATION: QUESTIONING, USE OF THE LIBRARY, HISTORICAL RESEARCH, AND FORM

This chapter introduces the student to four basic skills: critical analysis of the textbook, generating historical questions, using the library, and proper citation form. While it covers the basics, the information provided is not a substitute for actual library work or a complete style manual. Consequently, we suggest that you consider additional or different library exercises and that you recommend students buy one of the style manuals we have cited. We also recommend making clear your own preference for citation form.

ASSIGNMENT(S)

The five assignments listed are interrelated and we recommend using all of them.

Assignment 1 begins the process of historical questioning and critical analysis by requiring the student to raise a series of questions not answered in the textbook. It also serves as the base for the other four assignments. If graded, it will give you an early opportunity to identify those students who have serious problems with grammar and/or conceptualization.

Assignment 2 requires the student to take some sort of library tour and complete a library exercise. Since every library has its own organization, we strongly recommend using a tour and exercise specifically geared to your library. Usually, your library staff will already have or will be willing to prepare such a tour and exercise. The exercise provided at the end of this chapter can be used if you prefer, but it is limited to the card catalogue and four reference works. Answers to the questions asked follow:

1. *Daughters of the Promised Land*. Boston, 1970.
2. The call numbers will vary from library to library and are dependent on the system used. Ask your librarian for the specific answers appropriate to your library.
3. Laws in behalf of child welfare and of more rights for women.
4. Many state papers.
5. Chapter 33, "Rise of Anglo-America." Charles E. Banks, *Winthrop Fleet*, 1930, under sub-heading 33.2.5.3, "Puritan Migration and Massachusetts Bay" (p. 638).
6. 4657; Greene, Jack P., "Foundations of Political Power in the Virginia House of Burgesses, 1720-1776," *William and Mary Q., William and Mary Quarterly,* 16 (4), 485-506, 1959.
7. The answers depend on your library holdings; ask your librarian to check.
8. Yes; yes; yes; no.
9. U.S. politics and government, colonial period, ca. 1600-1775.

Assignment 3 asks how many of the questions generated in assignment 1 could be answered by consulting only reference works and which of those reference works should be consulted. Theoretically, *all* the student questions could be answered by consulting the historical encyclopedias and biographical dictionaries discussed in the chapter. The answers, however, would be quite thin and should in turn lead to deeper questioning and research.

Assignment 4 requires the student to use reference works to find two books and two scholarly articles relevant to the questions asked and to decide which of the two works in each category would be most appropriate to answer the questions raised. The *Harvard Guide* would be the easiest reference work to use, though numerous others could be substituted. Selection of the most appropriate book and article should be based on the annotations available in *America: History and Life* and/or the *Book Review Digest*. Appropriateness should be determined not only by content, but also by the comments in these volumes regarding the quality of the work in question and how recently it was published.

Assignment 5 asks the students to find the works chosen in assignment 4 within their university library and to cite them in correct footnote and bibliographic form. This assignment requires the students to use the card catalogue and explore the different sections of the library as well as practice correct citation form. Class discussion of this assignment will enable you to talk about the organization of your particular library.

ADDITIONAL QUESTIONS TO CONSIDER

Question 1 concerns shortcomings in the text revealed by the questioning assignment. Discussion of the issues raised in this question should reinforce the importance of critical analysis of what is being read in class as well as the biases inherent in all secondary works. In a textbook, those biases are of course compounded by the survey nature of the work, but you may wish to emphasize, even at this early date, the concept of conflicting interpretations and the myth of "objective" history. One effective way to do this is to ask your class to realize the extraordinarily large number of events taking place in the world at any particular moment and then to figure out what guidelines a historian would use to determine *which* of those events to include in a text.

Question 2 asks when footnotes should and should not be used. We have found it imperative to reemphasize in this regard the importance of proper citation and the danger of plagiarism involved in ignoring such citation. Many students do not know what plagiarism is, and a detailed explanation, we find, is necessary. In many cases, you can use the definition provided in your university or student handbook. In other cases, you may prefer to define and explain the term in your own words. One method we find effective is to compare student plagiarism with commercial plagiarism and to point out the serious legal consequences of both.

Even when students do understand what plagiarism is, they are often unsure about what to footnote. The essentials are given in Chapter 1, but you may wish to discuss this at greater length and/or invite questions.

When emphasizing the importance of footnote form, we have found one method to be particularly effective. The biblical basis of the Salem witchcraft trials was, of course, *Exodus* 22:17, "Thou shalt not suffer a witch to live." Ask everyone in the class who owns a Bible to bring it to the next session. At that session provide different students with different forms of the appropriate citation, each one incomplete and/or misleading in some way (e.g., chapter and verse listed in reverse order, no mention of chapter or verse or of edition, publisher, or year). The ensuing confusion in finding the verse illustrates very clearly the importance of proper form.

Question 3 asks how to go about preparing a preliminary bibliography for a research paper. While you may prefer to save such a discussion for later in the semester, the fact that the students have just finished exploring the library provides a good opportunity to "rehearse" for a real paper. Answers regarding which reference works to consult and in what order, how to use the card catalogue, and what would lead to the addition or deletion of specific works depend, of course, on the topic chosen.

CLASS / SECTION ____________ NAME ____________________

Chapter 1

ANSWER SHEET

1. Compose six questions on a Colonial era topic that are not answered in your textbook. Each question should begin with a different word of inquiry (what, when, where, who, how, why), and all should deal with the same general topic.

   a. "What" question:

   b. "When" question:

   c. "Where" question:

   d. "Who" question:

   e. "How" question:

   f. "Why" question:

2. Take your list of questions to the library. If a librarian-guided or self-guided tour is available, take it. If not, examine the library areas and reference works discussed in this chapter and complete the exercise given at the end of the chapter. Your instructor may collect this exercise or provide you with answers.

3. How many of your Colonial era questions could be answered by consulting only reference works? ____________ Which ones would you use?

4. Using the appropriate reference bibliographies and indices, find at least two books and two scholarly articles that would provide detailed answers to the questions you have raised. Then make use of the abstracts and book reviews (or summaries) available to choose the one book and one scholarly article that would be most appropriate for answering your questions.

CLASS / SECTION ____________ **NAME** ________________________

5. Use the card catalogue, the stacks, and the periodicals section and/or the periodicals list to find the book and the article chosen. Cite each in correct footnote and bibliographic form, and place the appropriate call number in the left margin. If your library does not have the book or article, choose another.

   Book in proper bibliographic form:

   Book in proper footnote form:

   Scholarly article in proper bibliographic form:

   Scholarly article in proper footnote form:

LIBRARY EXERCISE

1. Look in the subject catalogue under "Women—History." Find the book by Page Smith. What is its title, place of publication, and date of publication?

   Title: ____

   Place of publication: ________________________________

   Date of publication: ________________________________

2. In the author/title card catalogue, find and write down the call numbers for the following reference works:

   Dictionary of American History: ________________________

   Dictionary of American Biography: ______________________

   Harvard Guide to American History: _____________________

   America: History and Life: ____________________________

3. Locate the *Dictionary of American History* and read the article on women's suffrage. What notable early results of the Women's Suffrage Amendment of 1920 does it mention?

4. Locate the *Dictionary of American Biography* and read the entry for Dolly Madison. It indicates that during the evacuation of the White House in 1814 she salvaged a portrait of George Washington and what else? ______________

CLASS / SECTION ____________ NAME ____________________

5. Locate the *Harvard Guide to American History.* In Volume 2, which chapter lists books and articles on English colonization of the New World before 1688?

____

What is the title of the chapter? ____________________________

What is the author, title, and date of the first *book* listed under the subheading that deals with the establishment of the Massachusetts Bay Colony? ________

____

6. Locate *America: History and Life.* Take out the retrospective volume covering the years 1954-1963 (Volume 0), and turn to the heading "House of Burgesses" in the index at the end of the volume. What number is given for this entry? ____________ Locate that number in the main part of the volume and write down the following:

Author: ____

Article title: ____

Journal abbreviation: ____

Full journal title: ____

Volume number: ____

Issue number: ____

Pages: ____

Date: ____

7. Does your library own this journal? __________________________

How did you find out? ____

Does the library own the volume you need? ____________________

If so, where is the volume located and what is its call number? __________

____

8. Turn back to the index section at the end of Volume 0 of *America: History and Life.* The article you found in question 6 may be listed under additional subject headings to give you other points of access to the same information. Which of the following subject headings will lead you to the same article you found in question 6 (look for the same entry number):

Virginia—aristocracy: ______________________________.

Virginia—provincial and colonial government: __________________.

Provincial and colonial government—Virginia: __________________.

Colonial government: ____.

9. To locate a book in the subject catalogue on colonial government in the United States, what is the *best* subject heading to use? ____________________

Chapter 2

COLONIAL SOCIETY: ANALYZING PRIMARY SOURCES AND WRITING

The first part of this chapter provides a brief explanation of primary sources and their importance and introduces the student to the limitations, biases, and questions asked of these sources. Excerpts from eleven different primary sources in colonial history are reproduced at the end of the chapter to illustrate the diversity of material available to the student of history, as well as to provide a basis for the assignment. These sources range from traditional, official documents to literature and art.

The second part of the chapter offers an equally brief explanation of the importance of good writing. As in Chapter 1, the information provided is not a substitute for a complete style manual, and we again suggest that you recommend for purchase one of the manuals listed and/or one of the writer's guides discussed in this chapter. We also suggest recommending the purchase of a dictionary.

ASSIGNMENT(S)

As in Chapter 1, the four assignments listed are interrelated, and we recommend requiring all of them. Each one, however, can be assigned individually. Assignment 1 asks the student to examine the primary sources reproduced and to see if the evidence they provide supports or contradicts information provided in the textbook. Assignment 2 requires the student to summarize the contents of each source, an important skill that is emphasized in the next chapter. Assignment 3 requires that either the student or you choose one of the sources and that the student generate four historical questions from it. The aim is to get the students to begin to analyze sources via the same questioning process used in Chapter 1. If you wish to have a comprehensive discussion in class, we recommend assigning specific sources to different students so that all the sources will be covered. You may, however, prefer to limit analysis to a few of the sources provided or to let the students make their own choices.

Assignment 4 is the first writing assignment in this volume, a brief statement (about 100 words) on the reliability of one of the sources. As with the first assignment in the previous chapter, it will illustrate early in the semester which students have serious problems in terms of grammar and/or conceptualization. In completing this essay, students will come up with specific information and conclusions about one of the sources that they can use in class discussion, information and conclusions that will tend to reemphasize the fact that the reliability of a source and the questions asked of that source are interrelated.

The eleven sources reproduced have been chosen for their variety of form as well as content. Only four are traditional, "official" documents: John Winthrop's 1630 "City Upon a Hill" sermon (Source 3); excerpts from the 1770 Rhode Island General Assembly Proceedings (Source 4); Seventeenth-century laws of the Virginia House of Burgesses (Source 5); and a 1712 letter from the governor of New York to the Lords of Trade (Source 9). Martha Emmons' will (Source 8) is official, but hardly a traditional source. Along with the Rowlandson captivity narrative (Source 7) and the excerpts from the Byrd diaries (Source 10), this document illustrates the types of written sources used by historians who explore everyday life and values within the colonies. The remaining four sources are not documents at all in the standard sense, but they are clearly important and revealing primary sources: a Puritan gravestone carving (Source 1); a Connecticut folk-saying (Source 2); a Paul Revere portrait (Source 6); and a Benjamin Franklin woodcut (Source 11). The topics explored by these eleven sources include death, scarcity, religion, private property, community, education, commerce, boundaries, local politics, sexual relations, slavery, relations with Indians, and intercolonial affairs.

Each of the sources raises as many questions as it answers, and each can be questioned as to its reliability. As stated within the text, such questioning of reliability is often related to the questions asked of the source. Source 9, for example, may well be an accurate account of how the governor of New York perceived a slave insurrection but an inaccurate account of how the slaves perceived it. Similarly, Revere's portrait of King Philip in 1772 may illustrate nicely how eighteenth-century colonists perceived this Indian leader while bearing little physical resemblance to the individual who had lived a century earlier. Winthrop's 1630 sermon is probably an accurate assessment of the ideals held by the Puritan leadership, but it offers no evidence about what life was actually like in early Massachusetts Bay.

The variety of information and questions arising from these sources should provide plenty of material for varied student questions and essays.

ADDITIONAL QUESTIONS TO CONSIDER

Question 1 simply asks the students to be prepared to discuss for all the sources what they have written regarding one. This should lead to a fuller discussion in class and provide the students with additional information to answer question 2.

Question 2 asks if there are any general rules for determining source reliability and if any primary source can be completely reliable. Since reliability is partly determined by the questions asked of a source, the answer to both questions is no. Nevertheless, within given contexts, some general rules can be emphasized. For example, one should always question the possible biases of an author and the distortions that can result from the passage of time between the event in question and the actual creation of the source. One should also examine the purpose of the source, when it was created, and how that purpose might affect reliability.

Question 3 continues the logic of question 2 by asking the student to generalize about how primary sources should be used to write good history. In addition to questioning the reliability of each source and recognizing the link between reliability and the questions asked, the student should realize that sources need to be checked against each other for accuracy and generalizations. The good historian must thus amass many sources, analyze them, and compare them before reaching any conclusions.

CLASS / SECTION ______________ NAME ______________________

Chapter 2

ANSWER SHEET

1. Primary source chosen or assigned: ______________________________________

2. Four historical questions generated from source:

   a.

   b.

   c.

   d.

3. Using the questions listed, write a brief statement (about 100 words) on the reliability of your source. Remember that the accuracy of a source is partly determined by the questions asked of it.

LIVES OF THE AMERICAN REVOLUTION: ASSESSING EVIDENCE AND SUMMARIZING

Although this chapter can be used easily without prior reading or completion of the preceding chapters, the skills discussed are, in effect, more complex versions of skills previously introduced. Students are provided with biographical sketches of nine prominent individuals from the Revolutionary era and nine quotes from their writings, one for each individual. They are asked to summarize the information provided in these quotes, to use those summaries to match each individual to his/her quote, to reproduce one of the summaries, and to write a 100-250-word essay explaining why they matched a specific author to a specific quote. In completing this assignment, they are thus once again questioning and analyzing both secondary and primary sources, summarizing, and writing an essay. This time, however, the analyses and summaries are comparative in nature and are to be used to arrive at specific answers. Moreover, the essay is longer and more complex than the brief one they wrote in Chapter 2. Our own students generally begin to see with this assignment the cumulative effect of the skills approach on their work.

ASSIGNMENT(S)

As in previous chapters, the assignments listed follow each other logically, and we recommend requiring all of them. You may, however, prefer to ask your students to answer in writing only one or two of the three assignments and save the other(s) for class. The explanation that follows is appropriate for either method.

Assignment 1 asks the students to use their summaries to identify the author of each quote. In assignment 2 they reproduce one of their quote summaries, and in assignment 3 they write a 100-250-word essay explaining why they linked that quote to a specific author. To insure that all quotes and individuals are adequately covered in class discussion, we recommend assigning specific quotes to individual students.

Within the chapter, we emphasize the need to go beyond the literal meaning of quotes in order to complete this assignment. We also recommend a process of categorization and elimination, explained below, for matching quotes to specific individuals.

The correct answers are listed below and are followed by an explanation of one way to conduct class discussion of this assignment to maximize key lessons. In both discussing and grading this assignment, we emphasize not the number of correct answers to assignment 1, but the correctness and extent of the summary for assignment 2 and the logic and grammar exhibited in the essay for assignment 3.

The matches have been designed to be quite tricky so as to emphasize the fact that individuals do not always behave in a "logical" manner, and your students should not be expected to match each quote to its author correctly. They should, however, be able to summarize competently and correctly and to use those summaries to reach logical, even if incorrect, conclusions.

QUOTE	AUTHOR
1	Henry Laurens
2	Thomas Paine
3	Samuel Seabury
4	John Dickinson
5	James Otis
6	Thomas Hutchinson
7	Mercy Otis Warren
8	Gouverneur Morris
9	Moses Brown

Begin by asking the students to state the correct author for each quote. In every class we have taught, the students have at least five different answers for each quote. The verbalization of these answers often leads to both giggles and a more relaxed atmosphere in class, for each student can clearly see that he/she is not the *only* one to arrive at an incorrect answer. You may wish to reemphasize at this point what we have already stated in the chapter, that whether students answers are correct is not nearly as important as *why* they made the choices they did.

You may also wish to let your students argue among themselves, to see if they can arrive at the correct answers via such argumentation. If you prefer to lead the discussion, ask or explain how to categorize the nine individuals. We use four categories: radical, tory, moderate, and neutral. Paine and Otis are the only radicals, while Hutchinson and Seabury are the only tories and Brown is the only neutral; the other four are all moderates. One would thus expect to find two radical quotes, two tory quotes, one neutral quote, and four moderate quotes as one reads and summarizes the excerpts. Many of your students will insist, however, that the quotes do not break down in this way, an insistence based largely on literal and/or incorrect reading and summary.

Quote 1, for example, is *not* a tory oath of loyalty. Rather, it is an individual's statement that, while he is loyal to his king, that king has been misled by advisers. The author's agreement to take up arms, he makes clear, is a move against those advisers, not the king. This is obviously the statement of a moderate. Quote 2, on the other hand, is vehemently antimonarchial and clearly belongs to a radical. Going through all the quotes in this way, 2 and 5 can be identified as radical, 3 and 6 as tory, 9 as neutral, and the rest as moderate.

Summaries of the quotes further reveal that 9 belongs to Moses Brown. In addition to calling for neutrality, it also alludes to pacifism, names Newport as well as Boston, and uses Quaker terminology. *All* of these factors should be mentioned in a good essay on this quote.

Similarly, quote 2 belongs to Paine because of its antimonarchism, its emphasis on reason, its implied attack on Christianity, and its inflammatory style. Quote 5 belongs to the other radical, Otis, a fact made clear not simply by a process of elimination, but more importantly by the logic in the quote and its emphasis on the superiority of natural law. For the tories, quote 3 is Seabury's, because of its religious themes as well as its emphasis on support of monarchy, while 6 is Hutchinson's, because of its call for parliamentary force against "mob rule" in Boston.

Such a process of elimination leaves four moderates to be matched to their quotes. As previously stated, quote 1 belongs to an individual who opposes parliamentary taxation, but not monarchial rule from Britain. Quote 4, on the other hand, recognizes parliament's right to regulate trade for the good of the entire empire but insists that parliament has no right to legislate revenue bills. This was John Dickinson's position, as stated in the biographical sketch, and the quote is thus his. Quotes 7 and 8 belong to individuals who clearly fear "the mob," beliefs that go with both Gouverneur Morris and Mercy Otis Warren. By eliminating them, quote 1 belongs to Henry Laurens.

Deciding how to match quotes 7 and 8 with Warren and Morris is the most difficult distinction to make. The crucial difference between the quotes and the individuals is attitudinal. Quote 7 emphasizes citizenship virtues in such a way as to display a trust of the ordinary citizen, a trust not manifested by Morris. Quote 8 would thus be linked properly to him, and 7 would belong to Warren.

ADDITIONAL QUESTIONS TO CONSIDER

Questions 1 and 2 call for oral summaries of the quotes and oral explanations of choices and are covered in the preceding explanation. Questions 3 and 4 deal with the lack of direct correlations between socioeconomic status of the nine individuals and the stand of each on the issue of independence. In question 3, the students are asked what factors, aside from wealth and class, might explain the stand each took, and in 4 they are asked if these factors would provide sufficient evidence to disprove a class analysis of the American Revolution. Additional factors include religion, personal experiences with British rule and/or colonial rebels, personal temperament, political position, sex, place of birth, and education. The importance of these factors certainly casts doubt upon the validity of a narrow class analysis of the Revolution, but 9 cases are insufficient to support such a broad conclusion. Moreover, the socioeconomic elite of the colonies provided leadership for each segment of opinion—tory, moderate, radical, and neutral. Discussion of this fact provides you with an opportunity to discuss broad vs. narrow economic interpretations of history in general and of American history in particular.

CLASS / SECTION ____________ **NAME** ____________________

Chapter 3

ANSWER SHEET

1. Give the author for each quote:

QUOTE	AUTHOR
1	____________________
2	____________________
3	____________________
4	____________________
5	____________________
6	____________________
7	____________________
8	____________________
9	____________________

2. Reproduce a summary of one quote.

   Quote chosen or assigned: ______________________________

   Summary of quote:

3. 100-250-word essay explaining why you chose a specific author for quote summarized in #2.

Chapter 4

THE FOUNDING FATHERS AND THE AMERICAN STATE PAPERS: DOCUMENT ANALYSIS FROM THE CONSTITUTIONAL ERA

In this chapter students analyze specific documents within the context of their time and use the information they have acquired to complete one of three alternative assignments: answering a series of constitutional questions regarding hypothetical situations; linking specific passages in the documents read; or analyzing those documents to explain why their authors later became political opponents. The documents are the Declaration of Independence, the original Constitution, and the Federalist papers. Four of those papers are reproduced at the end of the chapter: numbers 10 and 51 by Madison, and numbers 15 and 23 by Hamilton. While these papers deal with different issues, all of them refer to problems of the Confederation and how the new Constitution can solve them. You may assign all four papers or a smaller number. In our classes, we use Federalist 10 and the hypothetical situations assignment and save the alternative assignments for class discussion.

ASSIGNMENT(S)

Assignment 1 consists of basic preparatory work for dealing with any of the other assignments. It involves summarizing the contents of the documents read, defining key terms (i.e., *democracy, republic, confederation, federation*) as used by the Founding Fathers, and noting the actual provisions of the Constitution in terms of powers, checks and balances, and so on. We do not request submission of any of this material, but you may wish to do so.

Assignment 2 involves choosing or being assigned one of four hypothetical situations and using the knowledge gained in assignment 1 to answer four questions about that situation. All four situations are based on events that actually took place during the 1780's and 1790's. They thus provide a link to next week's readings as well as a comparison between constitutional theory and what actually took place. We recommend assigning different situations to different students, so that all the situations will be covered, and asking the students in class to explain their answers for each situation.

Situation A: This is Shays' Rebellion with a twist—the militia joining instead of dispersing the rebels. Thus, the measures the rebels would demand (question 1) are exactly the ones that Shays' group did demand: an end to mortgage foreclosures, paper money, debt relief, and so on. The illegality of such measures (question 2) would stem from the prohibitions in the Constitution against violation of contract obligations and the coining and printing of money (Article I, Section 10), as well as the supremacy of federal over state law (Article VI). Federal powers to stop the mob (question 3) would include the executive's right to call out the militia and send in troops (Article II, Section 2), congressional legislation, and federal court rulings. Madison would argue (question 4) that this faction could never gain enough national adherents to control any branch of the government because of counterfactions and the voting filters in the Constitution and that even if it could take over the House of Representatives, it could not win the other branches for many years because of the different tenures for different offices.

Situation B: This is the Jeffersonian perception of Hamilton's fiscal system of the 1790s with a few twists. Specific actions to rectify the situation would include the executive (question 1) firing his appointees in the treasury or refusing to follow their suggestions, and the legislative branch (question 2) rescinding appropriations measures and enabling legislation as well as impeaching treasury officials (Article I, Sections 2, 3, 8). The powers of the judicial branch (question 3) would include trials for criminal activities but not declaration of federal laws as unconstitutional, since judicial review is not written into the Constitution. If all federal branches had been bribed into inactivity (question 4), citizens could turn to the division of powers by initiating a constitutional amendment in the state legislatures (Article V).

Situation C: This holds for both Britain and Spain during the 1790s. Presidential action without calling a special session of Congress (question 1) would include diplomatic negotiations with the power(s) and the mobilization and use of the military forces of the United States (Article II, Section 2). Congressional actions short of war (question 2) would include new military appropriations and economic retaliation (Article I, Section 8). If the president and Congress disagreed as to proper action (question 3), the president could try to act by a broad interpretation of his powers as Commander-in-Chief (Article II, Section 2); Congress could try to block the executive via new, specific laws; and/or there could be a stalemate. If both branches agreed that war was necessary (question 4), Congress, not the president, would have responsibility for the declaration and ensuing legislation to raise and finance an armed force (Article I, Section 8).

Situation D: This is based on the undeclared naval war with France and the Alien and Sedition Acts of 1798-1799. Dissenters could clearly turn to two branches of the federal government for aid (question 1), the legislative and the executive. They could request (question 2) congressional repeal of the laws outlawing dissent or presidential refusal to enforce them. The question of judicial power is unclear without expressed provision in the Constitution regarding judicial review, but individual judges could subvert the laws in specific cases via rulings based on definitions and technicalities. If these branches refuse to act, state legislatures (question 3) can file formal protests, begin the amendment process, and/or elect new senators at the proper time. The other legal recourse of dissenters (question 4) consists of their constitutional rights in court (Article I, Section 9; Article III, Sections 2 and 3).

Assignment 3 is a more traditional alternative to 2 involving identification of the specific problems of the Confederation era, a matching of those problems to the relevant constitutional provisions and Federalist papers passages, and a statement as to whether the Constitution did prevent a repetition of these problems and why. The answers are to a degree subjective and depend on what you have emphasized and assigned as well as the students' own beliefs regarding later American history. When we discuss this assignment in class, students who argue that the problems did not disappear tend to cite the rise of corporate power and technology as factors the Founding Fathers could not envisage. We often counter with a tory argument—that the real problem is amendments that have made the Constitution a more democratic document and that have thereby replaced checks, balances, and "Republican virtue" with "mob rule."

Assignment 4 asks for an essay comparing the Madison and Hamilton Federalist papers and explaining how these papers illustrate disagreements beneath the surface that would soon emerge. This is a difficult assignment and should be given only to your better students. Essentially, Madison is primarily concerned in his papers with the issues of justice and liberty, with domestic problems, and with establishing a system of government that can be effective without being tyrannical. His answer is the system of checks and balances, and throughout Federalist 10 and 51 there is a persistent emphasis of the need to *control* government. Hamilton, on the other hand, consistently emphasizes the lack of power within the existing government, not the need to control any new government with additional powers. Indeed, in both Federalist 15 and 23 he often talks in terms of unlimited powers and the importance of coercion. Implicitly, he also emphasizes foreign policy, speaking of the humiliation the United States presently suffers in international affairs and choosing military affairs as his example of the unlimited powers a national government needs to meet whatever external threats arise. While these differences should not be overstated, they clearly reemerged during the 1790s.

ADDITIONAL QUESTIONS TO CONSIDER

Question 1 asks the students to identify the actual events on which the hypothetical situations are based and to compare the answers they gave with what actually happened. As previously noted, discussion will provide a link to next week's readings as well as a comparison between constitutional theory and what actually took place.

Question 2 asks how and why the actual constitutional system today differs from what was envisaged in 1787. As previously noted, students often cite technology and corporate power, and we often counter effectively with the tory argument that "democratic" amendments have destroyed the checks and balances system and created a form of "mob rule" abhorrent to the Founding Fathers.

Discussion of these issues will in turn lead into a discussion of question 3, which asks the students to read the constitutional amendments, to discover why each one was added, and to analyze the repercussions of each. This question is worthwhile should you wish to bring the constitutional issues up to the present, but it does require knowledge of later American history, and you may therefore wish to lecture on it instead.

Question 4 deals with the relationship between the Constitution and the Declaration of Independence and provides an opportunity to discuss conflicting interpretations on this era in American history by noting how some scholars like Beard view the two documents as contradictory while others see them as complementary.

CLASS / SECTION ____________ NAME ____________________

Chapter 4

ANSWER SHEET

1. On your own, summarize the key points in the Federalist papers. Define the differences its authors would make between a democracy and a republic and between a confederation, a national government, and a federal government. Compare and contrast the different constitutional provisions relating to checks and balances.

2. Hypothetical situation chosen: ____________ (A, B, C, or D)

   Answer to question 1:

   Answer to question 2:

   Answer to question 3:

   Answer to question 4:

CLASS / SECTION ____________ NAME ________________________

ALTERNATIVE ASSIGNMENTS

3. Identify the specific problems that emerged under the Articles of Confederation and for each one cite the relevant passages in the Federalist papers and constitutional provisions designed to prevent a repetition. In retrospect, did these provisions prevent a repetition as the Founding Fathers had anticipated? Why?

4. Write a brief essay comparing the Federalist papers by Hamilton and Madison and explaining how these papers illustrate disagreements between the two that would soon emerge.

Chapter 5

THOMAS JEFFERSON AND THE PROBLEMS OF INTERPRETATION: INTERPRETIVE ESSAYS FROM OUTLINING TO REVISION

This chapter concentrates on the problems of interpretation and essay writing. In addition, students are introduced to chronology, cause-and-effect relationships, outlining, and revising. All of these skills are discussed in relation to Thomas Jefferson and the historical controversies surrounding him. The student assignment, their largest and most complex up to this point, is to research and write an interpretive essay on some controversial aspect of Jefferson's career. Successful completion of this assignment, they are informed, will involve making use of all the skills previously discussed in this volume as well as the ones introduced in this chapter.

We consider this assignment one of the most important in the entire volume. Consequently, we devote two full weeks to it and ask each student to see us individually with an outline and rough draft of his/her paper. In addition to synthesizing skills previously discussed, the assignment forces the student to come to grips with the subjectivity of historical analysis and to research and write a full historical essay for the first time. The assignment divides the process into six specific steps, thereby enabling both you and the students to note progress and problems and to make corrections whenever appropriate. In addition to setting important standards for later essays, this assignment emphasizes skills that are applicable to essay examination questions, and we have found that completion of the assignment has an important, positive "carryover" effect on examinations.

Successful completion of the assignment does require a good deal of explicit instruction and guidance from you. In the following paragraphs, we will explain our method of providing such instruction and guidance, as well as alternative methods.

ASSIGNMENT(S)

Assignment 1 asks each student to select a thesis statement as a basis for researching and writing an interpretive essay. Five examples are provided in this section, and the students are asked either to choose from that list or to devise a thesis statement of their own. You may wish to assign one of the five to the entire class, to divide the five among the class members, to give the students completely free choice, or to devise your own statement for the class to use.

Assignment 2 instructs the students to complete appropriate research. Here you may require specific readings on Jefferson in addition to the textbook (we use Morton Borden's essay on Jefferson in his *America's Eleven Greatest Presidents*) and/or tell the students to make use of the library as they see fit. In large classes, we strongly recommend putting essential works, such as Dumas Malone's biography of Jefferson, on reserve so that the entire class can use them.

In assignments 3 and 4 the students are instructed to compose an outline of their paper and a two- to three-page rough draft of the paper from that outline. They are also advised to revise this draft as discussed within the chapter.

In assignment 5 the students are instructed to present this outline and rough draft and to meet with you, the teaching assistant, or another member of the class to receive commentary and criticism. We have each student meet with us individually for approximately 20 minutes and have found these meetings to be extremely worthwhile. In addition to the personal contact, they can give you insights into the thought processes of your students and the opportunity to correct errors at an early stage. In general, we have found that correcting such errors via questioning (e.g., "What are you trying to say here? This sentence says the following to me. Is that what you really want to say? What about this piece of evidence?") is more productive than giving the student a minilecture on his/her outline and draft. If this method is too time-consuming for you and/or a teaching assistant, some of the objectives can be accomplished by having each student meet with and receive criticism from another member of the class. If you use this method, we advise providing each student with a list of questions to consider while reading the outlines and rough drafts, as well as some guidance regarding what to say.

Assignment 6 involves using the comments and criticisms received to produce and submit a final copy of the paper, along with the original outline and rough draft. You may choose to grade simply on the basis of the quality of the final paper or to take into account the degree of improvement from the first to the final draft.

Assignment 7 offers an alternative assignment, a critical review of a book about Thomas Jefferson, and a brief explanation of how to research and write such a review. Should you wish to use this alternative, we recommend assigning specific, interpretive works that can be reviewed critically by undergraduates and then following the same procedures outlined for the interpretive essay.

ADDITIONAL QUESTIONS TO CONSIDER

All four additional questions to consider concern the problems of historical interpretation. Students are asked to be prepared to defend their individual conclusions and the opposite conclusions, to explain why they consider their conclusion to be valid, and to analyze how and why individuals can reach different conclusions based on the same evidence. In class, we find the most effective way of dealing with this issue is to get a debate going between students who took opposite positions on the same thesis statement. As the debate proceeds, the instructor should request specific evidence to back up generalizations and should note that evidence on the blackboard. If the papers were done correctly, the same evidence will have been used on both sides of the argument. (You should reemphasize in this regard our point that one must account for, not ignore, contradictory evidence.) The different conclusions reached depend on how that evidence is organized, evaluated, and explained. In thesis statement b, for example, whether or not one agrees that Jefferson succeeded because he adapted Federalist methods to Republican ends, one must deal with the Federalist methods and the Republican ends; disagreement emerges only in the assessment of his success or failure, and the degree to which the means subverted the ends.

Recognition of this fact should lead into a detailed discussion of how and why historians disagree, and some students may very well conclude incorrectly that *any* historical conclusion is defensible. You may choose to address this issue now or to wait for the detailed discussion of interpretations in Chapter 10.

CLASS / SECTION ______________ NAME ______________________

Chapter 5

ANSWER SHEET

Use this as a cover sheet for your *final* essay draft.

Thesis of essay:

Brief outline:

CHANGING MATERIAL SOCIETY: USING STATISTICS AND GRAPHS

With the completion of the assignment in Chapter 5, the emphasis of this volume shifts from basic skills to different types of historical evidence as introduced in Chapter 2. In this chapter students are introduced to statistics and graphs; in Chapters 7-9 they are introduced to maps, historical artifacts, and literature. The chronological periods covered by these chapters overlap to some extent, and you may wish to delete some or cover them in a different order. The assignments have been so organized that they are independent and do not "build" on each other to the extent that the early assignments did.

Chapter 6 presents some very basic information on percentages and averages. Students are introduced to percentage increases and decreases, means, and medians. They are also introduced to graphs as a means of organizing and illustrating statistical trends.

ASSIGNMENT(S)

Assignment 1 consists of answers to specific percentage and average calculations requested within the chapter. You may choose to grade these or to provide the class with the correct answers. Those answers, and the appropriate calculations, are as follows:

a. Percentage of cotton exports in total U.S. exports in 1860: 60.75%.

b. Percentage increase of cotton exports from 1820 to 1860:

cotton exports in 1860	1,768,000,000
cotton exports in 1820	- 128,000,000
	1,640,000,000

result divided by 1820 figure and multiplied by 100:

$$\frac{1,640,000,000}{128,000,000} \times 100 = 1281.25\%$$

c. Percentage decrease in cotton exports from 1860 to 1861:

The *incorrect* calculation is the 1860 figure minus the 1861 figure, divided by the 1860 figure and multiplied by 100, or 474%; reemphasize the impossibility of anything decreasing by more than 100%. The correct calculation is the 1860 figure minus the 1861 figure divided by the 1861 figure and multiplied by 100:

$$\begin{array}{r} 1{,}768{,}000{,}000 \\ -\ 308{,}000{,}000 \\ \hline 1{,}460{,}000{,}000 \end{array} \qquad \frac{1{,}460{,}000{,}000}{1{,}768{,}000{,}000} \times 100 = 82.5\%$$

d. Mean cotton production for plantations on Table I is total cotton production divided by number of plantations:

1541 divided by 15 = 102.7 bales

e. Median cotton production is the middle case, #8—81 bales.

f. Mean number of slaves is total divided by number of plantations—601 divided by 15 = 40.7

g. Median number of slaves is middle case, #11—30 slaves.

h. *Per capita* is a *mean* by definition and is thus 1541 bales divided by 601 slaves, or 2.56 bales per slave. If any of your students did not get the correct answer, ask them to define *per capita*. Also, reemphasize the inherent distortion of such mean averages, i.e., "per capita national income" includes children, people not working, etc.

Assignment 2 involves the creation of a time series graph for votes cast in presidential elections from 1824 to 1860. This is fairly straightforward, and the resulting graph shows a linear increase in votes cast.

Assignment 3 combines the skills of assignments 1 and 2 by requesting percentage increase for each election. The answers are as follows:

1828 $$\begin{array}{r} 1{,}156{,}328 \\ -\ 356{,}038 \\ \hline 800{,}290 \end{array} \qquad \frac{800{,}290}{356{,}038} \times 100 = 225\%$$

1832 $$\begin{array}{r} 1{,}250{,}799 \\ -\ 1{,}156{,}328 \\ \hline 94{,}471 \end{array} \qquad \frac{94{,}471}{1{,}156{,}328} \times 100 = 8\%$$

1836 $$\begin{array}{r} 1{,}479{,}799 \\ -\ 1{,}250{,}799 \\ \hline 229{,}000 \end{array} \qquad \frac{229{,}000}{1{,}250{,}799} \times 100 = 18\%$$

1840
2,403,719
- 1,479,799
923,920

$$\frac{923{,}920}{1{,}479{,}799} \times 100 = 62\%$$

1844
2,698,611
- 2,403,719
294,892

$$\frac{294{,}892}{2{,}403{,}719} \times 100 = 12\%$$

1848
2,871,906
- 2,698,611
173,295

$$\frac{173{,}295}{2{,}698{,}611} \times 100 = 6\%$$

1852
3,143,679
- 2,871,906
271,773

$$\frac{271{,}773}{2{,}871{,}906} \times 100 = 9\%$$

1856
4,053,396
- 3,143,679
909,717

$$\frac{909{,}717}{3{,}143{,}679} \times 100 = 28\%$$

1860
4,680,193
- 4,053,396
626,797

$$\frac{626{,}797}{4{,}053{,}396} \times 100 = 15\%$$

The greatest percentage increase in vote total occurred in 1828. This increase cannot be accounted for by the population growth shown on the graph in the chapter. Rather, as the textbook and lectures should have pointed out, the key factor is the ending of property qualifications for voting and the extension of the franchise to all white males.

ADDITIONAL QUESTIONS TO CONSIDER

These three questions deal with additional, broader aspects of the statistics discussed in the chapter. In question 1 a statistical analysis of the 1844 election should show that Clay could have won the election by carrying New York; Birney's votes probably cost Clay the state, since Birney got more than 5,000 votes in New York (the number Clay lost by), and most of Birney's votes came from northern Whigs. With this fact in mind, your students should question whether Polk's victory in 1844 was the mandate for expansion he interpreted it to be.

Question 2 requests the students to use additional statistics available in their text and/or in the reference section of the library to illustrate relationships between transportation improvement, economic development, westward expansion, and increasing sectionalism. If you believe the regular assignments for this chapter are too easy for your students, you may wish to provide some hypotheses and statistical evidence for testing.

Question 3 is a series of general questions, quite appropriate for class discussion, dealing with the reasons numbers are so often deceptive; the limits of statistics, charts, and graphs; and questions that should be asked whenever such evidence is used. The answers, obviously, depend on a host of variables, including the information one wants to discover, the reliability of the statistics, the biases and/or errors of the user, and so on. An explanation by you of the criticisms leveled against Fogel and Engerman's *Time on the Cross* is a good illustration of the problems that often arise.

CLASS / SECTION ____________ NAME ________________________

Chapter 6

ANSWER SHEET

1. Show calculations for each answer:

   a. Percentage of all U.S. exports consisting of cotton in 1860: ______

   b. Percentage increase in cotton exports from 1820 to 1860: ______

   c. Percentage decrease of cotton exports from 1860 to 1861: ______

   d. Mean value of cotton production on fifteen plantations: ______

   e. Median value of cotton production on fifteen plantations: ______

   f. Mean number of slaves on fifteen plantations: ______

   g. Median number of slaves on fifteen plantations: ______

   h. Per capita production of slaves on fifteen plantations: ______

2. Time series graph for presidential elections, 1824-1860 (attach a separate sheet of graph paper)

CLASS / SECTION __________ NAME ________________________

3. a. Percentage increase in voters during presidential elections:

1824

1828

1832

1836

1840

1844

1848

1852

1856

1860

b. Year of highest percentage increase ____________

c. Can population growth alone account for this increase? ___________

d. If not, what other factors might contribute to this increase?

Chapter 7

WESTWARD EXPANSION AND INDIAN REMOVAL: THE USE OF MAPS IN HISTORY

As previously stated, Chapters 6-9 emphasize the different types of historical evidence, overlap a bit in terms of chronological periods covered, and may be assigned independently of each other. This chapter deals with the use of maps as applied to the Jacksonian Era and the subject of territorial expansion. Instead of the traditional emphasis on territorial acquisitions from European powers and Mexico, however (issues that are usually mapped in a textbook), the information and evidence provided concern Indian removal and associated issues.

The five maps reproduced within the chapter provide data on free and slave population movement and density during this era as well as Indian removal. Included with these maps is a brief discussion of the basic map symbols and conventions: scale, longitude, and latitude; directional arrows and compasses; and legends. Also included is a blank outline map of the United States for the student's own use. Since the basic aim of this chapter is to teach students how to understand and use the maps in their text, our specific assignments do not require preparation of additional maps. You can easily design and add or substitute such an assignment, however, if you so desire.

ASSIGNMENT(S)

The basic written assignment is simple and straightforward, to prepare three questions for future research dealing with possible relationships between Indian removal and the other issues included on the maps. The aim is to get the students not only to read maps properly, but to combine and compare information on different maps in order to synthesize data and raise new questions.

Assignment 2 is an alternative assignment that is linked to the skill of hypothesis formation discussed in the next chapter. It asks the student to suggest at least three ways in which the evidence on the maps might support, refute, or refine the hypothesis that Indian removal was largely the product of slave and cotton expansion. That evidence suggests a reciprocal rather than a simple, one-way, cause-and-effect relationship between these factors. Students are also asked in this question what additional kinds of maps they would want to examine to test this hypothesis further. Such maps would include information on Indian removal north of the Ohio River and west of the Mississippi, the relationship of slavery growth to cotton production growth, and population, slave, and Indian movement for earlier and later years.

ADDITIONAL QUESTIONS TO CONSIDER

As previously stated, the four questions in this section can be used as alternative written assignments as well as subjects for class discussion. The first three can also be expanded to require the preparation of the maps discussed. Question 1 asks how to indicate on a map the relationship between the acquisition of territory from another nation and the later cession treaties with the Indians who lived in that territory, a task easily accomplished through the use of colors and years to indicate both processes. Question 2 asks whether a map illustrating date of entry and slave vs. free status of new states would be useful to understand the growing slavery conflict, and if so how. What would clearly be revealed in such a map is the sectional "balance" that was maintained at first via unofficial agreement and later by the Missouri compromise, and the breakdown of that balance in the aftermath of the Mexican War. Question 3 asks how a transportation development map could be used to interpret the population density information contained on maps 7.2 and 7.3, another example of symbiotic, cause-and-effect relationship. Question 4 is a broader question dealing with the limits of maps as an illustrative device. In theory, there are no limits, though placing too much data on the same map can make it too complex or cumbersome to be useful.

CLASS / SECTION ____________ NAME ____________________

Chapter 7

ANSWER SHEET

1. List three questions for future research based on the possible relationship between Indian removal and the factors included on the maps in this chapter.

   a.

   b.

   c.

2. *Alternative assignment*: Three ways in which evidence provided would support, refute, or refine the hypothesis that Indian removal was largely the product of expansionist energies related to a dynamic cotton economy based on slave labor are

   a.

   b.

   c.

   What additional kinds of maps would you like to examine for additional information related to this hypothesis?

Chapter 8

MATERIAL CULTURE IN ANTEBELLUM AMERICA: HYPOTHESIS FORMATION AND THE USE OF HISTORICAL ARTIFACTS

Continuing the pattern of the last two chapters, this chapter introduces the student to another type of historical evidence—artifacts from the "built environment," a phrase used by historic preservationists to describe the man-made world. It also introduces a new skill, hypothesis formation. The assignment requires the student to use that skill with artifacts of material culture. Reproduced at the end of the chapter for this purpose are some architectural designs by Andrew Jackson Downing, along with excerpts from the preface to the 1850 edition of his *The Architecture of Country Houses*.

ASSIGNMENT(S)

Assignment 1 requires the student to develop two hypotheses about how Downing's ideas and designs reflect the values of his age, and/or how the living arrangements within the designs provide evidence to challenge, support, refine, or revise the modernization hypothesis for Jacksonian America presented within the chapter. Many of our students hypothesize about the values inherent in the different designs for different social classes, which reflect economic stratification in Jacksonian America. They also notice the American effort to control the natural environment while living within it.

Assignment 2, which can either be assigned as part of the written assignment or simply used as the basis for class discussion, asks the students to realize the limitations of historical artifacts as sources by finding a bias or shortcoming in each of their hypotheses. The most obvious shortcoming is the use of a single source. Downing was not the only architect in antebellum America. Moreover, acceptance of his designs was not necessarily the equivalent to acceptance of his ideas.

ADDITIONAL QUESTIONS TO CONSIDER

Question 1 continues the questioning process begun in assignment 2 by asking the students to compare Downing's ideas with those expressed by Thoreau in the first chapter of *Walden* and to modify their hypotheses accordingly. Thoreau and Downing occupy almost opposite poles on the question of housing, and the first chapter of *Walden* suggests that an exaggerated sense of their need for shelter may partially explain why most men "lead lives of quiet desperation." Thoreau's own basic shelter on the shores of Walden Pond provides a striking contrast to Downing's designs and beliefs. If you do not wish to assign *Walden*, you can quote from it in class and then ask students to modify their hypotheses accordingly. This is a good opportunity to reemphasize a point made in the chapter about hypotheses, that they are neither questions nor conclusions, but tentative theories or suppositions designed to explain certain existing facts and to guide the researcher in the investigation of other facts. Modifying them in light of new evidence is thus quite appropriate.

Question 2 can be used as an alternative or additional written assignment or as a basis for class discussion. Each student is requested to reproduce another artifact from antebellum America and to hypothesize about what that item illustrates about society at that time. If your institution is located near a historical society or a museum, this assignment can provide an excellent opportunity for individual exploration of its holdings.

CLASS / SECTION ____________ NAME ________________________

Chapter 8

ANSWER SHEET

1. Two hypotheses about how Downing's ideas and designs reflect the values of his age, and/or how the living arrangements in those designs provide evidence to challenge, support, refine, or revise the modernization hypothesis for Jacksonian America.

   a.

   b.

2. Briefly describe (100-250 words) *one* bias or shortcoming inherent in any hypothesis about Jacksonian society that originates with Downing's designs.

Chapter 9

THE PROBLEM OF SLAVERY: LITERATURE AND BIOGRAPHY IN HISTORY

This chapter serves as a bridge between the issues, skills, and assignments in Chapters 6-8 and those in Chapter 10. Like Chapters 6-8, it discusses a specific type of historical evidence, literature, as that evidence relates to specific issues in antebellum America—slavery, reform movements in general, abolition, and women's rights in particular. Like Chapter 10, however, it concentrates on the issues of the slavery/Civil War era, discusses secondary sources (biographical in nature), and requires the writing of a paper based on individual research. You may assign the papers in both chapters, choose one without the other, or give your students the choice. They should, however, be required to read both chapters.

After a brief discussion of slavery, reform, abolition, and women's rights, Chapter 9 discusses the advantages of biographical study and the problems inherent in using literary source material. It then provides biographical sketches of two literary women whose lives were dramatically affected by the slavery issue, Harriet Beecher Stowe and Mary Chesnut, and reproduces excerpts from their most famous works—*Uncle Tom's Cabin* and *A Diary from Dixie*.

ASSIGNMENT(S)

There is a single written assignment, divided into four parts, for this chapter. Should you desire to omit this written assignment, then assign only parts 1, 2, and/or 3 as appropriate. Assignment 1 simply asks the students to read the Stowe and Chesnut biographies and excerpts. Assignment 2 asks them to choose a third individual whose life was affected by slavery and who left some sort of documentary evidence. Assignment 3 requires them to reproduce a piece of that evidence and research the individual's life. (You may wish to remind them of appropriate reference materials as discussed in Chapter 2.) Assignment 4 asks the student to write a two- to three-page biographical sketch of the individual, complete with footnotes and bibliography, and organized in such a way as to serve as an appropriate introduction to the document reproduced.

ADDITIONAL QUESTIONS TO CONSIDER

Question 1 addresses the role of biography in historical study. It asks the students what their research taught them about this era, what they consider to be the general strengths and weaknesses of biographical study, and why biography is such a popular form of historical writing. As discussed within the chapter, biographical study often illuminates the values, beliefs, and experiences of an entire society, not simply an individual. It is always dangerous, however, to generalize about an entire society on the basis of research into the life of only one person. Biography is very popular primarily because, in treating only one individual, it personalizes history in ways many readers appreciate.

Question 2 deals with the "Quadroon's Story," the chapter reproduced from *Uncle Tom's Cabin*. It asks what themes Stowe develops in this chapter, whether these themes reflected or helped to determine social values, and why the book had such a tremendous impact. This particular chapter was chosen not only for its vividness, but also because it contains so many of the themes Stowe chose to develop. Most notable in this regard is the fact that slavery threatened all the Christian values Americans held, the efforts of individuals notwithstanding. No matter how good or evil the motives and character of the people described, the results were devastating for the Quadroon, and the result was the virtual destruction of all her morals and values. In the chapter, Stowe thus reflects and attacks social values.

Question 3 asks the students what psychohistorical interpretations we may be suggesting in our biographical sketch of Harriet Beecher Stowe. These include the great influence of her prominent father and his preachings, the numerous frustrations and difficulties of her marriage, the personal losses she suffered and moves she experienced, and her own brush with death. Some of these influences, you may wish to point out, were quite common for people of that era while others were unique to Stowe.

Question 4 asks about the strengths and weaknesses of Chesnut's diary as a primary source in light of the fact that it was revised over a 20-year period. The answer lies in the C. Van Woodward quote provided with the question, a quote that emphasizes the diary's ability to recapture the feelings and essence of the time rather than the literal record of events.

Question 5 asks about the strengths and weaknesses of literature as a primary source. From the excerpts they have read, the students should realize that literature is able to illustrate vividly the moods, thoughts, and beliefs of a past era, and at times to critique them. But each piece of literature must be analyzed on its own, with all factors previously discussed being taken into account.

CLASS / SECTION ____________ **NAME** ________________________

Chapter 9

ANSWER SHEET

1. Individual selected: ______________________________________

2. Biographical sketch (500-750 words). Please begin your essay on this sheet.

3. Attach your primary document to your sketch.

Chapter 10

THE CAUSES OF THE CIVIL WAR: INTERPRETATION AND HISTORIOGRAPHY

This chapter asks students to complete a major written assignment and introduces them to one of the most important and complex of all historical skills—dealing with conflicting interpretations and historiography. Therefore, as with Chapter 5, we recommend devoting two weeks to it and having individual conferences with students when appropriate.

Although the problems of conflicting interpretations have already been introduced in Chapter 5, Chapter 10 provides a detailed analysis of one of the major historiographical disputes in American history, the causes of the Civil War, and requires the student to use previously acquired skills to arrive at and defend his/her own conclusions as to the causes of that conflict. The written assignment and questions for class discussion complement each other in this regard and form an integrated whole. There are, however, numerous ways to deal with this assignment, which are outlined in the following discussion.

The chapter consists of a brief discussion of the centrality of the Civil War to all Americans since 1865, the problem of historical interpretation previously discussed in Chapter 5, and the need for each student to be his/her own interpreter of the past. At the end of the chapter are ten brief, representative quotes from different schools of thought on the causes of the Civil War, followed by a historiographical essay that explains each school and comments on its weaknesses. The essay does not, however, place these schools within their historical contexts; that task is left to the student and you in class.

ASSIGNMENT(S)

Assignment 1 requires the student to read the quotes and essay provided and then to choose the interpretation or combination of interpretations that he/she believes to be the most valid. The first part of the written assignment is to explain that interpretation and why it is more valid than the others.

Assignments 2 and 3 offer options for completion of the essay. Assignment 2 requires choosing, researching, and writing about a major event, person, or idea from antebellum U.S. history to illustrate the validity of the interpretation chosen. As an alternative, assignment 3 asks the students to use statistics, maps, or items of material culture, as described in preceding chapters, to explain and develop their interpretations. In both options, the student must thus research a specific aspect of the antebellum era, organize that research to support an interpretation, and make use of many of the skills previously studied.

The essay, students are instructed, is to be three to five typed, double-spaced pages, should not exceed 1,500 words of text, and must include footnotes and bibliography. The decision about whether research must go beyond the required course readings and lectures is up to you and/or the students. We give them the option of completing additional research in the library or relying on what they have already read and heard. You may wish to make additional research a requirement, or you may insist that they use only the information already provided.

Unlike assignment 5, we do not have required individual meetings to go over rough drafts instead of a class session. Rather, we devote two class sessions to the following additional questions and offer students the option of meeting with the instructor individually to discuss outlines, rough drafts, and ideas if any of them so desire. You may, of course, follow this procedure or use the same procedure as in Chapter 5—required individual sessions in lieu of one class discussion.

ADDITIONAL QUESTIONS TO CONSIDER

If you devote two class discussions to this chapter, we recommend centering the first class on the mechanics of the paper and the issues raised in question 1. In that question students are asked both to defend their interpretation orally and to descibe the historical context in which this interpretation developed. Oral defense should lead to instructive class debate once again. Description of the historical context of each school of thought has been consciously deleted from our historiographical essay and quotes. The students are provided with dates for those quotes, and such dates should enable them to put together, on their own, a historiographical analysis that would explain the emergence and popularity of each school during a given era. It is far from accidental, for example, that the economic interpretation represented by Louis Hacker's quote was developed during the era of the Great Depression, that the moral issue represented by the Schlesinger quote arose after World War II, or that the psychological interpretation of David Donald was written during the "consensus" era of the 1950s and early 1960s. The shortcomings of each school discussed in the essay of course led to further interpretation, but the key point students should learn from this exercise is that historical interpretations are partially the products of the era in which they were written and that the historical questions asked and answers reached reflect the values of that era. History, it should again be emphasized, is thus a subjective discipline in which one's view of the past is partially determined by one's position in the present.

One obvious conclusion from such an analysis is that the interpretations chosen by each student were influenced by events in his/her lifetime. Question 2 asks the students to conduct a virtual historiographical analysis on themselves in this regard by examining the key beliefs and events in their lifetimes that may have influenced their choice of interpretation. While not easy, we have found such an analysis to be extraordinarily valuable. You may wish to begin with an example by offering a historiographical analysis of your own ideas.

At this point, if not earlier, some of your students may question the value of historical study. If they do not, we suggest that you do. For if all historical study is relative and subjective, the value or truth of any interpretation, or of any historical analysis, is called into question. Part of the solution to this problem lies in the answers given to question 3, which asks the students to account for any differences between the interpretation of the causes of the Civil War they held when they entered the course and the interpretation they hold now. Even without historical study, all individuals have implicit interpretations of the key events in the past, interpretations largely shaped by the society at large. Historical study often enables one to move beyond such culturally defined boundaries, though never completely. Moreover, ask your students to compare the first and last "slavery" interpretations discussed in the essay. In one way, that essay implies that historical interpretations of the Civil War have come full circle, that we now stand exactly where James Ford Rhodes did. On another level, however, the Davis interpretation of 1977 goes far beyond what Rhodes wrote in 1913 by incorporating other interpretations into a more comprehensive and valid interpretation, one that can account for all the factors, which other interpretations do not. In all of this, your own personal philosophy of history will come out.

CLASS / SECTION ______________ **NAME** __________________________

Chapter 10

ANSWER SHEET

1. Thesis statement:

2. Event, person, or idea selected: ______________________________

3. Brief essay outline. Attach the final draft of your essay to this sheet.